THIS IS GOD'S WORLD

This Is
God's World

By
Reuben K. Youngdahl

AUGUSTANA PRESS
ROCK ISLAND, ILLINOIS

THIS IS GOD'S WORLD

⟦ PRINTED
IN U·S·A· ⟧

AUGUSTANA BOOK CONCERN
Printers and Binders
ROCK ISLAND, ILLINOIS
1961

Dedicated to those noble servants of the Lord who are laboring among people in distant parts of the world and introducing them to the risen Savior. To Harold and Louise Faust and their children, Mark, Ann, Linda, and Stephen who typify by their unselfish service the love of these missionaries for their fellow men goes a personal word of dedication.

Preface

With the greatly significant advances made in scientific investigation and discoveries during the past several decades, what had once been vastly separated areas of the world have now been drawn together into a universe which can be encircled by jet-propelled transportation in only a few hours. People who, in a day not far behind us, were regarded as foreigners are now our close neighbors. The world has shrunk into a compact universe as men have continued to find more and more of the hidden secrets of God in scientific achievement.

Because we now find that we are living in a small world, we are confronted with the need to understand that world, and particularly to know about its inhabitants. It has been the privilege of the author to travel during the past ten years to numerous places in many lands where he could observe at firsthand the ways and patterns of living of various cultures. Throughout his journeys he has had as a primary purpose the relation of these observations to his audiences at home. Consequently the plan for this book had its inception when its author first set foot on foreign soil in 1949.

Through the following years some of these observations have been employed often in an attempt to help others better understand the small world in which they live and, even more, to know the people who populate it. The devotional messages which fill these pages are meant to bring the reader into lands he very probably has not yet visited and to meet people he has not previously known. Most of the incidents which are included have been personal experiences or observations of the author. Some have been related to him by missionaries. Others have come to his attention from his general reading.

We shall journey around the world during the coming year both figuratively and literally, for these messages have been arranged so that we will be making a flight scheduled as any travel agency might arrange a trip for us. As we journey together, may it prove to be an educational experience as well as a spiritually-enriching one. It is the author's prayer that as we visit these lands there shall be revealed to us a world in need. In the days of Christ men needed the love of the Lord and the work of His followers. In an even greater measure today does the world need this same love to save it from self-destruction.

It is likewise the prayer of the author that by the help of God each individual who reads this book may respond to its appeal for greater love and devotion by strengthening his own dedication to the needs of his brothers. Each one of us can be a missionary right in the very situation where we are found in our daily life. As we are confronted with the real needs of the world, may our response come not only in a prayer that God's work may be done, but even more in a willingness to give and share of our every resource for the alleviation of such need. At the same time let us not fail to thank our God for the blessings He has sent us. In this spirit of gratitude may our lives be led into an even deeper consecration for the service of the Savior.

To the following people I am deeply grateful for the assistance which they have given me during the preparation of this manuscript for publication: Miss Mahala Kemp, Miss Virginia Miller, Mrs. Carol Powis, and Pastor Clarence T. Nelson.

It is a turbulent and deeply troubled world in which we live. Days are filled with moments of fear and unrest. Many men do not yet know the life that is possible as a redeemed child of God. Can we determine our responsibility to the rest

of the world? Again it is the prayer of the author that these
messages may be used to draw more men closer to their Lord,
and that their faith will unswervingly proclaim:

> "This is my Father's world,
>   O let me ne'er forget
> That though the wrong seems oft so strong,
>   God is the Ruler yet."

Reuben K. Youngdahl, Senior Pastor
Mount Olivet Lutheran Church
Minneapolis, Minnesota

The earth is the Lord's and the fulness thereof,
  the world and those who dwell therein;
for he has founded it upon the seas,
  and established it upon the rivers.

Psalm 24: 1-2

Thou dost show me the path of life; in thy presence there is fullness of joy. Psalm 16:11

Today marks the beginning of a new and promising year. We stand now before the open door which invites us to journey into that unknown called tomorrow. The unseen challenges of the future lie before us. Equipped with a daring faith, we step forward into the adventures of a new year.

Now as one prepares to take a trip into the far beyond there is much work to be done in planning for it. First of all you must decide upon the places you want to visit and the countries you want to tour. Then you schedule yourself so that you can make the best use of your time. It is also important to read any books that are available in order to receive background information about the places you are going to visit on your journey. The most important task of all is to study maps and be familiar with the routes you are going to take.

Life is the most important journey of all that men ever take. We must prepare for it, too. One should carefully choose the places he wants to go. There are some places we visit that will bring us comfort, and some that will bring us sorrow. We must be sure that we make the best use of our time, for time in this life passes quickly. It is important to read about life and to study so that we know where we are going.

The Bible is God's blueprint after which we are to pattern our lives. The greatest journey is the one which leads through this world in the companionship of Christ and continues into the world to come. Everyone of us can afford this journey. The price isn't to be reckoned in dollars and cents, but rather in the giving of our life. When we commit ourselves to Him, He will direct us in the way through the coming year. We can live each day in the assurance that we never walk alone!

PRAYER THOUGHT: *Dear Lord, may we always travel together on this journey of life and be assured of entering that eternal home which Thou hast prepared for us.*

1

Trust in the Lord with all your heart, and do not rely on your own insight. Proverbs 3:5

When one travels by plane he is permitted to take on his ticket free of charge only a limited amount of baggage. Any additional weight that you bring aboard the plane you must pay for, and the price is steep. People who do a lot of traveling choose carefully the items that they are going to take with them, selecting only the most important ones, so that they will not need to pay for excess baggage. Sometimes they will pack and repack and weigh and reweigh their suitcases in order to be sure to come within the proper limits.

What a parallel for life's journey. Beware of excess baggage. Too many of us are carrying things each day that ought really be left behind, since they do nothing but cost us heavily. Our hatreds are excess baggage. We should conquer them, and forget them. The Lord said we should forgive others seventy times seven, by which He meant that we ought never cease to forgive our neighbor, but continually carry the spirit of love in our hearts.

Our jealousies are excess baggage. They do nothing but harm us and keep us from knowing happiness. Instead of wishing for things which we cannot possess we should thank God for all the things which are ours. In fact, there are many common blessings that we do not realize we have until we visit other countries and see how our neighbors must live.

Our fears and worries are excess baggage. Constantly the Lord told His disciples not to be afraid. He assured and reassured them that He had the power to overcome the world. As long as they stayed in His presence, there was nothing of which they had to be afraid. If He cares for the birds of the air and the flowers of the field, He surely will take care of you!

PRAYER THOUGHT: *Dear God, help us to eliminate from our lives the excess baggage with which we foolishly burden ourselves, and to carry only an abiding trust in Thy wisdom and power.*

"If you would enter life, keep the commandments." Matthew
19:17

For an American abroad one of his most prized possessions
is his passport. It assures him of the rights and privileges of a
citizen of the United States of America and also affords him
sure protection.

On the inside cover of every American passport are these
words: "This passport is a valuable document. Care should be
taken to see that it does not pass into the possession of unau-
thorized persons. If it is lost or destroyed the fact and circumstances of its loss should be reported immediately to the Department of State. Any passports in such cases can be re-
issued only after exhaustive inquiry."

It has often been my thought that a life commitment to God
is just like a passport. It is by far the most valuable possession
we have. It gives us entrance each day into greater living, for
"our citizenship is in heaven." But we can be thoughtlessly
careless and lose it, too. The prodigal son lost his when he
wandered into the far-off country. He chose to give up the
prized possession of his homeland, and went in search of the
freedoms which he thought were enjoyed out there. It didn't
take long for him to discover that he had really left his freedom behind only to find an irritating slavery to the evil habits
that laid hold of him.

Thank God that even as the prodigal on his return found the
wide open arms of the father so we, too, can regain our lost
status with Him, if only we are penitent. Returning in contri-
tion we can know with certainty that, because of our faith-
relationship with Him and because of what He has done for us,
we can live life here with a new sense of glory on earth. And
what is more, we shall finally gain entry into the glories of
heaven.

PRAYER THOUGHT: *May we hold fast to the valuable possession of our commitment to Thee, dear Lord, so that we will always be prepared to go home to eternity.*

3

"It is the Lord who goes before you; he will be with you, he will not fail you or forsake you; do not fear or be dismayed." Deuteronomy 31:8

When one is about to take off for a long journey, mingled emotions come into heart and mind. Of course, there is always the excitement in anticipation of seeing new places and meeting new people. But there is also anxiety as to what the future has in store. One wonders who the captain of the ship might be, or who is piloting the plane. One has to have utter confidence in the captain or in the pilot that he is capable of bringing us safely to the destination, in order to have peace of mind.

In the journey of life we can all personally know the Captain. This is not always true in the other travels that we take. But we may not only know our Captain; we can have complete confidence not only that He has been on this journey before and knows the way, but that He will lead us safely to the place where we want to go. The captain of our life is God.

What is your concern about the future? Are you worried that you will not safely arrive at your destination? There is really nothing about which to be concerned, if we will but put our trust in our heavenly Father. Now our children trust us as parents. Even in the midst of busy traffic they will cross the street with us, if we are holding their hands. If we will but stay close to God and go where He wants us to go, we shall surely reach the destination He intends for us each day. Finally we shall attain man's ultimate goal which is heaven above.

There are other voices that will try to lure you astray along the way. The broad way leads off from the narrow with wide inviting turn-offs. We must choose with care the one we follow, because there is only one way which leads to the place where we would want to be for an eternity. That is God's way.

PRAYER THOUGHT: *Dear God, we thank Thee for the wonderful confidence which we may have in Thy divine direction, and humbly ask that Thy guidance may never leave us.*

> Set your minds on things that are above, not on things that are on earth. Colossians 3:2

Standing in line at the Idlewild International Airport, I was waiting to weigh in for my trip abroad. As my turn came and I stepped to the counter to hand my ticket to the agent, I asked him about the weather. As he pointed heavenward, he said, "It is always beautiful up there!"

Many times while in flight the pilot will announce that they are about to climb to a higher altitude in order to avoid turbulence. It's a rule that the higher the plane climbs, the smoother the airways become. God has meant that we should live our lives on the heights. The closer we live to Him, the more smooth and more beautiful life will become. Regardless of outward circumstances, if we stay close to Him, it is "always beautiful up there."

Many are content to live on life's lowlands. Now this is a dangerous place to be. I have seen great rivers that have poured over their banks because of the swelling flood waters until streets and houses were inundated in those lowlands. People have tried to reclaim the few irreparably damaged things they have left after such a calamity. Their houses become silt laden and dirt encrusted, and many of their possessions are simply washed away.

It is important that you decide just where you want to choose to live. The ideals that you determine for your life, your hopes, your dreams, and your aspirations all dictate what your destiny will be, not only in this world, but also in the world to come. To be sure, God has appointed you to become the architect of your own life. But He would also like a part in choosing your building site. He knows how important this is for your future happiness. So why not choose to live on the highest plane? That is where God is. "It is always beautiful up there."

PRAYER THOUGHT: *Help us to keep before our eyes a vision of Thy will for our lives, dear Lord, and enable us to follow Thy guidance with complete trust that all will be used by Thee for our best spiritual welfare.*

"My presence will go with you, and I will give you rest." Exodus 33:14

Seated next to a stranger on the plane as we were making our international flight, I began talking with him about the wonders of our modern world and what staggering changes have taken place even in our lifetime. Isn't it true that more technological changes have taken place in the last twenty-five years than in the previous five hundred? Not many years ago it would have taken days to cross the ocean. Now in this jet age it is possible to fly across in a matter of a half dozen hours. I was relating what Captain Eddie Rickenbacker had told me only several weeks before. It was his opinion that soon we would be crossing the Atlantic Ocean in one hour and the Pacific Ocean in two hours.

Suddenly the plane lurched as we hit a bit of turbulence and then righted itself until our ride again became smooth. We sat there in silence for a moment, a silence broken only by a voice over the loudspeaker system. "This is your pilot speaking from the cockpit. We have now reached our cruising altitude of thirty-two thousand feet. The weather is fine. We should have a smooth journey along the way and we hope to be landing at our destination in a matter of a few hours." When the pilot had finished speaking, this new-found friend turned to me and said, "Isn't it reassuring to hear the voice of the pilot telling us that all is well?"

Life is likewise a journey. Sometimes as we travel along we are jolted by the turbulence of life about us. But if we take time to be still and attentively listen, we shall be able to hear the voice of the Pilot telling us that all is well. The great God has a steady hand on the controls and can safely direct us through this life into the future life He has promised for those who have accepted Him and remain faithful to their commitment.

PRAYER THOUGHT: *Lord, we pray that we will always take heed and willingly listen to Thy comforting voice coming through the confusion and distractions of this life.*

If we confess our sins, he is faithful and just, and will forgive our sins and cleanse us from all unrighteousness. 1 John 1:9

Before entering a foreign country one is required to check through the customs office. Sometimes the customs inspectors open your every piece of baggage in order to learn whether you are bringing contraband articles into the country. For example, some countries restrict firearms and narcotics.

All of us want finally to arrive at the destination of eternal life in heaven. Just so there are certain things that we cannot take with us each day, if we want to enjoy even a heaven on earth. And there are certain desires that we cannot have along when our final day comes, if we expect to get on through the pearly gates of heaven. Our entire life is exposed to God. He knows all things and He sees all things. There is absolutely nothing that we can hide from Him.

There is one thing above everything else that He doesn't want to find in our life, and that is love for sin. Now all of us are sinners and have come far short of any standards which He has made for us. None of us has the power to rid himself of his own sins. Must man therefore conclude, "I am caught in the horns of an impossible dilemma and there is nothing left for me to do!"

Thank God, however, man does have a way out! There is forgiveness in the great heart of God, and its only condition is that man daily repents and grieves over the things he has done wrong. Never allow your unforgiven sins to accumulate day upon day, or they will constitute a burden so great as to break you down. The call of the gospel is to come to the mercy seat of God to confess your sins and there receive the assurance of the great love of God who is not only willing to forgive your sins, but also to forget them. The divine invitation which was made possible by the nails on the Cross now invites from the empty tomb: "Come!"

PRAYER THOUGHT: *We thank Thee, Lord, for Thy grace which enables us to put down the burden of our sins and to take up the joy of Thy forgiveness.*

I consider that the sufferings of this present time are not worth comparing with the glory that is to be revealed to us. Romans 8:18

When in London, it was my privilege to hear one of the great preachers of our day, Dr. Leslie Weatherhead. He and his people had endured much tension and difficulty during the devastating bombings of the war. Yet in the midst of it all Dr. Weatherhead continued to preach the glory of the good news of the gospel of Jesus Christ. People swarmed to the church where he preached in order to hear him. In fact, one had to be on hand early on a Sunday evening to find a place to sit.

On this particular Sunday, this great messenger of God spoke on death. He set forth the beautiful promises of the Bible as he told of the glories that shall come to all of us, if we will only put our trust in Christ as a Savior. That day he interpreted the words of our Lord: "Let not your hearts be troubled; believe in God, believe also in me. In my Father's house are many rooms; if it were not so, would I have told you that I go to prepare a place for you?"

He related an incident concerning one of his parishioners, a shining Christian saint who was now lying on her deathbed. He said, "I went to her hospital room and held her hand as I prayed that she might continue to have faith while in this valley of the shadow. As I stood there, a radiant smile came over her face. She drew her hand from mine as if to say, 'Don't hold me back!' "

The glory which she foresaw at this moment awaits all of us who in simple, childlike faith accept Jesus. What lies beyond no eye has seen and no ear has heard. We the living have not had revealed to us the secrets of that heavenly home. Yet, of one thing we can be sure: God will be there waiting for us when He calls us away from this world. He has invited us to live with Him forever, if we but choose to follow His way here.

PRAYER THOUGHT: *We pray, dear Lord, that we will so build our lives on this earth that we may some day live in the glory and majesty of Thy eternal kingdom.*

Unless the Lord builds the house, those who build it labor in vain. Psalm 127:1

The city of London was unmercifully hammered by bombs during World War II. The House of Commons was almost completely a shambles. After the war was over Englanders thought it should be rebuilt according to the original plans. But the old blueprints were nowhere to be found, even after a thorough exhaustive search.

However, they finally were uncovered under very odd circumstances. The government made an appeal for old papers that might be used in the process of manufacturing munitions. People rummaged through their old attics to answer the call. An architect member of an old firm, rummaging through stacks of old files, made a marvelous discovery. Among the dusty papers he discovered the long sought for plans of the House of Commons. He took them to the authorities who verified them as being authentic. Today a visitor can see the House of Commons rebuilt according to its original plan which had been so long lost and then so curiously recovered.

The parable here is almost self-evident, and it is one which would be well for us to consider for our everyday living. The world is being torn apart, and we do not know how to rebuild it. The reason for this dilemma is that we have laid aside the age-old plan of God. Our lives are in need of help, but in many homes the Holy Bible which has the only workable plan for living has been relegated to some cluttered corner. God's blueprint for the reconstruction of life must be seriously followed, if we are to have peace. His blueprint for eternity clearly indicates to us that by building a life of faith resting in His promised strength we shall never need fear to face Him on that last day.

PRAYER THOUGHT: *Teach us, gracious God, to follow Thy plan and to build on Thee as the foundation of our lives, going often to Thy Word for guidance.*

"There are those who rebel against the light, who are not acquainted with its ways, and do not stay in its paths." Job 24:13

The setting for this particular incident happened to be London. Welfare workers found an 85-year-old hobo living in an abandoned sewer drain. Immediately they decided that something had to be done about this strange situation. They arranged to move him from his wretched living quarters to a comfortable home for the aged, but the old man refused to move. "I am happier here," he drawled as he stretched out on his bed of straw in his narrow hide-out. So he stayed there until his day of death.

This situation seems unbelievable. Why would a man prefer the smut and dank smells of a dirty sewer to sunshine and clean fresh air? But aren't there people just like that about us today? They prefer their sinful ways rather than living in the light of God's love.

Christ comes to offer His children two great opportunities. One of these is eternity, a chance to live for ever and ever with Him in the mansions eternal. Those who accept this opportunity live in the constant knowledge that they are saved forevermore. In this company of people there is no fear of death, for death has been swallowed up in victory.

The second opportunity and the one most often overlooked is the way of life that Christ offers His children on earth. So many people say, "Excuse me for the time being. Maybe when I'm older I'll consider becoming a Christian." These people forget what they miss by not becoming a Christian today. The Christian way of life is the only way that will bring to its travelers abiding peace and joy. Today commit your life to Him. If you do, you will have a wonderful journey through life and a still more wonderful future in heaven.

PRAYER THOUGHT: *Dear Lord, we are thankful that we have the opportunity to share in the blessings which belong to those who know Thee as their guardian and guide in this life and in the life to come.*

"The winter is past, the rain is over and gone. The flowers appear on the earth, the time of singing has come, and the voice of the turtledove is heard in our land." Song of Solomon 2:11, 12

A Christian pastor in London has told about visiting a poor widow who was occupying a bleak small garret room in a dirty slum area of the city. Among her few possessions was a clay flower pot in which grew a stunted geranium plant. She faithfully watched this little plant with tender care. On one of his visits to her room the pastor asked why she took such careful pains to keep the puny plant alive. "It keeps telling me," she replied, "that God is here."

All about us each day there are miracles created by the hand of God. Winter comes and with it falls a mantle of snow that covers the earth. One wonders about how the roots of the grass of the warm summer days can now survive. And yet there comes spring when the earth is kissed by the sun's warm rays, and the rains descend, and the green mantle once again covers the earth. The trees which have appeared dead now break forth into bud and soon are adorned in all their leafy finery. The seeds which have been lying dormant in the cold ground break forth into green stems and beautiful flowers. These are all miracles which we so often forget. Let them remind us each day that God is here and very near.

Beyond that which is without, there is a voice within that reminds us that God is very near. As we live each day in an abiding relationship with Him we can trust that voice. It will tell us what to do as well as what not to do. Likewise, it will give us the assurance that we are not alone in the world, but that we are in company with an unconquerable partner who is the almighty God himself. God is here.

PRAYER THOUGHT: *Teach us, almighty God, to look for Thy miracles as they are evidenced in the wonders of earth and nature, so that they may remind us that we are never far from Thy love and grace.*

"I will show him how much he must suffer for the sake of my name." Acts 9:16

In walking among the English people along the streets of London, one is surrounded by the rich historical background of this nation. Among the countless outstanding personalities who had an influence in molding this history was the great navigator, Sir Francis Drake. When he needed sailors for his expeditions, he recruited young men along the coast of England. He did not tell them that life on the English sea vessels would be easy. Rather he told them the most harrowing experiences of the sailors of the deep. He related to them some of the narrow escapes he had experienced in the years of his sailing. When his tales were finished the young men usually became so excited they actually ran away from their comfortable homes to join Drake on his dangerous expeditions.

The Lord is constantly recruiting people to help Him in the building of His kingdom here upon earth. He does not promise an easy way to those who hear His challenge and follow after Him. The world which is the Lord's competitor does promise a way of ease. "Broad is the way that leads to destruction," says the Scripture warning.

The Lord has said, "If any man would come after me, let him deny himself and take up his cross and follow me." If we are following in the footsteps the Lord has planned for us, we have embarked on a very exciting journey. There are unquestionably going to be risks and perils along the way. There are crosses that must be faced. There are the jeers of the mob to be endured. There are temptations to be resisted. There will be heartaches from being misunderstood. But above everything else there is a grace that comes from the power of the Almighty which enables us to endure. This grace helps us to endure and emerge victoriously.

PRAYER THOUGHT: *O Lord, we pray that we may not choose the comfortable rut of worldly endeavors, but rather that we may be given the strength to endure the hardships of this world, in order to build Thy kingdom among men.*

"Watch and pray that you may not enter into temptation."
Mark 14:38

A number of years ago the entire dome of St. Paul's Cathedral in London, of Christopher Wren fame, had to be replaced at an enormous expense because dry rot had developed in its timbers. The workmen used every scientific method available to determine the cause of this premature decay. After careful research they discovered that a small fungus had found its way into the wood and had slowly deteriorated the wood fibers, thus at length destroying the strength and the glory of the structure.

Sin operates in much the same way. If we are not on the alert, it can enter into our lives so quietly and imperceptibly that we are all unaware of it until collapse exposes the spiritual decay which has set in. Frequently we are careless about the little things in life. We don't think they are very significant. We make one compromise, believing it will not matter much. And then we are led to make a second and a third, until finally the spiritual tissues of our lives are destroyed, thus enabling the evil one completely to destroy us.

That man is wise indeed who is daily alert to the temptations that surround him. Even the smallest of sins is yet a sin in the sight of God. Don't let it get a foothold on your life, because if you do it may very well ultimately destroy this temple of your body which is meant for God. Many a person could trace his ruin to a weak moment when he succumbed. Many an individual could also trace his peace of soul to that moment when he felt the grave depths of his sin, and turned penitently to God. Then he found forgiveness, restoration, and a new power to face life. These gifts are ours because of God's love.

PRAYER THOUGHT: *Precious Lord, may we ever be on guard against the insidious forms of evil which seek to enter our souls unnoticed in order to destroy them, and may we always seek to build up our strength in Thee.*

He who speaks the truth gives honest evidence, but a false witness utters deceit. Proverbs 12:17

It was in London where I noticed that a florist put on display in his flower shop a beautiful arrangement of artificial flowers. They were made so artfully that it was easy for the untrained eye to mistake them for living ones. Somewhere in the bouquet, however, there was one real flower. A notice on the vase challenged passersby to pick out the living blossom. Many of them stopped by to decide which was the live flower, but very few of them could distinguish the real from the artificial.

Very often we Christians work and act too much like the people of the world. In observing our actions, people unfortunately cannot always tell that we have committed our lives to the Master. We act one way while in the company of the friends of Jesus and another way while we are in the fellowship of the worldly. In reality we are being two people in one. Surely our fellow men must at times be confused. It is sometimes difficult to see through the veneer of life and thus to separate the artificial from the real.

However, even though we can confuse our fellow men about our real loyalties, we cannot hide our real self from God. He knows the difference between the Pharisee in us and the publican. He sees deep into our hearts and can tell whether we are merely going through the forms of religion without putting our beliefs into honest practice. If our faith means to us what it should, we will want to live it in our daily lives. Indeed, it will be an inseparable part of us. God's power set in our lives by faith is the only power that can help us meet and conquer the many problems we face each day. Draw near to Him and live in His plan.

PRAYER THOUGHT: *Dear Father in heaven, we pray that we may be genuine Christians in all that we do, so that we give true witness to our faith in Thee and do not mislead others by revealing false exteriors.*

14

When I sit in darkness, the Lord will be a light to me. Micah 7:8

While traveling in England I was told about a wonderful incident which can show us how adversity and misfortune can be turned into prosperity. It is good for us to remember that although God does not cause bad things to happen, He still can use them not only to His own glory, but to the glory of those who are afflicted.

This instance comes out of World War II. A young man had been hailed as a promising artist. Then he was drafted into the armed services as a pilot. After England became embroiled in the world-wide controversy, he was involved in an accident in the course of duty. Now he lay in a hospital with both his legs crushed. Moreover, a skull fracture had severed an optic nerve leaving him stone blind. Fighting courageously for his life, after a long time walking on crutches, he left the hospital.

Back home he was busily arranging blocks on a work table. "Since I can't paint any more," he said smiling through his blindness, "I am going to try building houses." Today he is one of Britain's foremost architects. That young man could have spent his years wallowing in self-pity, but God gave him the faith to develop his artistic talents despite his blindness.

Whenever we come to what appears to be a dead-end street, we should look around. God will always provide for us another avenue, a road that leads somewhere. No man is ever defeated until he thinks he is. Even then, with the power of God operative in one's life, there can still be failure, for men are sinners and often refute God's will. But if, drawing on His strength, we still keep pressing on, we can be sure that ultimately we shall find the open door into the land of abundant living.

PRAYER THOUGHT: *Whenever we come to the dead-end streets in our lives, Lord, help us to remember that, with Thy help, they can become the throughways on the road of salvation.*

Love one another with brotherly affection. Romans 12:10

When I was in England I was told about an incident that happened during the past world war. Three Minnesota GI's were on their way one Christmas Eve to downtown London. If they had been at home they would have gone to the church of their choice, because they were Christian boys. As they were driving along in their jeep they noticed a big building. Above the entrance was a sign which read, "Queen Anne's Orphanage." Underneath were these words: "Here are orphans whose parents were killed in the bombing of London."

They decided to stop and spread a little Christmas cheer. As they entered the building they found no Christmas decorations nor any presents, but just a group of lonesome children huddled together. They shared what few things they had which included some trinkets, a few odd coins, and an assortment of pencil stubs, pocket knives, and keepsakes. Finally one of the GI's saw a little fellow sitting in a corner by himself. He walked over to him and looked into his clear, blue eyes as he asked him this question, "And sonny boy, what do you want?" Without any hesitation the young lad replied, "Please sir, please sir, I want to be loved!"

From the mountainous regions of North America to the dessert areas of northern Africa to the place where you live this is the universal cry, "I want to be loved!" It is the one and the only language which all people of all backgrounds and of all lands can understand. It is the language which our Lord spoke and lived. If we speak and live this language of love we shall not only be helping to build a better world, but we shall be doing the will of God and hastening the coming of His kingdom among all men.

PRAYER THOUGHT: *Help us, dear Lord, to use only the living language of love in our relationship with others, and to bury the dead language of indifference.*

He will set me high upon a rock. Psalm 27:5

One stormy night a sailing vessel was battered and wrecked off the rock-strewn shore of Cornwall, England. Everyone on the ship drowned except a young Irish lad. He was tossed about by the rolling waves until finally he was thrown high on a jagged rock. There the pounding waves reached for him. Miraculously, however, he did not drown or freeze.

The next morning searchers hunting for any possible survivors along the beach found him through their powerful glasses. Immediately launching a boat they rowed out to that rock where the boy was isolated. By this time he was almost dead from cold and exposure. Tenderly he was lifted to the lifeboat and brought ashore.

Upon being given every medical attention and good food, after a few days he felt much better and soon was physically strong enough to tell about his experiences. One newspaper reporter asked, "Lad, didn't you tremble on that rock in the great storm?" He smiled and said, "Tremble? Sure I trembled, but that rock didn't tremble once all the while."

For all of us there will come times when, up against the anxieties and terrors of life, we will be afraid. These moments of fear become more intense when we look to ourselves. We sense a deep inadequacy to face the storms of life. There is, however, a source of power available for each one of us. It has been tested throughout the centuries. It is the power of Almighty God. The foundation of our salvation is the Rock of Ages. Upon the Cross God demonstrated that He was not only willing to die for man, but also willing to offer him a sure refuge for his life that would stand unshaken, no matter how fiercely the storms of life might rage.

PRAYER THOUGHT: *Almighty God, whenever we come face to face with our own inadequacy in overcoming the trials of life, we are comforted by the knowledge that Thou art a sure and strong source of strength which is ever ready to help us.*

Thou, O Lord, hast not forsaken those who seek thee. Psalm 9:10

Stories coming out of England in the wake of the recent war continue to give evidence to the power that comes from faith in God. If we are to have the staying power of faith, we must trust in Him not with an air of indifference and nonchalance, but with a passionately determined choice. So it is that we really come to know Him. "You cannot saunter through the gates of the kingdom with hands in pocket," said a wise Christian. And he is so right!

Consider the philosophy of a woman living in London during the terrible blitz bombings. While the whole city was living tense with fear, she appeared to be trustful and calm. Someone asked her, "How can you possibly maintain such a serene spirit?" She replied, "When I go to bed at night I pray God to take care of me. And then I believe that He will. Then I say that there is no reason for both of us to stay awake, so I go to sleep and let God take over."

We need to realize that God stays on duty every day, twenty-four hours a day. Is this the measure of our faith? Do we really believe that God's powers are unlimited? Will we trust Him to work in us to solve our every problem? Will we heed His plan for us?

He never yet has let anyone down. We can believe in Him. Over and over again He has proved himself. He has performed miracles in unnumbered lives in every generation. You have seen them happen, and so have I. He touches a life with His wonder-working right hand. He stills the storms and gives the peace that passes all human comprehension. He will do it in your life, too. Now let God into your heart.

PRAYER THOUGHT: *Teach us, Lord, to cease from living in anxiety and care about the future, and to place our trust fully in Thy power and wisdom.*

"Show kindness and mercy each to his brother." Zechariah 7:9

A poor old lady often walked the streets of an English town. Wherever she walked she kept her eyes downcast always looking for something. Occasionally she stopped to pick up an object and put it in her apron. One day a policeman halted her and asked her what she was doing. Then she opened her apron which was full of broken bits of glass, nails and other sharp objects she gathered from the street. "I pick them up every day," she said, "because I have discovered that many barefoot children come this way and, you see, they might cut their feet."

What a different world this would be, if each one of us would have that kind of deep and simple concern for our fellow men. There are many people who by the example of their lives are forever throwing sharp objects into the streets of life that can hinder and hurt. It might be only a careless word spoken, an untruth, a sharp word that hurts and condemns.

There are others who do not intentionally try to bring misfortune upon their fellow men; but like the priest and the Levite in Jesus' familiar parable of the good Samaritan, they simply pass by, absorbed in thinking only of themselves and their petty needs, completely oblivious to the welfare of their fellow men. Then there are those like this old woman constantly seeking to use their every resource to make it easier for fellow wayfarers along life's way.

Jesus during His entire lifetime went about doing good. He was forever putting His genius to work in making life more abundant for all He met. His hand of mercy was ever extended to those in need. The old woman of whom I spoke was but following the steps of her Lord as she went about doing good. Now you go and do likewise!

PRAYER THOUGHT: *Teach us, Lord, not to harden our hearts against the misery and need which we see about us, but to seek out every way in which we may show compassion to others as we follow Thy example of love and mercy.*

The Lord is near to all who call upon him. Psalm 145:18

A pastor in a certain village in a rural part of England visited one of his parishioners who had become ill. The parishioner said that he found it very difficult to sense the presence of Christ in his sickroom. The pastor then suggested that they place a vacant chair by the man's bedside. He said, "Now when you pray just imagine that Jesus is sitting in that chair by your side." An almost unbelievable change soon came into the life of this man. Whenever anyone came to visit him he would ask about this vacant chair. If anyone made as if to sit down in it, the sick man would say, "That chair belongs to the Lord. He always sits there and we often talk to each other during the day."

One day the pastor received a hurried call to come to the home of this same man immediately. His friend had taken a sudden turn for the worse. He rushed to the home, only to find that the man had just passed on to his eternal glory. The pastor found him in his bed with his hand outstretched and resting on the vacant chair. It was as though God sitting close to him had bent over to say, "Yea, though you walk through the valley of the shadow of death, fear no evil, for I am with you." And trustfully in the moment of release the sufferer had reached out his hand.

Is the presence of God that real in your life? When your faith gets that robust, there is real power for living. There is nothing at all finally of which to be afraid. The Lord is closer to you than the very breath that you breathe. He is present with all the glow and radiance of His person to keep you going. Let Him be your ever-present friend and comfort in all of your activity and living.

PRAYER THOUGHT: *We pray that we might be ever mindful of how close Thou art to each of us, dear God, if only we seek Thy presence through faith and prayer.*

Be strong in the Lord and in the strength of his might. Ephesians 6:10

In the days just before the French Republic collapsed under the onslaught of the Germans, Winston Churchill was called to the French conference rooms for counsel. He said to the French generals, "These are your armies? Where then are your reserves?" They replied, "We have none." He knew then that the future of this Republic was doomed.

What about your life? Do you go on living day after day without attempting to build up reserves for the more critical moments that may unexpectedly come? Life cannot be lived forever on a placid sea. There are days of calm, to be sure, but there are stormy days also. It is then that we need the extra reserve we have afforded for ourselves by our growing faith in the Lord in order to keep the boat of our life stabilized. It is then that we need a power beyond our own to keep us going.

It is the promise of God that there are available for us spiritual resources unlimited. The great creative God did not place us in this world to face life all alone. A great scientist once said in effect, "One of the reasons I came to a religious faith is the fact that I could not believe that a great God would create children in a world like ours and then leave them alone. So I turned to God and I discovered the power that I needed for daily living."

How are your spiritual reserves? Are you each day in contact with Him who has the power to give you all that you need? For every burden He will send us the strength to bear it. Are you daily attuned to Him in prayer? Are you allowing Him to come into your life to rule and direct it? Are you walking in the way He has planned for you to go? Are you building your life for eternity?

PRAYER THOUGHT: *Dear God, we pray that as we encounter the battles of life we shall not be without the full reserves of faith, and that we may daily remain close to the store of power and strength which comes from fellowship with Thee.*

It is good to give thanks to the Lord, to sing praises to thy name, O Most High. Psalm 92:1

Over the doorway of a little chapel in England have been inscribed these two words: "Think-Thank." On seeing this inscription, one must pause before entering. What significance do these words have for the Christian? We must think about our blessings. So often we fail to do this. We are prone to complain and grumble over that which we do not have. We become envious and jealous of those who possess more than we. We are so unwilling to count our blessings and then to see how wonderfully blessed we have been because of God's love for us.

Let us think for a moment today of only a few of these gifts from God. Think of what your life would be like if Christ had not been born. Think of how hopeless your situation would be if He had not given His life upon the cross where He died for your sins. Think of how dark the future would be if He had not conquered death and risen from the grave. Suppose you had to live this day alone. Suppose He had not promised to be with you always, even to the close of the age. Suppose you had to walk life's uncharted course alone and depend upon your own power and resources to handle whatever difficulties might come your way.

But, thank God, as we think upon these things we know at the same time that God did send His Son into the world, that He did die upon the cross, that He did raise himself from the dead. Let us thank God for all He has done. Indeed, when we think even for a brief moment about how completely dependent man is upon the mercies of God, we are led to do nothing else but fall upon our knees in gratitude for His love. We are richer than kings, for we have been called to be the loved children of a great God. To that almighty God we send our prayer of thanks this day.

PRAYER THOUGHT: *Teach us, gracious God, to reflect on the matchless gifts of grace which we have received from Thee; and as we think on these things, let us also thank Thee.*

Then he showed me the river of the water of life, bright as crystal, flowing from the throne of God and of the Lamb. Revelation 22:1

Two desert Arabs met in England while there for a visit. They were fascinated by the many things they had never seen before. The modern gadgets and conveniences on every hand were entirely new to them. It was a totally different world into which they had stepped.

What fascinated them most was that they could turn a faucet and water would pour out. They toyed with that faucet, never ceasing to be amazed that even hot water would pour out. They begged their guide to get them two such faucets, so that they could bring them back to the Arabian desert. The puzzled guide asked, "What would you do with these in a desert?" They answered, "Then we can have hot water back in Arabia."

These men had made the mistake of failing to see that back of the faucet were the pipes, the pumps, the filter, the endless channeling from the water sheds, as well as the workers and the millions of dollars invested all in order that water might freely flow.

Your life and mine can be likened to a faucet. If we attach it to air pressure only, nothing comes forth. If we attach it to the business and social world, there is only a sizzle and a sputter when we turn it on. When we attach it to God's infinite reservoir of greatness and mercy, tremendous blessings flow forth. There is an endless supply of life-giving water adequate to satisfy our every need. We need not worry that the well might go dry. For we are always in touch with Him who has the capacity not only to set the springs flowing, but ever to renew them. The water that we draw from His well is satisfying for He has said, "Whoever drinks of the water that I shall give him will never thirst."

PRAYER THOUGHT: *We thank Thee, Lord, that we are able to drink of the pure and sweet water which comes from Thee, which is able to quench every human spiritual thirst.*

This is the gate of the Lord; the righteous shall enter through it. Psalm 118:20

Travelers in Norway always remember the beautiful and silent fjords, with the grand mountains rising all about them, and the beautiful cascades of water making music as they hurry down the cliffs to the open sea. As you board a boat and sail along on one of these walled-in streams, you can stand on the deck of the vessel and see the channel ahead of you. All of a sudden it looks as though it were coming to a blind end. It would appear that you are sailing straight into the mountain ahead. You are confident that if the boat keeps going as it is now, in a few hundred yards it will crash against the side of the mountain. But just when progress seems impossible another channel opens up around a bend in the stream which you have not seen before, and the boat moves out into yet another unexplored fjord of enchanting beauty.

As we reflect on this experience, we discover here another parable for life. Men travel along the pilgrimage of life. It seems as though we come head-on into an unsurmountable mountain which might be disappointment, sorrow, sin, or even death itself. But if we travel life's way with God, we shall always find another opening that leads into far more glorious living than we have ever known before. Many people have discovered that at the very time when it did not seem worth while for them to keep on striving, God had brought renewed hope into their life in a way they had not been able to foresee. Behind every door that closes to us there is another one that stands open to new opportunities and encouragements. And even when it comes to the end of life that gate will swing open, allowing us to travel from this world into a far more breathtakingly beautiful world to come.

PRAYER THOUGHT: *Almighty God, we are thankful that as we travel through this life we have Thy blessing and guidance to lead us out of peril and into pathways of glory.*

Happy is he whose help is the God of Jacob, whose hope is in the Lord his God. Psalm 146:5

One of the greatest souls in the church history of Norway was Bishop Eivind Berggrav who has now passed on to eternal glory. He bravely resisted the Nazis at the time of World War II during their occupation of his country. The Nazi officials were afraid to do him bodily harm because of the great following the bishop had. On the occasion of my visit with him in Oslo he related to me a parable concerning his interpretation of death.

A father went with his son one day to visit a nearby town. On the way they had to cross a weak old bridge. The son was obviously frightened as he looked down at the rapid and swirling waters below. Apparently the son had worried all day long during their visit to the neighboring town because he knew they would have to cross this same bridge on the way back home. He knew it would be dark by that time; he was desperately afraid.

Late afternoon came when father and son started their journey home. The father could sense the nervousness of his son, so he picked him up in his arms and carried him along the journey. It wasn't long before the tired lad was fast asleep in his father's arms. When the boy awakened he was very surprised to discover that he was home, that it was morning, and that the sun was shining brilliantly. Along with his father he had gone safely on the way.

Said Bishop Berggrav, "So it shall be at the end of my life. In the twinkling of an eye I shall be with God. There is nothing of which to be afraid," he continued, "so long as I am in the presence of Him who has power over life and power over death. He is able to conquer even the greatest enemy of mankind." In that hope we may all live, if we but continue to have faith in Him.

PRAYER THOUGHT: *We thank Thee, Lord, for the everlasting arms which carry us through the shadowed valleys in our lives as we place our trust in Thee.*

Come and hear, all you who fear God, and I will tell what he has done for me. Psalm 66:16

Bishop Eivind Berggrav, of whom we spoke yesterday, was at one time during the last world war under Nazi guard. When visiting with him in Norway before his recent death, I was told how his eleven-man guard was changed constantly to keep them from coming under his spiritual influence. The Nazis knew they were dealing with a man who knew Christ at first-hand and they dared not take any chance with him. They knew that such a man of strong faith may merely by his character influence his guards to change their loyalty from the Nazi philosophy of Europe to the kingdom of God. What a powerful witness the bishop was to the thousands of people in his own country of Norway and throughout the world as he refused to capitulate but chose rather to hold fast in his faith.

How wonderful are the lives of those who like Bishop Berggrav can say, "I have tried God's promises; I have committed my life to Him. He is able to do all that which He has promised me. He has not disappointed me, for He is with me in times of happiness and in times of despair. If I call on Him when I need Him, he is there. When I pray to Him, I know that he is listening, and out of His love He will send an answer."

Each day we read about some manufactured product, what it is to do and why we should purchase it. There are advertising campaigns going on all the time. It is always more effective when someone witnesses to what the item has meant to him personally. So it is with our Christian faith. When we commit our lives to God, we shall know that His promises are true. Others, seeing that we have tested these promises, will be led to a renewed faith in the Lord as well.

PRAYER THOUGHT: *Teach us, almighty God, to trust the witness of those who testify to their faith in Thy power; may we renew our personal commitment to Thy will for our lives.*

Do not enter the path of the wicked, and do not walk in the way of evil men. Proverbs 4:14

In northern Europe is found the habitat of a strange little animal called the lemming. This rodent looks something like a field mouse. It has a brownish-colored fur, black beady eyes, small ears, and a short tail. One of the most amazing things about the lemming is its foolish shortsightedness in following others of its kind.

At regular seasonal intervals of the year it seems that one lemming says to another, "Let's march to the sea." That word of restlessness is passed along until soon a great company of lemmings starts the march from the higher plateaus down to the sea. This journey might take from one to three years. It is a strange phenomenon indeed, for there seems to be no obvious reason for this mass migration. It is a death march, for almost all of the animals, numbering into the thousands, perish along the way. Those who do survive long enough to reach the coast foolishly follow their companions, plunging over the rocky ledges into the waters, and are drowned.

Many people are as foolish as that in establishing the pattern of their lives. They are easily persuaded to follow the voice of the crowd. Rather than taking the time to investigate where they might be going, they just wander along, not thinking of the fact that their ultimate destiny might be complete tragedy. Plunging blindly into situations which may have the inherent possibility of degrading one's character or harming one's spiritual life, people yet are attracted by the ways of the evil one. Wise is the man who keeps in constant touch with Him who has said, "I am the way, the truth, and the life." This is the road that leads somewhere, for it leads to everlasting life with God. He who believes in the Lord and is faithful to Him will never die.

PRAYER THOUGHT: *May we never foolishly follow the voice of conformity, dear Lord, but instead may we heed Thy call and set our life's journey only on the road to eternity.*

"I am the good shepherd. The good shepherd lays down his life for the sheep." John 10:11

In a certain town in the mountainous rural countryside of Norway one is able to visit a church that has an especially beautiful tower. Near the top of the tower is the carved figure of a lamb. This seems to be a strange location for the figure, but when one asks about the symbolism of the statue he is told this true story.

Many years ago when the church was being built, one day a workman fell from the scaffolding around the tower. The men who were working with him saw the fall and naturally were fearful that their friend had fallen to his certain death. They scrambled down to the ground as quickly as possible, expecting to find his body dashed to pieces or his bones crushed and broken. To their amazement and surprise he was virtually unhurt. It so happened that a flock of sheep was being driven past the building site at the time of the fall. Miraculously the workman had fallen on the back of one of the lambs. The animal was crushed to death, but the man's life was saved.

The carved figure of the lamb was later placed at the top of the tower to commemorate this event. Its purpose was also to remind all people who passed by or who entered that church for worship that the Son of God came to this world to give His life for His flock as the Lamb of God. He came to die that we may live forever, if only we place our faith in Him. He became our sacrifice for sin. This Good Shepherd was not forced to give His life. No one took His life from Him. Voluntarily because of His great love for us He said, "I lay down my life for the sheep." Those sheep are we who have learned that a life of faith is the greatest blessing we can know and the deepest joy we will ever understand.

PRAYER THOUGHT: *Merciful Jesus, may we be continually grateful that Thou didst sacrifice Thy life in order that we might be saved from our sins and receive eternal life.*

The free gift of God is eternal life in Christ Jesus our Lord.
Romans 6:23

Out of Sweden comes the beautiful story of a little boy wandering about among the gardens of the royal palace. Being a very shy little lad, he finally gathered up all his courage and turned to the gardener to ask if he would sell him some flowers. The gardener rebuked him sternly, saying these flowers were only for the enjoyment of the royal family and not for the commoners of the country. The youthful prince standing nearby heard the little boy's unusual request. Immediately he cut and gathered together a large cluster of flowers and handed them to the lad. When the grateful boy offered to pay the prince, he turned to him and said, "My father is not a merchant who sells; my father is a king who gives."

What a beautiful description of God this gives us! Our heavenly Father delights in giving blessings to us daily without cost. Salvation is free. Of course, it is costly in the sense that God's Son had to die upon the cross in order to make it possible. But we cannot buy it with gold or silver or precious possessions. We merely accept it in faith, believing that Christ is our Savior, and knowing that His promise is true.

God's love to us abounds every day, as is seen in the multitudes of blessings we are given, so many of which we take for granted. We are surrounded by God's love. It is a love that will never let us go, for He is a faithful God. God's power and strength come to us every moment that we live. Indeed, He sustains our very lives. He gives us the capacity to overcome any of the difficulties that we face in life. How grateful we should be to know that we are children of a King who gives and keeps on giving until eternity is ours.

PRAYER THOUGHT: *We thank Thee, heavenly Father, for the free gift of salvation, for which we can pay no price but only accept as a testimony to Thy matchless love and generosity.*

This slight momentary affliction is preparing for us an eternal weight of glory beyond all comparison. 2 Corinthians 4:17

It was while I was in Amsterdam that I heard about a man who listened each day to the music of the chimes coming from a church tower there and filling the air with sweet melody. When his curiosity had been so aroused that he really wondered at this, he went to the custodian of the church and said, "I would like to see how this beautiful music is produced." The next day when it was once again time for the chimes to be played, he was admitted into the chime room where a musician was about to go to work. While in this room the man could hear no melodies. The only sound was the thump and the clatter of the keys as they were struck. While beautiful music floated out over the city from the tower, the thump and the bang of the keys was yet necessary to make it.

There are times in life when we are so close to situations that all we see is the pain and heartache of it all. We even become so tense and worried, we begin to blame God for our sad state. We cry out that our faith in God will depend upon His getting us out of our predicament resulting in the way that we think it should be.

However, as time goes on we begin to hear the sweet sounding music that is born even out of these desperate situations in living. Scripture is indeed again true when it states that in everything God works for good with those who love Him. God sometimes chooses strange and very wonderful ways to reveal His love to His children. He saves us from what could be our destruction. We cannot judge future results by present happenings. Out of our Calvarys there may come glorious Easters, bringing the dawning of new days of hope and victories which we had never thought were in our future.

PRAYER THOUGHT: *Help us, gracious God, to look beyond the present chaos and confusion into the future, where we may see the glorious rainbows of victory and know that Thy ways are best.*

A wise man is cautious and turns away from evil, but a fool throws off restraint and is careless. Proverbs 14:16

In Belgium may be found the ruins of an old fort once thought to be impregnable, one an enemy could never take. This fort even in ruins is an impressive sight. Its concrete and steel walls are ten to fifteen feet thick and bristle with guns mounted on movable turrets. If one were to come upon it as it once was, untouched by the ravages of war, one certainly would have said, "No army exists that could swarm it. The defenders behind those stout walls are perfectly safe. This impregnable fort is a protecting shield to all people living behind it."

But history tells us that the fortress fell to a mere handful of German paratroopers. Dressed in the uniforms of Belgian soldiers, they rushed up to the guards of the fort shouting, "The Germans are coming!" In near panic they opened the gates to receive them. Once within they immediately set about to overpower the guards. Then they threw open the main door to their comrades who followed them in strength. Accordingly, this fort was conquered from within without its guns ever firing a single shot.

Beware of wolves that come to you in sheep's clothing. Each one of us has the possibility, with the help of God, to raise up a fortress around his soul. But no matter how deeply committed we may be as Christians, we are always in danger of yielding to temptation and falling into sin. So many voices are raised to deceive us, trying to get us to open the door just a wee bit that they might press in. After one compromise, a second is always easier. Instead of listening to the voice of the evil one, give your ear to the voice of the Good Shepherd who leads you along the paths of righteousness.

PRAYER THOUGHT: *Dear Lord, we pray that we may not open up the fortress of our soul to the forces of evil, but that we may receive only Thy presence, and listen to Thy voice, guiding us in the way in which we should go.*

"I am not alone, for the Father is with me." John 16:32

Many people have been killed in recent years not only by the horrors of war, but also as martyrs for their religious faith. Because of it there are many children who not only do not have homes, but who do not have living parents. Naturally they are lonely boys and girls.

One day I observed a group of German refugee children standing in line. They were being registered as they walked past a desk. There a man asked them their names and wrote these down. Among these children there was one little girl who caught my attention. She was wearing a torn dress. Her hair was uncombed, she had a dirty face, and tears were streaming down her cheeks. As she came to the desk to be registered, the man there asked her what her n a m e was. Through her tears she sobbed, "I'm nobody's nothing! I'm nobody's nothing!"

How many people there are in the world today who have that same feeling. They are lonely, for they feel that no one loves them or is concerned about them. No one cares. The feeling of not belonging and of not being attached is one that cuts deep into the heart.

Anyone who has rooted his faith in Christ knows that this will not happen to him. We are children of God. No power can destroy Him or take Him from us. We have been promised that we are fellow heirs with His Son Jesus! He will never leave us alone nor forsake us. If we choose Him, we can constantly be in His presence and know that in Him we have a friend closer than any brother. He is one who not only understands us, but also has the power to help us. No Christian need ever say, "I'm nobody's nothing." Everyone of us is important in the all-knowing sight of God. In every heartache Christ yet stands by our side.

PRAYER THOUGHT: *Dear Lord, we thank Thee for the wonderful feeling of "togetherness" we have when we know that we belong to Thee.*

"Whoever denies me before men, I also will deny before my Father who is in heaven." Matthew 10:33

The communists have tried every conceivable means to drive East German people to relinquish their faith in God. They have set up a system deliberately calculated to alienate people from their faith. Many of these people are Lutherans whose youth were instructed in confirmation courses during their early teens. Therefore, the communists set up competing classes teaching young people about how ridiculous it was to believe in God and indoctrinating them in the ways of atheism and Marxian dogma. But they do not wait until the children become teen-agers to put their propaganda program into practice. In the public schools, dominated by the communists, they try in every way to undercut the faith of children whose parents have remained true to their Christian faith and have sought to keep alive in their children a love for Jesus Christ and a desire to worship.

In one school the teacher used this device in order to ridicule God and praise the dictator who at that time was Stalin. She said to her class of little ones, "First I want you to pray to your God. I want you to shut your eyes and pray hard. Ask your God for a candy sucker and see what happens." The children prayed as they were instructed; of course nothing happened. "Now," she said, "I want you to pray to Stalin and ask for a candy sucker." When they shut their eyes a sucker was placed on each of their desks. When they opened their eyes there was the candy.

But God is not mocked. Whatever a man sows that shall he also reap, and those who sow the seeds of distrust in Him will suffer. Those who have faith in Him, even despite persecution and ridicule, will be eternally blessed not only here on earth, but in the life to come. What are you doing now to prepare your own soul and the souls of others for eternity?

PRAYER THOUGHT: *Dear Lord, we pray for strength that we may be steadfast when we meet opposition and ridicule because of our faith in Thee.*

He who looks into the perfect law, the law of liberty, and perseveres, being no hearer that forgets but a doer that acts, he shall be blessed in his doing. James 1:25

Costly gifts can either bring blessings or lead one to tragedy. Their value is dependent upon their use or abuse. The gift of freedom is a blessing, if it is used for the glory of God. On the other hand it will bring tragedy, if it leads to complacency. This is especially true of religious liberty.

Visiting East Berlin I saw many old stately buildings that had been bombed and reduced to rubble because of the ruthless ambitions of men. All that remains now are weed-grown heaps. But in the midst of that destruction and desolation now stands a chapel which Lutherans with the help of American friends have erected there. The women and children of the congregation have worked diligently to clean the brick gathered from the old church and other destroyed buildings, in order that the workmen might have materials with which to construct a place of worship. Now that it has been completed, the church is filled to capacity three times each Sunday by these faithful Christians. On the other hand, there are cathedral-like churches all over the free world that stand almost empty on a Sunday.

One asks the question, "Must Christ's church suffer persecution in order to be appreciated by His people?" This question is pertinent in relation to our own land and city. When we take the priceless gift of freedom to worship for granted, we are already sowing the seeds of disintegration. Each day we should thank God for allowing us to worship Him according to the dictates of our conscience and pledge to Him anew that we will be ever loyal to Christ and His gospel, so that this freedom may be preserved for generations yet to come.

PRAYER THOUGHT: *Gracious God, we thank Thee for the religious freedom which we enjoy and pray that we may preserve this framework of liberty by continuing in a deeper loyalty and dedication to Thee.*

The eyes of the Lord are in every place, keeping watch on the evil and the good. Proverbs 15:3

Many people have seen at firsthand the tragedy resulting from the division of the city of Berlin. In fact, a situation of total and hopeless tragedy would seem to be the story for this divided Germany with the communists controlling a part of it, and the rest of it in the free world. Those who have visited the two sections of Berlin see here a contrast that is almost unbelievable. In the free world the city is almost completely rebuilt and looks new. It is humming with production and industry. The economic conditions have vastly improved.

But when you walk into East Berlin, you have a very peculiar experience. Turning down a street called Stalin-Allee, which is one of the main streets, you see beautiful buildings fronting each side. But back of these impressive structures you find bombed-out buildings and rubble. Proud Stalin-Allee is a sham street. It is like putting a prince's coat on a dirty beggar.

Isn't this a striking parable of life itself? Many of us put on a good front to our associates. We try to mimic a favorite friend or acquaintance, or we pretend to be a person who is not our real self. However, the impression we leave does not give a true reading of our characters.

We may be able to fool our neighbors, but there is One who has an all-seeing eye. From God you can hide nothing! He sees past the thin coat of personality veneer and deep into our real selves. Each day each man needs to take an honest look at himself as he is exposed before the eyes of the Almighty. It is very difficult to live for very long pretending that you are something you really are not. Why not let God change you into what you should be and the person He would want you to be?

PRAYER THOUGHT: *Gracious Lord, we know that with Thee there can be no pretense nor artificiality, and we are grateful that Thou art able to change the ruins of our lives into an enduring structure for Thy kingdom.*

For freedom Christ has set us free; stand fast therefore, and do not submit again to a yoke of slavery. Galatians 5:1

There are many living in the eastern zone of Germany who are extremely unhappy with the restricted kind of living they have known since the communists took over the government. Among them at one time was a fine devoted couple who had fled this zone at the risk of their lives. The man had been a very successful businessman. He had owned a tailor shop, and at one time he had as many as twenty people working for him. He owned his own home and had completely furnished it in just the way he and his wife wanted it. They had lived in this community all their lives.

But after the communists moved in to set up their rule, these people lived under constant fear. They were harassed and needled by the communist police day and night. No private detail of their life was their own. The sense of fear finally became too much for them to endure. They decided that to continue in such a life was unbearable. So they fled, leaving all their material possessions behind and setting out in search of freedom.

But what is the worth of material things in comparison to the priceless value of freedom? Most of us have not known slavery such as communism has thrust upon its subjects. We do not realize the extreme physical anguish and mental torture many people must endure in the world today. Will we consider that their fate could be ours, too, if we forget to rest our lives upon the foundation of faith in God? Only by reexamining the godly foundation upon which our country was founded, and by renewed dedication to Christ, can we escape a like slavery. In our shortsighted negligence of the things of God, we stand in the possibility of losing them. Rise up, children of God, and use your faith for the building of your heavenly Father's kingdom.

PRAYER THOUGHT: *May we learn to place a higher value on the freedom we possess, dear God, and to strengthen our resolve to lead lives of deeper dedication to Thee.*

"The Spirit of the Lord is upon me, because he has anointed me to preach good news to the poor. He has sent me to proclaim release to the captives and recovering of sight to the blind, to set at liberty those who are oppressed." Luke 4:18

A certain small village of Germany was very badly bombed during the last world war. But the courageous people set out to clean up the rubble and soon were hard at work rebuilding. They were a goodly number who volunteered to help rebuild the church. When they were ready to complete the chancel the workers looked around for the statue of Christ which had stood upon the altar with hands outstretched inviting people to prayer. They found various pieces of the marble statue and had them pressed together. Although they sifted the rubble piles they could not find Christ's hands. However, they put the statue upon the altar as they had reconstructed it. Underneath was set this sign: "Christ has no hands but our hands to do His work today."

What a challenge this should be to each one of us! The Lord lived a perfect life. He spoke as no man has ever spoken. He went about doing good. He was not only man's Savior from sin, but He was our example for living. In response to the question, "Who is my neighbor?" He told the story of the good Samaritan concluding it by saying, "Go and do likewise."

Have we followed in the pathway along which He wants us to go? There is so much to be done in the world today, and yet there is so little time to do it. There is much to be done even in your own community. People are lonesome, and need your companionship. People are living in darkness, and need you to bring them the message of Christ who is the light of the world. There are people who sense their sin and need to be told of Christ who is the Savior from sin. You are the only gospel this world will read. Christ has no hands but your hands to do His work today. Will you accept the challenge?

PRAYER THOUGHT: *Gracious Lord, help us to be more willing to give not just of our money but of our selves to further Thy work.*

"In Thy hand are power and might; and in thy hand it is to make great and to give strength to all." 1 Chronicles 29:12

At the bottom of the Rhine River there is to be found a heavy iron cable. Hugging the bottom, it makes its way from shore to shore through the swiftest currents and rapids that are to be found along the whole course of this river. By grabbing this cable in their powerful gripping claws the heavy barges make their way without incident slowly steaming against the current. Other boats are frequently shipwrecked in the great storms, being blown by the wind and turned by the currents upon the rocks. But in the center of the stream as if unmindful of the storm, the barges brave every difficulty and slowly move up the current, because they are connected to an unseen guide line.

Life, too, has its storms and currents. But we are offered God's unfailing strength to rise against the storms, to keep abreast of the currents, and to sail steadily on to the harbor on the other shore. Let me, then, take hold of the cable of God's power and strength, for then I shall be able to defy whatever tide or current comes against me. But if I thrust aside the offered hand I am lost. No one has the power and the strength to go it alone through this turbulent life. Nor is it necessary for him to do so. The power and presence of God are available for each one of us, whatever our need might be.

It was Martin Luther who wrote, "Miracles take place, not because they are performed, but because they are believed." In the limited understanding of men some of the things that God is able to perform seem impossible. But our faith has told us that with God all things are possible. Believing that truth, we can face life as brave saints, for we carry with us the assurance that God is at our side, our source of help and strength.

PRAYER THOUGHT: *Everlasting God, may we ever call upon Thee to receive the power and strength which will enable us to withstand the turbulence of this life.*

38

"I will trust, and will not be afraid." Isaiah 12:2

The plight of many children around the world is greatly disturbing. Who shall be able to tell the whole story of how they have suffered through these last years because of sickness, malnutrition, and just pure loneliness? In so many countries, because of persecution and war, many thousands have been separated from their parents to wander about as homeless waifs.

The story is told of a certain group of refugee boys and girls who were plagued by an acute sense of insecurity. They had been separated from their families for a long time. They were desperate for love and the feeling of belonging. Now they had gone for days without food. They had reached the point where they cried themselves to sleep at night, because they were afraid to think of another morning without anything to eat. This persisted even after they were safe in an orphanage.

Now, when my daughter was little, and resisted being put to sleep at night, all she needed was to have her favorite doll brought to her. It was a similar plan that the workers used successfully with these orphaned children. They placed a piece of bread beside each child's bed. When the child went to sleep at night he was sure of something to eat when he awakened in the morning.

There are many children in this world dying not of physical starvation, but of spiritual need. Without any family rooting they have nothing to anchor to in the storm. No wonder they are pierced with fears when their resources are so pitifully insufficient for facing the next day. Yet all the time there stands One waiting by their side, assuring them that they won't have to face the new day in their own strength. God is able and willing to face life with them. With Him they can be more than conquerors, if they will only trust and obey.

PRAYER THOUGHT: *It is so comforting, gracious God, to know that we do not have to face the problems and perils in our lives alone, but that we have always with us the quiet strength of Thy presence.*

The God of Israel, . . . gives power and strength to his people.
Psalm 68:35

Out of the Second World War have come thrilling and nearly unbelievable accounts of reconstruction. One of these stories regards the great rose window of the Rheims Cathedral which was shattered into thousands of fragments in an air raid and bombing. People who were interested in the restoration of the church laboriously spent time to gather all the fragments they could find. They stored them away in a secret hiding place. When the war was concluded, skilled and trusted glass workers took these fragments and with painstaking care fitted them into a new pattern. The great rose window was finally reconstructed. The shattered glass was once again created into an object of new and glorious beauty. Again the light of God's sun could shine through this place of inspiration to help bless the souls of mankind.

Here is a parable of what God's creative power can do for you. If you feel that you are a broken person, in ill-health or defeated spirit, if your dreams and goals are shattered, if your spirit has been crushed with heartache and disappointment, God who is the skilled and trusted worker can take your life and recreate in you faith and poise and vitality. The promise of Scripture is "that they who wait upon the Lord shall renew their strength." Daily we should claim this promise. His resources are at all times available for us. Behold, He makes all things new. Because of Him, there need be no people without hope. When problems seem almost impossible of solution God has the answer. Would that we were more patient and let Him work things out for the best. God will heal and restore broken lives, if we but allow Him that opportunity. "If any one is in Christ, he is a new creation," is the assertion of the Apostle Paul.

PRAYER THOUGHT: *Almighty God, we know that nothing is impossible for Thee, and that Thou art gracious and powerful even to repair the shattered fragments of a broken life and mold anew a life full of happiness and hope.*

Beware lest you be carried away with the error of lawless men and lose your own stability. 2 Peter 3:17

There is a saying that goes the rounds these days: "Relax and keep your blood pressure down. Avoid anything that makes for nervous tension." This is not to make us run for cover to our comfortable homes and there live in physical ease. We are not to hide from life because we fear it is too much of a struggle. Life cannot be that easily made free of trouble. In fact, in adjusting completely to one's environment there are dangers. Conformity may lead to weak-kneed living. In failing to defend the right, we may be overrun by the wrongs of the world that so often seem so strong.

When the Nazis overran some of the countries in Europe, including Germany, some of the citizens of this country said, "We've got to be willing to adjust ourselves to the situation at hand and to those who are in power. A man must live!" Such people were known as collaborators. What then finally happened? When the country was liberated the collaborators faced trials at the hands of their countrymen who had refused to go along. Some of them who resisted had suffered long years in the concentration camps rather than to belie their basic beliefs in freedom or to give up their faith in Christ. Now some of the collaborators swung as stiffened corpses from the very gallows they had ordered built because they had conformed to the situation.

It is so easy in life to take what appears to be the easy course, to agree when you should be disagreeing, to remain silent when you should speak out for Christ. When we fail to stand up for what is true, we are in grave difficulty, because we put our soul in jeopardy. As children of God it is a part of our responsibility to live as loyal witnesses of the power and mercy of God. His charge is, "Be strong in the Lord."

PRAYER THOUGHT: *We pray, precious Lord, that we will not compromise our faith by following the easy road of conformity, but rather that we will stand firm as dedicated witnesses for Thee.*

"He who loses his life for my sake will find it." Matthew 10:39

Many heart-rending stories of courage have come out of the occupation of Germany by the Nazis. One of these is about a certain Protestant pastor who refused to give up his preaching of the gospel of Jesus Christ. The Gestapo came to his home one night and said, "Don't you know that we will throw you in a concentration camp if you continue to preach?" He replied, "That may be true. But I will still be faithful to my God." In a short while they put him in a concentration camp.

He noticed, however, that here were wooden walls. So he shouted his message from behind the blockade. Then the Gestapo came to him and said, "We will give you one more chance. If you promise to stop preaching we will give you release." "What's the alternative?" asked the pastor. "You will be shot at sunrise," was the quick reply. "I will choose the latter," said the pastor. The amazed Gestapo officer turned to him and said, "You don't have to decide now. We will give you three days to make a definite decision." Those three days came and went. Once more he was asked, "Have you changed your mind?" "No," was the staunch reply. At the next sunrise he was shot.

How many of us would be willing to pay such a great price for our faith? We have not yet been called upon in our day and in our land to die for it, but are we willing to live for it? Right now that is more important. Every day God challenges us to go forth and work in His vineyard. Let us resolve to serve Him faithfully. As He died to make men holy, let us live to make men free—free in the knowledge of salvation in Christ.

PRAYER THOUGHT: *May we daily renew our pledge to live only for Thee, precious Lord, and to serve Thee in complete loyalty and faith even unto death.*

Yield yourselves to God as men who have been brought from
death to life. Romans 6:13

Following the Second World War in many European communities, living conditions were extremely difficult to endure.
Food was scarce, and unemployment was prevalent. Ruined
homes and buildings lay all around. The future was dark and
uncertain. Yet glowing testimonies of hope came from those
for whom life had meaning. These were the brave souls who
still saw the powerful Christ towering above the ruins of man's
inhumanity to man in war. These were the ones who acknowl-
edged that a country, like a life, could be rebuilt with His
wonder-working power. Today we have seen it happen as the
free nations on the continent have set their economics back
into working operation.

A gentleman in the twilight of life who had lived close to
the Lord throughout his years, and had experienced many of
the horrors of war, turned to me and said, "It is my daily
prayer that those who follow after us might be better than we
are. They cannot be any happier, for even under severe circumstances we have known a deep peace of soul. But I pray
that they might be better. May God give them and us courage
to face the future."

Such faith gives testimony to the power of the living God.
The only way the world can become better is for people to be
changed by the power of God who alone has the capacity to
rebuild lives. With rebuilt lives the world will then know lasting peace. But it is only the yielded heart that God finds possible to change. Willingness to surrender to His will is the
prerequisite to a renewed spirit. Then what about the future?
We may trust that in His hands we will be safe, not necessarily spared from troubles, but given the strength to endure
them.

PRAYER THOUGHT: *Help us, God of life, to surrender our
hearts to Thy keeping, so that by Thy love and power we may
be transformed and at peace.*

As therefore you received Christ Jesus the Lord, so live in him, rooted and built up in him and established in the faith. Colossians 2:6, 7

A guide was taking a group of tourists through an old castle deep in Germany. Moving about from one room to the next, he was telling them about the glories of centuries ago. Finally he came forth with this statement: "This castle has stood for six hundred years. Not a stone here has been touched. Nothing has been altered and nothing replaced. The structure you see now is the same as it was when it was built in the Middle Ages." Nothing has been done to repair this building.

Scripture tells us that we are temples of the Holy Ghost, for in us the Lord dwells, and through us He accomplishes His work among men. We, too, can allow our building to go into disrepair as had been the case with this old historic German castle. Without the power of almighty God, our lives become ramshackle and tumble down. Unless we practice vigilant care, life in reality could eventually run down hill into ruin and degradation.

There isn't a single day but that every one of us commits a long line of sins. We all fall short of ever deserving the mercy of God. But the Lord has offered us a way in which we can repair our lives, if we only choose to use it. He has assured us that if we confess our sins, He will surely forgive them. He will build up anew the weakened places in our life's structure.

Rather than to run the risk of having life completely fall apart or cave in, is it not better for us each day to use the power of the Builder who is so close at hand to help us in that which we need most? Each one must decide whether he wants to use the continuing skill of the Grand Architect who framed our lives. He alone has the foresight, concern, and ability to help us so to build that our lives will be saved for eternity.

PRAYER THOUGHT: *Teach us, our great God, to maintain the strength of our souls by repentance of sins which can otherwise cause our lives to collapse into decay and despair.*

44

He has made known to us in all wisdom and insight the mystery of his will. Ephesians 1:9

Sometimes hardship and disaster are the conditions from which blessings are born. At the time all seems futile, yet amazing it is that so often what is best for us can come because of our trouble. One of numerous incidents which prove this truth to us is that from a community in Germany where stood a beautiful Lutheran church. The cathedral was damaged during one of the air raids of the last world war. The bell tower served as a huge chimney. As the smoke rushed upwards, driven by the fire below, the bells rang loudly. People said it was as though God were reminding them of the penalty for their sin and the judgment of God. Soon after the fire had spread its flames, the bells plunged to the ground in a mighty crash and lay stilled.

But the Word of God is not silenced today in this little community. The parish has rebuilt this church, which is used again for Sabbath worship and instruction in the spiritual truths. In the course of making repairs on the walls, the workmen came upon certain colorings showing beneath the plaster that had cracked and peeled because of the heat from the fire. After removing the plaster they uncovered some outstanding paintings from the thirteenth century, their colors as fresh as they were on the day when workmen covered them years ago.

When disaster comes into our life we must patiently wait to let the Lord work out what is best for us. Blessings may very well come out of our suffering, wonderful blessings which we would otherwise not have received. It has been said that every knock is a boost, and that behind every closed door there is another one open. Let us resolve with patience to trust in the Lord's good workings and have faith in His promises for the future.

PRAYER THOUGHT: *May we always seek to find Thy purpose in every misfortune which befalls us, kind Lord, and wait patiently for the light of Thy love to dispel the clouds of darkness.*

Set the believers an example in speech and conduct, in love, in faith, in purity. 1 Timothy 4:12

Switzerland is one of the most beautiful countries in the entire world. As one goes out into the villages, one finds many houses that have been built more than a century ago, and yet the occupants have used every means to maintain and beautify them. Flower boxes which grace practically every window ledge are neatly trimmed and well ordered. They are aflame with beautiful flowers that witness to the tender care given.

As I viewed these pleasing scenes, I thought about many people and the ways they conduct their lives. So often we put artificial flowers in the windows of our lives. We pretend to be someone that we really are not. It is a genuine effort for man to pose as a self other than his real self before his fellow men. Why not resolve to be honest and put the flowers of sincerity in our heart? Let us be what God wants us to be to our fellow men instead of this sham window dressing that exacts so steep a price!

Let men see in our lives the flowers of forgiveness, our willingness to forget the wrongs that have been done to us, and the will to give a man another chance, even though he may have grievously hurt us. Let God see in the window box of our life the flowers of appreciation. Instead of always complaining, let us take stock of all the things for which we can be grateful, and so let our lives express constant thanksgiving to God. Let the flowers of understanding be permanently displayed. Let us not judge our fellow men until we have tried to put ourselves in their position and have walked in their footsteps. Such a life glorifies God, and exhibits the depths of Christian love. This is the man who knows and walks with the Lord.

PRAYER THOUGHT: *Dear Lord, we pray that we may be arrayed with integrity and sincerity as we go about witnessing for Thee; help us never to put on the artificial exterior of a false Christian.*

I will instruct you and teach you the way you should go; I will counsel you with my eye upon you. Psalm 32:8

In Switzerland a traveler has told of this experience. He drove out into the countryside, but after he had gone some distance he became confused in his directions and uncertain about whether he should continue driving on this road. Finally he stopped a lad playing by the roadside and asked where a certain village was. He received a very significant answer from the boy. "I don't know where the town is, sir, but there is the road to it." All the while he pointed in the direction the man should go.

There are many things that we as Christians do not know even about our faith and the matters of the kingdom of God. For example, we do not know where heaven is, but we know the road to it. In Scripture our Lord reminds us of the fact that narrow is the road which leads to life. The only reason that many of us find ourselves confused and bewildered and lost in this business of living is that we don't follow the voice that God has provided to direct us in the way that we should go.

The Lord has not made it difficult for any of us to find peace in this life or to know the eternal security that shall be ours forever. He freely offers us both of these as gifts from Him. The only condition He stipulates is that we follow Him. If we refuse to do this and instead go the broad way, we cannot expect to arrive at the destination that He has provided which will bring us the joy that we are seeking. His is the only way that leads to eternal life. Though we do not know what the future has in store, we need not be afraid if we walk life's way with God. We don't know the place of heaven, but let us make certain that we are on the road that leads to it.

PRAYER THOUGHT: *Show us the road to eternal life, dear God and Father, and guide us daily on this path, that we may travel confidently through the unknown and into the glory of Thy heaven.*

The day of the Lord is coming, it is near. Joel 2:1

A traveler spent the night with his guide in a chalet high up in the Swiss Alps. He was awakened early in the morning by thunderous crashings and rumblings. Becoming very frightened, he finally went to the next room, aroused his guide from his sleep, and asked him, "What's happening? Is the world coming to an end?" Calmly the guide replied, "No, it is not. There is nothing of which you need to be afraid. What is happening is this: When the sun starts coming up on the other side of the mountain, its rays touch the snow at the peak, causing this snow to hurtle down the mountain. Then the warming rays play upon the surface of the glacier and cause the ice to crack with loud reports. This is what you hear. It is not the end of the world. It is only the dawn of a new day."

Many times we become frightened by the happenings of a single day. We hear of wars and rumors of wars. We see man's bitterness toward man, and the deep hatreds of nations toward other nations. We become fearful and afraid. We are distressed because things do not seem to be working out as we would like.

But God's world is not ultimately to be ruled by human force or by any man-made and godless system. On the contrary, our hope is ever that He shall reign supreme. This world will end when God determines that it shall. All will work out in His time and plan. In this attitude of trust we can live, unshaken by any fears regarding the future, for we are certain that God's plan is the best one, and that it shall be fulfilled. Each day as we live with Him, He allays our fears as He says, "Don't worry, it isn't the world coming to an end. It is only the dawn of a new day." "Lift up your heads, your redemptionn draws nigh."

PRAYER THOUGHT: *Teach us, almighty God, to be unafraid of the power of earthly forces, and confident in our knowledge that ultimately Thou shalt reign supreme over all the world.*

Our help is in the name of the Lord. Psalm 124:8

There is a famous story told in Switzerland which concerns a little hunchbacked keeper of a halfway station on a mountain climb and a big strong mountain guide named Jim. One day as Jim was leading a touring party on a climb, they stopped at the halfway station. Conversing with Hunchy, he discovered that his friend had never been to the top of Jungfrau, one of the glorious mountain peaks in the Swiss Alps. He turned to him and said, "Hunchy, tomorrow you are going with me because you have missed one of the most glorious sights of God's creation." Hunchy looked askance at his frail body and said, "Jim, it is impossible, I haven't the strength. I cannot possibly make that climb."

Jim was persistent. The next day he came to Hunchy and said, "We are going to begin." They started the climb, and for a while all went well. Hunchy would get tired, but Jim would put his strong arms around him and help him climb over the rough places. When they were almost to the top Hunchy was ready to quit, but Jim picked Hunchy up in his arms and carried him to the peak. There Hunchy surveyed the beauty about him, dropped to his knees and cried, "Jim, if it hadn't been for you I would never have made it!"

Along life's journey the great Christ is beside us all the way. Without Him we cannot ever make progress successfully, for our own strength is not enough to keep us going on. When we falter, He persistently picks us up and gives us strength to continue. He encourages us to persevere even though at times our trials may be nearly unbearable. Each step upward puts us a bit closer to our goal, the wide vistas of heaven, that God is yet preparing for His own.

PRAYER THOUGHT: *Precious Savior, we thank Thee that Thou art always ready to help us over the rough places in life and to encourage and guide us toward the new lands of eternity.*

The Lord will guide you continually. Isaiah 58:11

Rome is a city of much historical interest, for it was once the center of a highly advanced civilization, both politically and culturally. This "Eternal City" has many beautiful parks and lovely gardens. One particular day some tourists were being guided through a few of these interesting places. Among them was a little girl who was along with her parents. Late in the afternoon they came to a dense garden where the tall trees cast dark, heavy, and foreboding shadows. The guide sensing that this little girl was frightened, turned to her and said, "You don't need to be afraid. I will not take you any place where I have not been before myself." After that the fear seemed to leave the little girl's heart, for she said several times to her parents, "I am not afraid now. The guide has been here before and he knows the way."

So indeed, followers of the living Christ have a guide who knows the way all through life. We can walk confidently into any day, unafraid of any problems or troubles that may lie ahead of us, if we stay close to Him. This does not mean that all along the way the path will be smooth. But it does mean that when we face mountains of difficulty there is a proven guide who will help us scale them. With any moment of trial and with any heartache He will give us sufficient endurance and hope to walk through. Above all, He will give us the assurance of His loving presence. When there are troubles to endure there is One who is ever ready to say, "My grace is sufficient for you." Believe Him and ever live in that promise! The Christ of resurrection morning stands before you as your friend now and on into eternity.

PRAYER THOUGHT: *May we as Christians be continually fortified by our knowledge that, no matter where we go in this life or what task lies before us, we are ever blessed by Thy love and strength, Almighty Lord.*

Whatever your hand finds to do, do it with your might. Ecclesiastes 9:10

Each time I go to Rome I visit the ruins of the famed Colosseum. There I try to visualize what took place many years ago. I envision thousands of people in the stadium cheering for blood of the victims with the same gusto as we cheer at a football game today. Then I look to the arena's edge and think of the dens that were there, where were kept the famished lions roaring out their eagerness to tear apart their human prey. I look over to another side and think of the dungeons where the prisoners were kept. These were the Christians of that early era. Just before they were led to their certain death, they would be asked the question, "Do you want to keep your faith and lose your life, or will you give up your faith to save your life?" Think of the many brave souls of the past whose faith meant more to them than life and who were willing to pay the supreme sacrifice in order to prove to the world that the Lord of life stood with them even through their afflictions.

As this picture comes into mind, I think of my own life and the lives of the people with whom I rub elbows today. Would we be willing to make such a sacrifice? Thank God that we have never yet had to face such a hard choice. But we have been asked from time to time to contribute of our means to Christ and His kingdom.

Everyone has a life to give. Everyone has time, talents, and means. These are things which have been given to us as a trust. Some day we shall have to give an account of our stewardship, and the One to whom we shall give account keeps the record of what we have done and said straight. If the Christians of our day would only recapture a little of the enthusiasm and devotion of the first century Christians, unbelievable things would happen in God's world.

PRAYER THOUGHT: *Help us, dear Lord, to restore in ourselves the unflagging zeal and devotion which should be characteristic of a true follower of Christ.*

For the sake of Christ you should not only believe in him but also suffer for his sake. Philippians 1:29

One of the innumerable places of significant historical interest in ancient Rome is that of the catacombs. Here one finds silent and vivid testimony from the days when Christianity was a living and fighting force among the early Christians in Rome.

As you drive down the Appian Way, a short distance beyond the Chapel of Quo Vadis, you arrive at a small entrance. You are given a lighted taper and then told to follow a Trappist monk down some stone steps. Suddenly you are in the exact surroundings of first-century Christianity. As you stand there your thoughts race back to what activity very possibly took place here. Communion was celebrated, baptisms were held, and marriages were sealed. Here were buried the bodies of martyrs secretly brought into the catacombs. Everywhere are symbols of the early church, including the cross, the lamb, and the light. One cannot stand there without feeling the daring of those Christians. It was dangerous then to be a professing Christian. Yet they were willing to challenge the pagan world and to stand firm in their faith.

We are too frequently tempted to believe that Christianity, instead of being something costly, is a pushover. There will always be those who oppose the Lord. There will be those who claim they do not need any power other than their own. There will always be people who will ridicule those who avow that they are followers of the Lord's way. Unless we are willing to fight for our cause which we know is right and also sacrifice for it, we stand in danger of losing it. Let us be challenged by the courageous faith of those who have gone before us and who have made far greater sacrifices than we will ever be called upon to make.

PRAYER THOUGHT: *Gracious Lord, may we find a challenge in the devotion of those early Christians who witnessed for Thee by complete self-sacrifice, and resolve to renew our dedication by greater faithfulness.*

"You are my witnesses," says the Lord, "and my servant whom
I have chosen." Isaiah 43:10

On the Appian Way, immediately outside the city of Rome,
there stands a little chapel. Legend says that this is the place
where Peter the disciple of Christ had a remarkable experience. It happened during the time of the Roman persecutions
of the Christians. Peter was afraid the officials were going to
take his life. He decided that the best thing for him to do
would be to flee from the city. So he escaped down this road
leading out of Rome.

At the particular place where I stood one day legend says
that Peter came upon the Master. Naturally he was greatly
surprised to meet Him there. He asked Christ the question,
"Quo vadis?" which is to say, "Where are you going, Lord?"
The Master replied, "To Rome to be crucified anew." Immediately Peter knew what He meant. As long as Peter didn't have
the courage and conviction to stand up for his faith, the Lord
would have to go back to Rome and be crucified there again.
Legend goes on to say that Peter, utterly ashamed of his cow-
ardice as he had been that time earlier in his life, turned and
went back to Rome. His last request was that he be crucified
with his head down and his feet up, since he felt undeserving
to die in the same manner in which the Lord had died.

Frequently we must admit that we lack the courage and conviction to stand strong against temptations. We are easily discouraged and disappointed. We try to run away from the persecutions that face us, because we are afraid to stand up and
be counted as children of the Lord. Each time we fail to trust
our Lord we help in the age-old process of re-crucifying Him.
Let us resolve each day to witness fearlessly in behalf of Him
who is the King of all kings. The Lord was not ashamed to die
for us. How can we dare to be ashamed to live for Him?

PRAYER THOUGHT: *Lord, help us to reflect that courage which
Thou didst reveal on the cross as we witness everywhere for
Thee.*

"When I am lifted up from the earth, [I] will draw all men to myself." John 12:32

There is a beautiful old church in Italy where stands an alabaster pillar. Tradition says that this pillar has been preserved from the ruins of Solomon's temple. Now it is used as a support for the high altar of this church. The pillar is cut in a lovely shaft of graceful proportions. It blossoms out on the top into an exquisitely carved capital. Standing bravely in its place, it bears much of the weight of the large altar. Therefore, it has great practical value, as well as being a beautiful piece of art.

In shifting our thoughts again to our lives in the kingdom of God, does not Jesus mean we shall be beautiful in our living as well as strong in His service? Like this pillar, we are to be radiant witnesses as well as diligent servants. Perhaps too few people take enough pains to make goodness attractive to others. At times we may confuse goodness with piety or even with vanity.

The Lord said, "And I, if I be lifted up from the earth, will draw all men unto myself." Christians ought to have more of our Lord's drawing power. In watching us live, others should be prompted to ask, "What he has I, too, need for my life." Our prayer should be that we be forgiven for being poor advertisements of our faith. When we don't give evidence by our living that we have any reason to rejoice in the promises that God has given us, He is very sad indeed. The joy of our faith should be the contagious kind that will be enticing to our co-laborers. If we truly believe what we profess, we cannot help but be attractive witnesses. Because of our deeds and our testimony, in an unconscious way others will be brought to the Lord. Such is our daily challenge to be strong in His service and to be faithful to His commands that we love others.

PRAYER THOUGHT: *May we daily advertise through our lives the power of Thy love and grace, gracious God, so that others may be drawn to Thee through our witness.*

"Come, let us join ourselves to the Lord in an everlasting covenant which will never be forgotten." Jeremiah 50:5

The setting is war-torn Italy. Because of the bombings and war combat, many little children were left orphaned and homeless. This incident concerns one of these many helpless youth.

An American soldier, hurrying down a littered street one day, noticed a little boy dejectedly sitting in the ruins of what only a short time before had been his home. In a friendly tone he called out, "What's your name, sonny?" The boy answered with a half-hearted smile, "Tony." What child could be happy who had so recently lost both his parents in a bombing attack? The soldier brought the lad with him back to the camp where he was outfitted in an extra uniform and cap.

When the order came one day that all the refugee children would be sent to live at a special camp for them, the soldier explained to Tony what was going to happen to him. "Tonight after the bugle sounds taps I want you to march over to the jeep just like a brave soldier. I will drive you to a place where people will take good care of you." Night came and the boy obeyed every instruction. Bravely and with all the courage he could muster he walked to the jeep. Then he could stand it no longer. Bursting into tears he sobbed, "I can't go! I belong to *you!*"

Would that our relationship to God were as unseverable. All of us stand in need of daily forgiveness for our failing in loyalty to our God. He himself never turns His back upon us, but yet how often we flinch in our dedication to the kingdom of God. When the world tries to show us that its ways are the best, we are much too readily convinced. Yet how much deeper and more lasting are the joys of those who have made the commitment to pattern their lives after the way of the Lord. They have an unshakable faith in the heavenly Father.

PRAYER THOUGHT: *We pray, dear heavenly Father, that we might possess the joy of complete dedication to Thee, for it is through such loyalty that the richest rewards of faith can be received.*

"Come to me, all who labor and are heavy-laden, and I will
give you rest." Matthew 11:28

When passing through the city of Milan one recalls an incident which had taken place many centuries before. Lazily
stretched out beneath a fig tree in a garden lay a young man.
He had lived a wild dissolute life, tasting every forbidden fruit.
Now he was engaged in a struggle with himself and his soul.
Like the prodigal son, he had come to the end of his wander-
ings. He had thought that earthly things could satisfy him.
Now all seemed in vain. Seeking escape from his desperate
struggle, he cried out, "How long? Will not the answer come
tomorrow? Is there not some way to end my uncleanness? Is
it impossible for me to find a new beginning for my life?"

As he lay there entangled in his dilemma, there came the
voice of a child singing, "Take up and read." Opening a book
at his elbow, St. Paul's Epistle to the Romans, he read these
words, "Put ye on the Lord Jesus Christ, and make not provi-
sion for the flesh in the lusts thereof."

Suddenly we see the prodigal Augustine come to his senses.
Through this encounter with Christ he was changed to one of
the holiest of saints of the early church. From that day until
now he bears witness from his own experience that man is forever restless until he finds his rest in Christ. There is no other
way to be happy than to trust in the Lord and obey Him. This
day, as you hear His voice, resolve to give a reasonable answer.
You too will know the peace that God gives.

Precious is the moment of awakening. In Michelangelo's
work, "The Creation," Adam reclines, leaning on an elbow with
his hand hanging limp and lifeless. In sharp contrast, God, dynamic with power, stretches out His hand toward Adam, His
forefinger alive. This same God reaches just now for you!

PRAYER THOUGHT: *We pray that we may come to the foun-
tain of Thy forgiveness, gracious Lord, so that we may be
cleansed from our sins and find the peace and rest which only
life in Thee contains.*

56

"Do not lay up for yourselves treasures on earth, . . . but lay up for yourselves treasures in heaven." Matthew 6:19, 20

The great cathedral of Milan has a triple archway. Over the first arch is carved a rose. Beneath it are inscribed these words: "All that pleases is only for a moment." Over the third arch is a cross. These words are carved above it: "All that troubles is for a moment." Above the great center archway appear these significant and inspiring words: "That only is important which is eternal."

All that which pleases is but for a moment. Certainly the author here is referring to the fleeting pleasures of life. So many people spend so much of their time seeking those things which satisfy for a moment and then vanish away even more quickly at a touch. Life at its best is but a brief span of time. During the years we live, we have many important decisions to make. One of the greatest that should be made is to put first things first, to determine what things in life should have the greatest value.

All that troubles is for a moment. Here is a word of encouragement to those who are weary, worn with cares, and sad. One need not search for very long, as they may be found by the score out on the highways and byways of life and right in the middle of everyday situations. They are tempted to give in because they cannot see a way out of their problem. And yet, like the storm clouds in the sky, trouble disappears and it is sunlight again.

That only is important which is eternal. "Lay not up for yourselves treasures on earth, . . . but lay up for yourselves treasures in heaven." This life is but a preparation for a greater life to come. We have been enabled by the mercy of God to build it well on the solid foundations of trust in Him. All else in life must take a secondary position in relation to our preparation for life in eternity.

PRAYER THOUGHT: *Teach us, merciful Lord, not to place too much importance on the fleeting things of earth, but rather in this life to prepare our souls for eternity.*

"With us is the Lord our God, to help us and to fight our battles." 2 Chronicles 32:8

When in Italy I learned of a certain incident which happened during World War II. As the army of invaders was
about to strike at Sicily, General Dwight Eisenhower stood
with his staff on a hill overlooking the harbor of Malta. As he
saw the great armada of ships resting there, he straightened
his body and saluted the men that made up this striking force.
It was a still night, and the moon was shining clearly. One
could even hear the dip of the rowing oars. Then without comment the General dropped his head for a period of silent
prayer.

After that prayer to God upon whom he trusted as his supreme commander, the general thought it best to explain his
feelings to his staff. He turned to them and thoughtfully said,
"There comes a time when after you have used all the technical knowledge available and every conceivable means of stra-
tegic planning, and there is nothing more for you to do, the
only alternative remaining is to turn the whole matter over to
God and let it rest there. Then one must have faith to believe
that everything will turn out all right."

Here in a few short phrases from the lips of a great world
personality is the secret for victorious living. God expects us
to do all we can with our own resources. We cannot just sit
idly by, expecting to push some button, and then have miracles
occur. Still, miracles will occur when we do the best we can
with the resources we have been given, and then turn our
lives completely over to the Lord. His power is always sufficient. We may not attain what the world calls victory, but we
shall always have spiritual strength to emerge victorious.
There even in the so-called defeats of life we may discover
some of the greatest blessings we have ever known.

PRAYER THOUGHT: *Almighty Lord, may our dedication to
Thee be complete and sincere; may we receive Thy strength
and aid which empower us to emerge victorious from the battles of life.*

"Thou dost keep him in perfect peace, whose mind is stayed on thee, because he trusts in thee." Isaiah 26:3

In a certain palace in Florence, Italy, there hang side by side two paintings. One represents a stormy sea. The waves are menacing and wild. The clouds are black and foreboding. Lightning zigzags across the sky. In the raging waters a human face appears wearing an expression of utmost agony and despair.

The other painting also represents a storm-tossed sea. It too has black and threatening clouds. But in the midst of the waves a rock rises against which the white-crested water dashes in vain. In the clefts of the rock are to be seen patches of green grass, some trees, and even sweet pastel-shaded flowers. In a sheltered cove in the heart of these a dove sits calm and unruffled on her nest, unperturbed by the wild fury of the storm around her.

The first picture represents distress. It sets forth the sorrow and heartache of the world where all is helplessness and despair. Man is in anguish because he has let his fears cloud his faith. His dilemma seems too much to endure. He cannot save himself. The second painting is a beautiful representation of peace. It depicts the fact that the Christian is set down in this world and is not spared its sorrows and burdens. But still, he is not of the world. In the midst of chaos there is to be found an unruffled calm. There is in the Christian's heart the peace that passes all human understanding, because in the midst of life's thundering storms he finds security in the everlasting love of God. Such security is ours for the asking. We may receive it from the hand of God the Father Almighty. His greatest pleasure is to answer our prayer and give us calm in our souls.

PRAYER THOUGHT: *Merciful God, we thank Thee that, even though we live in the midst of confusion and unrest, we can be at peace and feel secure because we know Thee and Thy saving mercy.*

Abstain from every form of evil. 1 Thessalonians 5:22

Athens is a beautiful city with many places of historical interest. Of course, one of the most famous of these antiquities is the Acropolis. At the foot of the Acropolis stand a few beautiful Corinthian pillars. These are all that remain of the once famous temple of Olympian Zeus.

The Athenians today point to these pillars with pride. They are works of magnificent architectural beauty, and the people have done everything possible that they might continue to be preserved. To their great surprise and regret, however, they discovered one morning that one of these pillars had crumbled to the ground. Visitors can still see these scattered and broken pieces about the others. The catastrophe occurred not because a storm had shaken the pillar, or because vandals had been around. The reason for the fall was found in a colony of ants. These little insects had found a small crevice where one of the drums of the column joined another. They had forced an entrance and gradually had eaten away at the cement until at last the pillar crumbled into ruins.

Sometimes what we regard as the little things in life do not seem important. Yet they are, whether for good or for evil. We commit what we call "little sins," but our conscience isn't bothered very much by our errors. However, our little sins, if carelessly neglected or disregarded, can keep growing into bigger sins, until finally we find ourselves in serious trouble. We at last discover that this progressive growth of evil in our lives has been happening to us in a very quiet and unobtrusive way. Is there, then, no hope? Indeed, yes, for God's love is so broad He takes us into His forgiving arms when we realize our failings and penitently confess our error. His love cleanses away the stains and restores renewed hope.

PRAYER THOUGHT: *Merciful Lord, teach us to be watchful lest the things we call little sins in our lives eventually cause our souls to be overrun with evil.*

They who wait for the Lord shall renew their strength. Isaiah 40:31

The streets of Athens carry a lot of traffic, since taxicab rates are quite reasonable. Many people use them rather than purchasing their own cars. Therefore, it is frustrating sometimes to drive through this hilly city, since waits at stop signs are so long. I was quite amused one day when our car became involved in a traffic snarl. Coming to a halt, the taxi driver turned off the car motor, sat back and relaxed. At the second red light he did the same thing. Every time we were halted in our progress it was the same ritual.

Then my thoughts went back to America's busy streets. Coming up to a light as it turns red, I usually race my motor as I await the amber signal so that I can rush away to my destination. Of course, the reason the Athens taxi driver turns off his motor is to save gas.

By the same token we would save a lot of energy in life, if we figuratively did the same and put to positive use these waiting periods. All of us come to stop signs in life. There are days in which the road ahead seems to come to an abrupt end. But what we cannot see is that there is always a way out, if we only will have faith in Christ. Rather than expend our energy fretting about when our circumstances will change, wouldn't it be better if we regenerated our resources by communicating with Almighty God, receiving renewed powers for the demands of daily living?

For the man who puts his trust in the Almighty there is always a way out of any situation. "Underneath are the everlasting arms . . ." These sure arms of God have never yet failed men. Furthermore, His promise is that they never will.

PRAYER THOUGHT: *Almighty God, teach us the folly of trusting in our own powers, and instead enable us to trust in the marvelous strength which we can receive through quiet communion with Thee.*

"For you shall go out in joy, and be led forth in peace." Isaiah
55:12

While eating in a hotel restaurant in Athens, I watched a
man on his round of duty. His job was to push a little cart on
which there were vases of beautiful flowers and place one of
these vases on each dining table. I thought to myself, "What
a pleasant task he has as he goes about trying to brighten and
add cheer and beauty to someone's life."

Then I thought of a childhood experience which has always
stayed in memory. It was during those days before the city
streets were lighted by electricity. There were then gas lanterns on poles that lined each side of the avenue on which my
family lived. At eventide came the man we children called
"the lamplighter" with his flaming torch. He would go down
one side of the street lighting lamps along the way and then
up the other side. Wherever the lamplighter went he left a
trail of light behind him.

No matter what our situation in life might be, there isn't any
one of us who cannot do the very same thing in life. Let the
radiance of your faith be aglow. There are all too many in this
world today who go about deliberately blowing out the lights
of hope in other people's lives. Too many are critical of their
fellow men as they are looking with searching eyes for the bad
things instead of the good. How much better it would be, if
we resolved each day not to let a single opportunity pass by to
share the kind of joy and happiness with our fellow men that
the Master shares each day with us. Indeed we would be doing
a bit to obey the command of our Lord to help make disciples.
Everyone has the opportunity to assist in making life more
beautiful and more joyful for someone else. Let us resolve to
answer the Master's challenge and serve Him as best we can.

PRAYER THOUGHT: *Gracious Lord, may we promote those
things in this world which are beautiful and good and which
bring cheer into the hearts of men, so that in this way we
might draw others into the joy of fellowship with Thee.*

We aim at what is honorable not only in the Lord's sight but also in the sight of men. 2 Corinthians 8:21

It is always an interesting experience to visit shopping centers in various parts of the world. Usually the merchants are so friendly and always eager to sell their goods.

One day I walked into a jewelry store in Athens where I noticed a display of beautiful crosses. Purchasing one of these, I asked the shopkeeper who was able to speak a little English whether I could pay for the jewelry in American dollars. He replied that this was acceptable. When I gave him the correct amount of money for the purchase, he took up a magnifying glass from under the counter, looked at the dollar bills and scanned them carefully to try to determine if they were counterfeit or real.

As I left the store I thought of the fact that walking the streets of life each day are people who pretend to be one thing on the outside, but are something quite different within. They wear a different face and disposition according to the group or situation they are in. Now frankly ask yourself this question, Is my life counterfeit or real? "As a man thinketh within his heart, so is he." We all at times pretend to be something we are not, if it seems to be to our advantage to do so. There is One who sees beneath the superficiality of our daily actions. He knows what we are thinking deep in our hearts.

That you might become what He wants you to be, think daily upon those things which are true, honest, pure, and honorable. Let the seed of His life be planted within you. Your life will then blossom into a beautiful garden. There will be no artificial flowers that have no root. Then you will know the real living that comes to those attached to the power of God.

PRAYER THOUGHT: *Teach us, gracious God, to lead lives of integrity, so that we will not be artificial Christians in our witness for Thee, but genuine and sincere.*

Bless the Lord, O my soul, and forget not all his benefits, who forgives all your iniquity, who heals all your diseases. Psalm 103:2-3

Tuberculosis has a high rate of incidence in Greece. Because the disease is so common, the country has a difficult time taking care of its own people who are thus afflicted. Besides this, however, many refugees come to this country from behind the Iron Curtain. A goodly number of these also are afflicted with tuberculosis. The government of Greece has no extra funds with which to take care of them. Consequently, for a while there was no place for these sufferers to go because they were unwanted burdens. When X rays were taken of some of these refugees, and it was discovered they were suffering from tuberculosis, they would be so upset that they would thereupon commit suicide. Finally a certain neighboring European country did open its door saying, "We will take care of you." This country then became a haven of hope for these depressed and unwanted people.

The great Physician says to us, "I am the door. My door is always open. Anyone who is in need can come to me for cleansing, and I will give him help." No one is ever excluded from the blessings of God. No matter how serious your spiritual disease might be, no matter how far away you might have wandered from the Father's house, the invitation comes to you each day to give up your evil ways and turn to Him who is mighty and able to help.

The greatest invitation ever extended to fallen men is that one which continually comes to us from our God, "Come unto me and I will give you rest for your soul." The Lord indeed is our haven of hope. His arms are constantly outstretched, as He offers to each and all of every age the invitation to come to Him. He only can give you the rest your soul needs.

PRAYER THOUGHT: *God of mercy, we pray that we may turn away from the spiritual diseases of evil and accept Thy invitation to come and be cleansed from our sin and receive eternal rest for our souls.*

"Choose this day whom you will serve." Joshua 24:15

Having previously arranged for an official conference in Athens, my appointment brought me to the tenth floor of an old building. When I stepped on the elevator I observed that an old man was operating it. I gave my floor number in English, hoping that he would understand that I wanted to get off at the tenth floor. He asked, "Are you an American?" to which I replied, "Yes." Tears immediately welled up in his eyes. On the way up he began to tell me the story of how he had lived in America for 30 years until he had become a citizen. In fact, as a White House chef he had cooked for President Wilson. Then before the elevator reached my destination the operator said, "But I gave up my American citizenship!" Lifting his head he sobbed, "O God, why did I do it?"

Every child has the opportunity of being accepted as a citizen of heaven. For us Christ has conquered sin and its dread power, has overcome death, and has promised that if we will but follow He will lead us to eternal glory. The only reason that we may miss getting to heaven will be because of our own choice. If man listens to the wrong voices, and follows along the wide pathways away from Christ, he simply will never reach the city of God.

Sometimes the things of the world look so very attractive. They don't seem too expensive, when actually to the discerning eye the price tags are very high. It is the most foolish of all bargains to gain the world but at the same time lose the Savior's love. Stay very close to your Lord. If we but remain in His presence, we can live each day confident that some blessed day our citizenship will be forever settled in the house of many mansions.

PRAYER THOUGHT: *We pray that we may choose the things of Thy heaven, gracious God, with which to guide our lives, forsaking the temporary pleasures of earthly rewards.*

"Know therefore this day, and lay it to your heart, that the Lord is God in heaven above and on the earth beneath." Deuteronomy 4:39

Istanbul is the only city in the world which is located on two continents. As we were traveling up the Bosporus one day, the guide said, "That part of the city is in Europe." He pointed to another direction and said, "That part is in Asia." It is a divided city which is under the administration of one and the same government.

As we sailed along in our boat, I kept thinking of what the guide had just said. Here we were traveling between two continents. We were in a border area, so to speak. But yet there was unity in government and a good harmonious feeling between the residents of the two sections. In a similar circumstance is our life here on earth. Actually we are living in a divided city. There is a very fine line that separates earth from heaven. We can call that fine line the valley of death.

God has meant that earth and heaven should have the same King. Heaven can be right here on earth, for it begins when we allow heaven's rightful Ruler to enter our lives. Now, to be in heaven is to walk eternally with God. When we accept partnership with Him, then our lives are secure, for we can depend upon Him for all things. He is our stout fortress against evils that we must face in this world. He helps us withstand temptations which daily attack us. He undergirds us in our sorrows. He gives us His power to keep going on when perplexing problems face us.

But He not only wants to be your King in this world, He also is absolute King of the world to come. Daily as we walk with Him, He whispers in our ears that one day we shall be with Him forever. Living in that assurance, we can patiently bear disappointments and experience the true happiness of loving and trusting the Lord.

PRAYER THOUGHT: *May we enter into complete partnership with Thee, dear Lord, and then being ruled by Thee, find our lives surrounded by the impenetrable fortress of Thy love and protection.*

Be sober, be watchful. Your adversary the devil prowls around like a roaring lion, seeking some one to devour. 1 Peter 5:8

The guide who had been chosen for us in Turkey proved to be a most interesting man. He told us of his people's love for America and their hatred for Russia. He was very friendly and accommodating to us in every way. One day as we were casually chatting I turned to him and bluntly said, "I am old." This was his quick reply: "Only the devil is old."

Since that day I have thought about his wise remark many times. The devil is as old as the Garden of Eden. He has been with man since the beginning of the world. He hasn't changed even a bit in his desire to keep people from living joyfully and knowing eternal glory. He is subtle; he is sly; and he waits at every turn on the road of life to try to influence men to take the temporarily attractive pathway that really leads nowhere. He tries to convince us each day to forget about God and to deny His very existence. He tells us it is unnecessary to pray or to take the time to be holy and live in fellowship with the heavenly Father. Why bother about being concerned for and loving our fellow men? If you don't take care of yourself, nobody else will, says he.

The more we try to grow in grace and in the knowledge of our Lord Jesus Christ, the more urgently he will attack us. When he sees that we are devoted in our spiritual growth, he is all the more eager to win us over to his side. The devil's most prized captives are those who once devoutly pledged allegiance to God and His kingdom. Therefore, each of us should watch diligently lest, influenced by this evil force, we do things dishonorable in the sight of God. Be strong in the Lord. His power alone is sufficient to bring you out on top as a conqueror over evil and the temptations of the world.

PRAYER THOUGHT: *Merciful Lord, may we seek daily to arm ourselves with faith in Thee, the only force which is powerful enough to overcome the influence of the devil.*

"I have set before you life and death, blessing and curse; therefore choose life." Deuteronomy 30:19

Just as it is an educational experience to visit shopping areas around the world, so it is also interesting to visit restaurants in various areas of the world and there find the amazing varieties of food. Even the familiar courses we know so well in America are prepared and served in a way different from ours.

While dining in Istanbul, I was fascinated one day by a dessert cart wheeled to our table. There were many shelves on this cart, all of which could be pulled out and displayed. On each shelf were many kinds of pies, cakes, fruits, and all sorts of fancy desserts. After we had made our choice, we watched the waiter go from one table to another, and observed how carefully the people viewed these desserts before making their final choice.

After all, it isn't so important what we eat. In fact, I'm certain that we proportionately spend altogether too much time poring over recipes and menus. But I was reminded thereby that our choices in life today determine our eternal destiny. We choose to go the broad way or the narrow, to travel the high road or the low, to follow the Lord or the evil one.

The voices of evil clamor loudly for our attention. Yet in the midst of all the tumult of the world today there is the voice of God saying to those who will listen, "Try me, and I will give you everlasting life. Take my road. Therein you shall walk in safety." As we face these choices each day, let us think carefully lest we sell our birthright to the inheritance of the kingdom of heaven for a life of pleasure and fleeting joys that last for only a moment in the light of eternity. What if you should gain the whole world, and lose your Savior?

PRAYER THOUGHT: *Gracious Father, we pray that we shall not be so vain as to feel that we can make the right decisions alone, but that we may call upon Thee to help us wisely choose those things which will bring us closer to Thee and Thy ways.*

"Behold, to the Lord your God belong heaven and the heaven of heavens, the earth with all that is in it." Deuteronomy 10:14

Previous to one of my journeys abroad I had by correspondence prepared for the confirmation of a lad whose parents had accepted a temporary assignment in Ankara, Turkey. He had completed his instruction by the time I arrived in Istanbul, and he and his family flew there so that I could conduct the confirmation service for him. We were granted the use of a quaint old church in that city. One of the most inspiring moments of my entire life took place there when I heard another young man confess that he believed in God his heavenly Father, that he believed in Christ as his Savior, and that he believed in the continuing presence of the Holy Ghost in his life. It was indeed moving to see the dedication in his face when he promised to remain faithful to the church and his Lord the rest of his life.

After the service we enjoyed dinner together in a lovely restaurant overlooking the Bosporus. Below us were moving the seagoing vessels. The young lad questioned me about what I had seen. After describing some of my experiences to him, he seemed to sense anew the greatness of God as he turned to me and said, "Pastor, what a world! What a world!"

Man has done many outstanding things in life. He has been able to invent the means of sending air ships into outer space. He has broken the sound barriers in flight. Gadgets, machines, and mechanical inventions of every type have been put together, but in spite of these achievements of our century, man cannot take God's place. Only God could make this world. And only God can save us into a greater world, a world to which He has gone to prepare for all His children who love Him and remain faithful to Him.

PRAYER THOUGHT: *We pray, dear Lord, that we shall not overrate man's importance in world achievements, but that we may maintain a true perspective, knowing that these things are possible only because Thou hast first ordained them.*

69

Be constant in prayer. Romans 12:12

Not only in Turkey but in all the other Moslem countries around the world you see along the skyline of the cities a large number of minarets—these slender prayer towers which point heavenward. Even the classic Massachusetts Avenue, the street of embassies in Washington, D. C., has its proud skyline pierced by a minaret. At the top of these spindly towers is always a balcony where a man can go at the specified time during the day to call out to people the hours of prayer. There are over 500 minarets in the city of Istanbul alone.

We were informed by our guide that in this modern day only a small percentage of the faithful respond to these prayer times. But there are those who do stop, whatever they are doing, spread their prayer rug, and perform their prayer rituals. One is reminded of the great privilege we Christians have to speak each day in prayer to the living God. How different life would be if we used more fully this outstanding privilege which is ours!

There exist countless unused powers in the world, such as the mighty flowing rivers and thundering waterfalls, that could be harnessed, and the resulting power turned into constructive good. Much good could be accomplished, if only men would be willing to work and expend the effort. But the greatest unused power I know of is the power of prayer. Each day every one of us can link our weak lives to a vast power that can revolutionize our thinking and make dynamic our acting. The praying man finds his fears turned into faith, his failures into victory. His shattered dreams are transformed by prayer into newborn hope. Prayer remains forever the source for the healing of man's troubled soul.

PRAYER THOUGHT: *Gracious God, may we respond to the privilege of prayer by using every opportunity to come to Thee and to receive that power which is the reward of faith.*

There will be richly provided for you an entrance into the eternal kingdom of our Lord and Savior Jesus Christ. 2 Peter 1:11

In one of the many beautiful hotels in Istanbul, overlooking the Bosporus, there are several lovely restaurants. As I was seated in one of these dining rooms one day, I struck up a conversation with a waiter. It was not long until I discovered he had applied to the government for a visa to leave his country and travel to Canada. He had successfully completed all of the required examinations, and his papers were all in order. Now he was eagerly waiting for the visa to come through, so that he could leave. He said, "Every time the telephone rings I wonder if it isn't someone informing me that now I can go to this wonderful new land. I can hardly wait for that day to arrive."

As he related his hopes and desires, I thought of the fact that all of us are destined someday to travel to another country. Whether it will be a place of eternal happiness or one of eternal fear depends entirely upon us and the choices we have made here. Each day there are examinations that must be passed, if we are to keep our visa in good order. We do not earn the right to possess a visa by what we do. Instead, it is a free gift from God who has given it to us through our Lord Jesus Christ. We can lose it and all the value it has, if we don't take proper care of it. If we will seek each day to do the Lord's will, ask His help against sin, and penitently confess our sins seeking His forgiveness, then we can be sure that we are ready when He comes to take us on life's most wonderful journey. That final walk through the valley of the shadow of death into the yet unseen land of eternal joy in heaven which God is now preparing for His own we shall make with the Lord at our side.

PRAYER THOUGHT: *We thank Thee, gracious God, for the free gift of eternal salvation and for that long-anticipated entrance into Thy heavenly kingdom.*

"They will see the Son of man coming on the clouds of heaven with power and great glory." Matthew 24:30

One of the show places of Istanbul is the Mosque of St. Sophia. It is a converted Christian church. In its day it was one of the most beautiful churches in the world. But now all of the Christian inscriptions and symbols have been whitewashed and in their place Moslem inscriptions and symbols have been overlaid.

As one stands under the great dome of this building one can see faintly the figure of the ascending Christ with His hands outstretched in blessing. This figure had been painted out, but now is appearing again through the surface, as the covering paint is flaking off.

The lesson this brings home is an impressive one. Christ is coming back. That was His own promise when He ascended into heaven to be with His Father again. Through the centuries men have attempted to hide Him, to speak all manner of evil against Him, and to throw His followers into prisons and concentration camps. But Jesus simply cannot be contained. The future does not belong to the would-be strong men and dictators of the world. The future belongs to Christ. "I will come again," He said, "and take you to myself."

His first coming into this world as a helpless babe was in great humility. He came as a man and offered His life upon the cross for the eternal redemption of His followers. He would use none of the heavenly powers to fend off His great approaching death at the hands of wicked men. But His return and His second coming will be a coming in great glory. No power or combination of powers can stop Him. He will come again to take His throne and to reign forever as King of kings and Lord of lords. Why not crown Him king of your life now?

PRAYER THOUGHT: *Gracious Redeemer, we pray that we shall not try to put Thee out of our lives, but rather that we might seek to be ever ready for Thy glorious coming on that day when Thou shalt establish Thy reign forever.*

Put on the new nature, created after the likeness of God in true righteousness and holiness. Ephesians 4:24

One day my wife and I stood inside the Mosque of St. Sophia. Our Moslem guide told us the true yet almost incredible story of what had happened in one corner of the building a number of years previous. When the building was constructed the workmen followed the design and placed in one section two pieces of plain marble. Identical in size they were placed side by side. After a number of years had passed one of the pieces of marble changed in its external appearance, for one could clearly see that the features of a face had become visible. It was the ugly, repulsive face of the devil with horns.

So also in a real sense, we are two different people living within the same physical body. The Bible describes it this way: "The old man and the new man." Life becomes for us, then, a constant battleground for one self continually seeks to conquer over the other. One wants to be humble, and the other wants to be proud. One wants to doubt, and one wants to have faith. One wants to follow God's way, and the other wants to stray down the way of evil.

This battle within the souls of men will continue as long as we live, for human nature does not change. Nor does the power of evil change, for it ever seeks to make inroads into the heart of a man, especially in the Christian. However, victory can be assured, if we allow Christ to come into our lives bringing strength to the new man. As the new man within us grows daily in the knowledge of Jesus Christ, he is so fortified within by the strength of the Almighty that he can not only resist, but also overcome and gain the victory. Such is the promise of the Lord. Such is the testimony of those who have tried His way, and unfailingly found that He is faithful.

PRAYER THOUGHT: *Dear Lord, help us so that the growth of the new man within us may increase so that with Thy help we may obtain the power which can completely overcome that old man in us.*

"The gate is wide and the way is easy, that leads to destruction, and those who enter by it are many." Matthew 7:13

The waters of the Black Sea flow through the Bosporus and the Aegean Sea down to the Mediterranean. In some places the water currents run at a speed of ten miles or more an hour. Those who sail boats on these waters say that, contrary to anything which one might suppose, it is much more difficult to guide the ship with the direction of the flow of the stream than against it.

So even it is in life. Many times it is much better for us to face up to some difficulty that confronts us, because then we would summon up every resource and power reserve to overcome it. It is very dangerous for us just to go drifting along with the stream of life. The skipper of the ship might become careless and think that the current will carry the boat itself. But if he tried this, the ship would like as not be dashed against the rocks along the coast. The relaxed drifting would catch the crew off guard. But when one is sailing against the flow of the current one must constantly be on the alert and wary of dangers.

Again we see a parable for our life. Some of us go drifting along with the uninhibited routines of the crowd. People fail to ask where they are going or anything about how they intend to get there. Suddenly we discover that we are in difficulty because life has no lifting purpose. It has lost its meaning. On the other hand, there is the Master's way. His is the upward climb. It doesn't appear always to be an easy way to travel, but it has great rewards for those who are willing to take the Lord at His Word. With the power of God behind us we have nothing to fear. Indeed, the greatest joy will be ours, a companionship with the Almighty.

PRAYER THOUGHT: *We pray that we may be spared from drifting carelessly along the easy currents of life, dear Lord, and that instead we will seek to follow the more difficult, but more rewarding, path to eternity.*

"He who endures to the end will be saved." Matthew 24:13

We traveled up the Bosporus one day, being permitted to observe, as we had done so often before, the beauties of God's creation. We were riding on a boat plying between two continents and heading toward the Black Sea. The guide was telling us about the friendly attitude of the Turkish people toward America. He said, "You will never know how much we appreciate the tremendous assistance which you are giving us in our time of need. We will forever remain grateful to you for all that you have done." He went on to relate how anticommunistic the Turks are and how they are using every possible safeguard to preserve their country from infiltration by the communists. Then he squared his shoulders and proudly said, "But I want you to know that one Turk can handle twenty Russians!"

Just as we were approaching the Black Sea the boat docked. There we got off and drove to where the waters of the Bosporus and the Russian waters meet. Then he pointed out a string of buoys that extended from one shore to the other shore. Commenting about this he said, "These buoys hold up a net which extends to the bottom of the waters. This net is in place from night to day to keep enemy submarines from coming into our territory."

Perhaps it would be good if from this situation we learned that we should set up a net around our lives to protect us from the enemies that are trying to subdue us and entice us away from God. There is the seductive enemy of materialism that wants us to wangle all that we can for ourselves without thinking of our fellow men. Then there is the enemy of popularity which wants us to drift along with the crowd. Be strong in the Lord and resist!

PRAYER THOUGHT: *Dear Lord, we pray that we may never become so ensnared in the net of evil that we will want to remain there, but that we may be strong and able to resist Thine enemies.*

You shine as lights in the world, holding fast the word of life.
Philippians 2:15, 16

On the drive back from visiting the shore of the Black Sea
our guide insisted that we stop to see the palace of the last
sultan. This structure is located very close to the Bosporus.
It is a beautiful building where as one enters the throne room
one sees the world's largest chandelier. Weighing four and a
half tons, it has four thousand light bulbs. As I stood there
gazing at it, I thought about how each single bulb had some
significance. None of them was too large, and yet the four
thousand bulbs together caused the throne room to be flooded
with dazzling light.

It was the Apostle Paul who referred to Christians as lesser
lights shining in the world in whose hands is the responsibility for setting aglow in the hearts of others a faith in the heavenly Father. Just as these chandelier lights, each of us has
meaning and significance in life, too. We may think that we
are not very important, but if we dedicate what we have to
God, our lives become of tremendous significance. Any ordinary talent and task can be sacred, if it is done in a spirit of
love and consecration to the Lord.

If all individual Christians would shine out with the light
of goodness, there is not enough darkness in the world to
shroud that light. If everyone who has dedicated his life to
God would resolve to let his light shine, no matter what the
circumstances might be, the darkness would vanish. The Lord
himself has said, "You are the light of the world." It is our
duty and our privilege to resolve to do just what many of us
have said we would do in that Sunday school chorus of years
ago, "This little light of mine, I'm going to let it shine!" Rich
blessings can come from a spirit of love and concern for the
spiritual welfare of another.

PRAYER THOUGHT: *We pray that we may never let the light
of our witness go out, dear Lord, but instead that we will keep
it burning brightly for all the world to see.*

"Thou art my lamp, O Lord, and my God lightens my darkness." 2 Samuel 22:29

When I was passing through Vienna, it came to my attention that above the entrance to a tunnel in the Austrian Alps
are written these words in the old Roman language, "In thee,
O Lord, do I hope." All travelers read this before they enter
the darkness of that tunnel.

A Christian is never spared the darkened tunnels in life.
No greater mistake can be made than to believe that, once
you have given your life to the Lord, you will travel only in
open sunny places and in full view of the beautiful valleys.
On the contrary, experience teaches us that those who give
themselves to Christ sometimes are tried even more than those
who do not have faith. But to His children God has given His
promise that He will provide for them the necessary strength
to meet temptation and to see through every problem.

The difference between the follower of Christ and the individual who is not His disciple is the fact that the Christian
through the power of his God maintains a faith that enables
him to endure the hardships of life. Every tunnel that opens
up to him he faces with the confident prayer, "In thee, O Lord,
do I hope." Never does he need to be afraid of traveling in
the darkness alone. He is the possessor of God's Spirit in his
heart and life. As we travel along we see glimpses of light at
the end of the tunnel, and we know that this is but a foretaste
of the great lighted glory of the land where we shall be with
God forever.

That little girl who often traveled with her parents left a
lesson for us when she told her mother, "I used to be afraid
of those dark tunnels, but I'm not any more because I know
there is light at both ends." The light of His eternal presence
is our hope. Let us live in that faith!

PRAYER THOUGHT: *We pray, God of light, that when we are
traveling in the tunnels of life we will keep our eyes on the
end of the tunnel where Thy light waits to receive us in the
radiant warmth of Thy love.*

Let your requests be made known to God. Philippians 4:6

In Vienna the post office department has developed a wonderful idea for weary parents. Now they can get bedtime fairy tales by telephone. In fact, Vienna has one of the most remarkable telephone systems in the entire world. There is very little one can't hear just by dialing the right number. Perplexed housewives can receive dinner recipes, travelers can get pertinent bus and train information, sports-minded individuals can be informed of skiing conditions or football results; and for musicians there is a perfect A tone.

The Christian has an even more remarkable opportunity. Through prayer he can communicate with God and receive from Him whatever directions are necessary for abundant living. The promise from Scripture is, "Ask, and you will receive." If you don't use the telephone in Vienna, you simply will not get the promised results. If a person dosen't pray to God, how can he expect to receive the blessings which Scripture has promised?

What is your need today? Is it strength for this day's task? Is it power to overcome obstacles? Is it faith to remove your doubts? Is it peace to calm your troubled soul? Is it hope that tomorrow will bring encouragement? These and many more unnumbered blessings can be yours, if you will only turn to the heavenly Father who knows what you need. Martin Luther translated the words of Psalm 46, "Be still, and know that I am God," as follows: "Be thou silent unto God and let Him mold thee." He is the one Friend who has never failed His children. He knows what is best for you. He always answers prayer, but sometimes not in the way we expect. Remember always, our heavenly Father knows just what is best for us.

PRAYER THOUGHT: *Dear Lord, may we fully use the wonderful opportunity of prayer, wherein we can receive the blessings of Thy wisdom and love by simply bringing our requests to Thee.*

Stand fast therefore, and do not submit again to a yoke of slavery. Galatians 5:1

Not many days after the Budapest revolution in Hungary, I was allowed to go into neighboring Austria. It was inspiring to see there in Vienna how loving hands had joined together in creating a new life for those who had escaped from the other side of the Iron Curtain. The International Red Cross operated teams in many temporary refugee camps to provide housing and food for these people. Many of the Hungarian refugees had walked long miles through muddy swamps to reach freedom here. They were transported in trucks to Vienna after they had crossed the border where they were given good secondhand clothing. After being registered they were placed in a camp where they patiently waited to go to the country of their choice to seek out a new life.

What price had they paid for this new-found hope? They had left behind nearly everything they owned except for a few valuable items like their rings and their razors which they sold along with whatever other meager things they could sell, in order to get to Vienna or some other city. As many as eight thousand came in a single day through the snow and freezing weather. This is only one part of the price that these people have been willing to pay for their freedom.

How fortunate we are to live in a country where we enjoy freedom that we are apt to take so much for granted. How fortunate we are to live in a land of the open church where we can find freedom to worship and the joy from following after Him who is the light of the world. To keep our faith, we must be more vigilant than ever before, in order to preserve to ourselves and our children those privileges which now we can treasure so dearly.

PRAYER THOUGHT: *Help us, loving Lord, diligently to guard and protect the freedom which is ours to worship and follow Thee in this land, so that we may never lose this great gift of liberty.*

The Lord has anointed me to bring good tidings to the afflicted; he has sent me to bind up the brokenhearted, to proclaim liberty to the captives, and the opening of the prison to those who are bound. Isaiah 61:1

It was my experience to stand one day at the Austrian border where many refugees were coming from Hungary. It is almost impossible for us in America to understand the intense drive for freedom made by those brave Hungarians who rose up to shake off the Soviet yoke of communism. It was as if a nation had shouted, "We will take this suppression no longer!" One can hardly sense the piercing heartache in merely reading about it. One can better see it by meeting these people in the disappointment of their lunge for freedom having been so brutally suppressed.

This is a typical example. One night a man came home as usual to his wife and four children. After the little ones had been put to bed he said to his wife, "Tomorrow we are leaving." Startled she asked, "For where?" He answered, "In search for freedom." She replied, "I have been hoping and praying that you would suggest this for a long time."

Morning came. They packed a few of their belongings in a bag and turned the key in their door, knowing that they might never see their home again. Boarding a train, they rode it as far as they dared. Then they started walking, the mother and the father each carrying two children. Through swamps they walked in the bitter cold of winter. They waited for the cover of darkness before they dared to escape across the line, there to stumble into the arms of their rescuers.

The only institution left in this world that can with a superior ideology combat communism and lay bare its empty boasts until tragedies like this no longer occur is Christianity. With its superior ideology of love, it can answer the longings of every heart and give the freedom that truly sets a man free.

PRAYER THOUGHT: *Dear Savior, help us to be strong and to endure as we carry the banner of freedom in Christ to those in sin's bondage.*

"Go into all the world and preach the gospel to the whole creation." Mark 16:15

Many heartbreaking memories of a trip to the Hungarian border during the ill-fated uprising in Budapest now come to my mind. One is the true story of a little lad who was awakened one morning by his parents. They dressed him in his warmest clothes. They filled his knapsack with food. Then they opened the door of their home and as they bade him farewell they tearfully said, "Son, you must not stay here. You must go for we don't want you to be a slave."

The boy went on all by himself, walking as long as he was able, crawling under barbed wire entanglements on hands and knees through rain-drenched fields. Finally he reached the border of freedom. He was fearfully tired and soon fell asleep.

Along came a Red Cross relief worker, and on finding him asleep in the ditch with a cap pulled over his face to protect him from the pitiless rain, he was taken at once to a shelter, dressed in dry clothes and given food. Men and women of good will took care of him. A family provided him with a home. Time will pass, but there still is the haunting memory of a child whose parents had become the victims of a godless government, and who had preferred to abandon their son rather than see him live as a slave under a communist government.

Should not instances like this challenge us to a greater willingness to bring the gospel of Jesus Christ to all men? His gospel really sets men free. Should we not be stabbed awake to an awareness of what our youth may have to endure because of our negligence in working for the Christianization of the world? Where we have failed, worldly power has now entered. The future of the world lies in the deeds of this generation.

PRAYER THOUGHT: *Lord Jesus, may we become ever more ready to bring the gospel of truth and love to all men, that they might know the glorious liberty which rightfully belongs to the children of God.*

Jesus said to him, "I am the way, and the truth, and the life."
John 14:6

As I waited in the airport at Vienna, about to take my first flight behind the Iron Curtain, beside me sat my new-found friend. Having a few fears in my heart in anticipation of the journey, I looked out the window to see a man in an ill-fitting uniform smoking a big black cigar, all too close, in my estimation, to the plane which was being fueled. I asked, "Who is that fellow?" The answer came, "He's the pilot of your plane." This fact didn't relieve me of any of my fears. Finally, when we boarded the plane I was amazed to discover that there were no seatbelts. Later when I asked the reason the answer was this: "That's just another demonstration of the freedom we allow our people here inside the Iron Curtain."

Then I asked myself the question, "What is freedom?" Is it our total privilege to do what we please? Was it freedom the prodigal had when he ventured forth into the far-off country to live as a libertine, wallowing in riotous living? No, instead he became sin's slave. He never knew freedom in the true sense of that word until he returned to his father's house and entered in again under the restrictions of his parental home. From the spiritual point of view, no man is free until he knows at last the only truth that makes a man free, namely Jesus Christ, who is truth.

A G string lying loose on a violin cannot give music. Only when it is in tension does it sing. A locomotive loose from the rails is on a rampage of destruction. Only when bound on the shiny rails does it pull its burden with profit. Unless we are willing to follow Jesus through our Gardens of Gethsemane, along life's narrow pathways, on to Jericho roads of selfless serving, can we discover the freedom, the joyous awards and the deep satisfaction we all want.

PRAYER THOUGHT: *Dear Lord, may we never follow after the way of false freedom, but continually seek Thy way, so that we may be eternally free in the knowledge of Thy truth.*

We are children of God, and if children, then heirs, heirs of God and fellow heirs with Christ. Romans 8:16, 17

Behind the Iron Curtain one is constantly made aware of the shortages of everything, even the necessities for everyday living. There is a shortage of adequate housing. Families are crowded together in a single room and have to share with three other families a kitchen and a wash room in the government housing projects. There is a shortage of certain foods. For example, fresh fruit is very rare and consequently expensive, so few commoners can afford it. Articles which Americans consider to be only the ordinary things of life are to Russians luxuries. There is a shortage even in the transportation facilities. People can be seen at all times of the day standing in queues a block or longer, waiting to get from one place to another. There is a shortage of good clothing. Most people haven't the income which gives them the opportunity of buying new things to wear.

As we stood at Red Square looking through the windows of the famous Gum Department Store, surrounded by hundreds of Russians doing the same thing, my friend said to me, "Only one Russian luxury is really cheap—window gazing." Here were people looking at things which they could not afford to buy. Then this thought occurred to me: We Christians need not be window gazers. God has invited us to come into the storehouse of His great kingdom and share everything that He possesses. No one of us is too poor to know the goodness of life with Him. He tells us that these things belong to us because we are joint heirs with Him, because we are His children and He is our Father. We all can be rich in the things that are of eternal value, for we are children of a God who is abounding in mercies.

PRAYER THOUGHT: *Teach us, God our Father, not to stand on the outside of Thy kingdom looking in, but rather to accept Thy invitation to partake of the inheritance of Thy children, which is eternal salvation.*

Because the creation itself will be set free from its bondage to decay and obtain the glorious liberty of the children of God. Romans 8:21

To my hotel room in Moscow one day, upon my personal invitation, came a Russian man who had been living in America for many years. But he left the United States in 1949, after the famous purge took place. The government officials were suspicious of him when he came back to Russia, but finally he was able to gain employment and advance to a good job. Our visit proved to be very interesting, for he talked very freely to me about some matters in which I had an intense interest. I asked him if there were any delinquency problems among the youth in Russia. He answered, "Of course there are, and I can tell you why. Both the mother and father from the family must work eight hours a day in order to make a living. If they are good party people, they go to the party meetings at night. Therefore, the children have many hours by themselves outside of time in school when they can roam the streets at will."

Without much difficulty one can read through the sentences he was speaking. It isn't only because the children are left alone in Russia to shift for themselves that they get into trouble. It is also because they are reared in an atheistic system which teaches that there is no God. What developed inner voice of conscience do they have to teach them the difference between right and wrong? In this country we have the opportunity of religious freedom where we can choose for ourselves the manner in which we will worship God. We still believe in a God who is the supreme power and must rule the hearts of men. Let us, then, put our faith to work and make it the activating force for good in the world that God has ordained it to be.

PRAYER THOUGHT: *May we never underrate the value of the religious freedom which we enjoy in this democratic land, precious Lord, but seek to strengthen the pillars of this freedom by the diligent practice of our faith.*

The Lord is the everlasting God, the Creator of the ends of the earth. Isaiah 40:28

Many churches and great cathedrals in Russia have now been converted into museums. They stand as mute sinister reminders of the appeal and even more of the great silencing power of atheism. These anti-religious museums pose the superiority of the state over against the message of the church and the freedom of the individual soul.

On one occasion a group of ordinary laborers was brought into one of these museums on a pre-arranged tour led by a communist Russian guide. He tried to explain to them the creation of all things by scientific knowledge and methods. Part of his speech was to tell them in as convincing a tone as possible that it was ridiculous to believe that God had ever made the heavens and the earth. Even this building they were now standing in was evidence of the feebleness of this Christianity business, he implied, for it finally went to the state, its rightful owner.

The group was then left without the guide as they went to one of the great art galleries. All alone they walked about looking at the numerous paintings. To their amazement, they came upon a painting of Christ hanging on the cross. They stopped. They gazed at the timeless expression of love upon His face. Suddenly something dramatic happened. One of the men took his soiled cap from his head and held it to his heart. The rest followed his example of reverence.

There is still a longing in the hearts of these people for something more than they now have. As Christians, we trust that God's voice cannot be silenced. One day He shall take His throne and reign forever. This is the world's only hope for the millions who now live in darkness and suppression.

PRAYER THOUGHT: *Almighty God, we know that no matter how clever the godless forces of the world may be, they can never erase the image of Thee which is carried in the hearts of men, for Thou art eternal and shalt rule forever with love.*

If you do suffer for righteousness' sake, you will be blessed.
1 Peter 3:14

While visiting in Russia, I asked permission one day to meet briefly with someone in the Soviet government whose responsibility was to be in charge of religious affairs for the country. In conversation with him I discovered that only those are allowed to preach the gospel who have previously been examined by the Soviet officials and authorities. As soon as a divine worship service is concluded, the worshipers must return to their homes. They are never allowed to gather in their homes for religious meetings. Nor are they permitted at their work to talk to anyone about their religion, nor in the trains, nor on the streets. To do so is to face a possible prison sentence of twenty-five years or longer.

No new churches are permitted to be established. The only churches that are open in Russia today are those that had already been organized prior to the coming of communist rule. The government in the words of the constitution has every right to propagandize against the church. Children are early taught about atheism in the schools. People who attend church can never attain to any responsible position in government. They must be content merely to exist.

Yet in spite of these rigid restrictions, there are still thousands of people living under the persecution of a godless government who are willing to make the sacrifices necessary to maintain their faith. These are the twentieth-century martyrs. How our feeble witness should shame us by contrast to that of these Christian friends behind the Iron Curtain. God needs soldiers of the Cross today who are unafraid of the world and who know positively that from Him is received the power to overcome the world.

PRAYER THOUGHT: *Almighty God, we pray that we will become more dedicated in the struggle for men's souls against evil, and that Thou mayest be able to use us to the extension of Thy kingdom.*

We are fellow workmen for God. 1 Corinthians 3:9

Nearly everywhere one goes in Moscow one sees people standing in long lines. They stand in lines to board the bus to go to work. They stand in lines to check in at the factory. They stand in lines at the department store to see what articles there might be to buy. They stand in lines at the cashier's desk to buy a ticket so they might purchase the goods.

One day I spoke with a Russian woman who explained to me her typical day. She would arise early in the morning and join these people in lines. Even in her own home, this was necessary, for her family shared a kitchen and a bathroom with four other families in the same building. She worked, as also did her husband, eight hours each day while the state took care of their children. She was a devoted communist party worker, for she went to meetings nearly every night each week. As she related the story of her life I thought to myself, "What a monotonous existence!"

It is indeed sad that one needs not go behind the Iron Curtain to find such monotony in life. There are those in our own country whose lives are so everydayish! They work to earn a wage to buy some groceries in order to feed their family. They earn money to pay for the rent and insurance. Then they start the treadmill of this "straw life" all over again.

But life can be so vastly more purposeful than this. We need not be just occupied in acquiring the shiny gadgets and artifacts of the world. The making of a living is important, but not just to receive things in life. We must also make a contribution. There isn't anyone who can't find some area of activity where he can be used to the glory of God. Such diversified living makes life worth while. And the man who can say with St. Paul, "For me to live is Christ," will want an eternity of that.

PRAYER THOUGHT: *Help us, dear Lord, to get out of the monotonous rut of self-centered interest and instead see that the purpose of our life is to serve Thee by helping others.*

"I give them eternal life." John 10:28

On one of my several visits to Moscow I was fortunate enough to have the same guide for a span of about eight days. By the time I was ready to depart, she had become most inquisitive about life here in America. It was difficult for her to believe that so many churches were open, and that multitudes crowded within them for worship each Sunday. As for herself, she was a devoted communist and a militant atheist, even though her one living grandmother was a Christian.

The day I was to leave Moscow I talked with her about some of the more important things in life, so I asked what meaning life had to her. She replied that this was to do the best she could at her job so long as she lived, making a total commitment of herself to the state. This it was easy to see was her god. So I turned to her and said, "Alexander, what happens to you after you die?" She looked hard at me and gave me this answer: "Nothing." Whereupon I followed with this question: "Wouldn't you like to believe that you would live forever in a much more wonderful place than earth?" She attempted no answer. In the meaningful silence I intuitively sensed what she was thinking. For she was living in a system where not only her job but her very life would be at stake, if she dared openly confess belief in God and in immortality.

How fortunate we are to live in a country where without penalty we may nurture the faith that makes life worth living and whets our appetite for eternity! How wonderful it is to live each day in the faith that there is a grand future for our life, more wonderful than anything we have known in the past. We Christians have a future to anticipate that is without pain, without sorrow, without separation—a future of unending joy!

PRAYER THOUGHT: *May we never cease in our thankfulness for the promise we have from Thee of the eternal life which will begin when this passing life is finished.*

Trust in the Lord for ever, for the Lord God is an everlasting rock. Isaiah 26:4

Most people who go to Moscow ask for permission to join the thousands of Russians who each day go to the mausoleum in Red Square which was built for the purpose of putting on public exhibit the preserved bodies of Lenin and Stalin. Russian scientists are said to have devised a special process of embalming whereby these bodies have been preserved. Their faces can be seen through the glass caskets. The Soviet Congress at the time of the death of Nikolai Lenin issued a statement containing this tribute: "He was the greatest leader of all times and all peoples. He was the lord of the new humanity, the saviour of the world."

It is significant that all of this is spoken in the past tense, for the glory of a dictator soon fades away. How different it is for the Christian to stand in the Garden of Joseph of Arimathea in Jerusalem and there find the empty tomb out of which Christ walked early on the first Easter morning. How significant it is that we can say that Jesus not "was," but "is" the greatest leader of the world, that He is the only Savior and the only Lord of all humanity.

This Jesus Christ is the same yesterday, today, and forever. The kings of this world come and go, and their power rises and fades away. They leave an imprint on the sands of time which is quickly washed away by new leaders and events. But the Lord whom we Christians worship is the Lord of all history. His influence shall never be erased. His power shall never be subdued. He is the changeless Christ in a changing world. He is the Rock of ages whom we can cling to and know that when we do, we are secure, no matter how turbulent the storms of life may be. He is the one and true Lord of all mankind.

PRAYER THOUGHT: *Eternal God, we are thankful that Thou art God for all eternity, and that when we put our trust in Thee no time or tide is able to keep us from the refuge of Thine everlasting arms.*

"He is the living God, enduring for ever." Daniel 6:26

From five thousand to twenty thousand people stand in line practically every day of the year in the Red Square in Moscow waiting for the opportunity to go into the mausoleum which houses the tomb of Lenin to view the bodies of their pioneer leader and other dead heroes. For me to join this group one day proved to be an unforgettable experience. It was a bleak day in the month of January when the weather was bitterly cold. We shuffled along at a tediously slow pace. It seemed as though we would never reach that doorway. When we finally did arrive, we saw the guards standing stiffly at strict attention. At long last we were past them, descending some stairs to a lower level. We were swallowed up by the never-ending queue which walked by the glass-sealed caskets of Lenin and Stalin. Both were attired in their military dress uniforms, both perfectly preserved as to body since their death. Lenin had died in 1924 and Stalin in 1953. As we filed past them my friend who was an American newspaper correspondent said to me, "These are the dead hands that still guide this nation."

It was a gruesome sight and a horrifying experience. Yet it pointed up to me our great privilege of being directed and guided by a living God. The God we worship is not found in a casket or interred in a tomb. He walks the streets of life today, not only to be the consoler of men suffering from man's inhumanity to man, but to be man's guide leading him into more abundant living. Ours is a living God who has been our help in ages past and who is indeed our hope for the years to come. In gratitude for what He means to us, let us resolve to serve Him each day and sincerely seek to glorify His name.

PRAYER THOUGHT: *Eternal God, we are thankful that we can have an abiding faith in Thee, for in Thee there is no beginning or ending, because Thou art steadfast and unchanging, enduring for ever and ever.*

None of us lives to himself, and none of us dies to himself. Romans 14:7

Accompanied by a close friend who had never before visited the Soviet Union, I traveled into Kiev. I told him of the reticence people felt in communicating with American tourists. They were held back out of fear that the secret police would be watching and listening. However, I was greatly surprised to observe how the attitude of the Russian people had changed since my previous visit there two years before.

After we had been assigned our hotel rooms, we were ushered to the dining room and there assigned a table. We two were the only Americans in Kiev that night. As we went into the dining room the band started playing, "'Yankee Doodle." A short while later there was the encore, "Oh Susannah!" On the table we found a small Russian flag and also an American flag. It was as though they wanted to tell us that at least the common people of that country were ready to share friendship with Americans.

There is a tremendous difference between the official attitude of the Kremlin and the thinking of the ordinary person on the street. If the people in Russia dared to speak out their real feelings, undoubtedly they would be as eager to rid themselves of their system of slavery as anyone could possibly be.

In America we must remember that we may have to pay a price to maintain the system of democratic freedom that we have. We must be concerned about all people, regardless of their racial background, skin color, or creed. We must daily live in such a way that we are putting into practice the democratic Christian principles which so easily can become mere lip profession.

PRAYER THOUGHT: *Gracious Lord, help us to place a higher value on the blessings of democracy which we enjoy; may we strive to maintain this freedom and encourage its growth by daily observance of the Christian principles which are the backbone of true democracy.*

When the righteous are in authority, the people rejoice; but when the wicked rule, the people groan. Proverbs 29:2

Kiev is a sizable city, located in the Ukraine inside the Iron Curtain. Upon my arrival there I was met by the guide who brought me to my hotel and assigned me a room. My guide informed me that he would be available to act as my interpreter for four hours each day, and that he would also have a car and a driver on hand to take me to the places which I was permitted to view. The rest of the time I would be on my own.

This was my first visit behind the Iron Curtain, and I did not know just how I would be received. Apparently we in America have been propagandized to believe that all Russian people are bad. The system is obviously bad, but the people are merely victims of their circumstances. There is very little that they can do to resist when they are living in a state that figuratively controls their every waking hour by force.

Many people I met that first time I visited Russia were unfriendly and indifferent. However, one man I shall long remember. He was an old gentleman who, no doubt, had lived for some years before the Revolution of 1917. Undoubtedly he remembered some of the freedoms long since lost after communism's rise to power. Every time I stepped on the elevator he was operating, if there was no one else around, he would give me a gracious smile and pat my hand. We could not speak the same language, and yet we shared the common language of friendship. In his own way, he was saying, "I want to be your friend. I want you to know that all of us under this system don't agree with its teachings." My friend, get on your knees and thank God today that you are privileged to live in America where freedom is your birthright.

PRAYER THOUGHT: *Dear Father in heaven, may we not take for granted the blessings of freedom which we can enjoy in this land because Thy name is honored here.*

You will go before the Lord to prepare his ways, to give
knowledge of salvation to his people. Luke 1:76, 77

One Russian Christmas Eve I was invited to speak in the
Baptist Church in Moscow. It proved to be one of the most
thrilling experiences of my life. The church was filled to capacity, with more than fifteen hundred people packed together
under a single roof. At that service I preached the same sermon that I had used at my own church in Minneapolis just a
few days before. It was a deep inspiration to hear these people sing the great hymns of faith. Now the church is one of
the very few places in Russia where the people can still sing
the hymns of faith.

At the conclusion of the service Bishop Jacob Zidkov, the
head of the Baptist Church in Russia, invited me to come to
the pulpit. The congregation then sang the hymn which they
always sang to guests from foreign lands, namely, "God be
with you till we meet again." When they came to the chorus,
"Till we meet at Jesus' feet," they all took out their white
handkerchiefs and waved them. Tears streamed down the
cheeks of nearly everyone in the congregation. I felt that I
could almost read the thoughts in their minds: "You can go
back to America, to the land of freedom, but we will not know
freedom until we meet you in heaven."

As I walked down the aisle, people patted me on my cheeks
and on my hands. Then I thought of all the unfinished business that the Lord has. There are many behind the Iron Curtain who have never heard of Jesus, and who have never been
told about the God of love. Many other people around the
world are unaware of the good news of the gospel. That day
in Moscow I silently said a prayer which I hope each one of
us will pray again today, "Lord, I want you to know that you
can count on me, you can count on me!"

PRAYER THOUGHT: *Help us, Lord, to search out the place in
life in which we can be of most service in bringing the good
news of salvation to others.*

"For this is the will of my Father, that every one who sees the Son and believes in him should have eternal life; and I will raise him up at the last day." John 6: 40

Many of the churches in Russia where people previously gathered for worship have now been turned into museums stocked with exhibits designed to turn the masses against all things ecclesiastical. They are only places of historical interest, setting up the state as the new god and the party leaders as apostles. There is at least one church, for example, where they have taken out the altar and put in its place a casket. The open casket displayed the half-decayed body of a human being. Each day as people filed by this casket all they saw was this body. The purpose of the government for doing this was to disprove to the people the doctrine of immortality.

Christians never did believe that the body as such will survive forever. The body is just the house in which we live briefly on our way home. How ridiculous to think that the sight of a lifeless body shatters our faith. The soul lives on for ever and ever. Our final authority for this exclamation mark to our creed is our Lord Jesus Christ who himself walked free from a grave and has never yet failed us in any of His promises. Not only has He given us a way of life to live on this earth which is the highest possible of all ways that a man can live, but He has also shown us the pathway that leads to eternal glory. We ought therefore to trust Him and believe His promise. Has He not said, "I am the resurrection and the life; . . . whoever lives and believes in me shall never die." We can each live confident in the hope that in heaven we shall walk with Him and live on and on. If ultimately we persevere in our faith we shall be citizens of heaven and members of the great church triumphant. "They shall see him face to face, and his name shall be on their foreheads."

PRAYER THOUGHT: *We thank Thee, gracious Lord and Redeemer, for the hope which we have of an eternal spiritual home where we shall live with Thee.*

"Holy, holy, holy, is the Lord God Almighty, who was and is and is to come!" Revelation 4:8

After much negotiating with the Russian authorities, it was finally agreed that I could drive with my guide out to Zagorsk which is a monastery where priests of the Russian Orthodox Church are trained. The distance requires about a two-hour drive from Moscow. While I was there, I had an audience with Alexis, the patriarch of the Russian Orthodox Church. He has unswervingly led his people on in the Christian way, in spite of the persecutions and hardships pounded upon them by the communist system. Since I could talk no Russian nor he English, we had to communicate through my Russian guide, a dedicated communist and an unbelieving atheist. When I asked him what the future of Christianity was in Russia, his reply came to me through the lips of my atheist interpreter in these words, "You cannot abolish God!"

At the beginning of time God sent this world spinning out in space and then crowned His work by creating man to live in it. He gave man only a very few restrictions. One of these was that man must obey God. Yet, nearly from the very beginning man refused to obey. He thought he could live unto himself, only to find that he was then in serious trouble. He had to learn the hard way that it is impossible to know the reality of life apart from God.

It is so true that, "you cannot abolish God!" He is the Creator and also the Redeemer of the world. He is its guiding hand and its source of unending love. He is its sovereign Ruler and triumphant King. Only as man himself makes the decision to let God run his life, can he find the way that leads to the abundant life of which God is the source and the merciful sustainer.

PRAYER THOUGHT: *Dear Lord, may we fully realize that, although we are alive physically, we are dead spiritually, unless we know Thee and Thy will for our lives.*

"Do not be faithless, but believing." John 20:27

It was of special interest to visit an old people's home in Moscow. They told me I was the first American tourist to make such a crazy request. Of course, the people in this home had been told of the coming of an American, and no doubt were carefully briefed beforehand.

In company with my guide and interpreter, we came to an old house located in the same block as a noisy factory. Each factory is to care for its old and outworn workers when they no longer can take care of themselves. We were courteously greeted by the matron of the home who showed us rooms where many people were asleep on cots. We finally went to the central dining area where we were seated. Sitting around us were some of the residents of this institution.

I was given the opportunity to ask questions. Then my interpreter said to me, "Our people would like to ask some questions of you." Several of them began to speak at once. They asked, "Why don't you provide homes for old people in America?" I explained that we had social security to permit most people to live by themselves, but that homes were provided for those who needed them. I added that even my own church was building a home to take care of elderly people. They became very annoyed. Some even came and shook their fists in my face belligerently saying, "It isn't true. We have been told that you don't take care of the old people in America."

Of course, it was useless to argue. But I pondered how so many people living outside the kingdom of God will not believe the Christian when he witnesses of the glorious provisions God has made for men. God's mercy is great, for our concerns are His concerns also. Let us then live as God's children, helping others to trust in the heavenly Father.

PRAYER THOUGHT: *May we endeavor to remove the doubt and unbelief of those outside the family of faith, merciful Lord, so that they might come to share in the inheritance of Thy guidance and care.*

Ungodly persons who . . . deny our only Master and Lord, Jesus Christ. Jude 4

The Russian system of Communism is dead set against God. Back in the year 1936 Lounatcharski, the Commissar of Education said, "We hate Christians. Even the best of them must be regarded as our worst enemies. They preach love to one's neighbor and pity, which is contrary to our principles. Christian love is a hindrance to the development of the revolution. Down with love for one's neighbor. What we want is hatred. We must know how to hate, for only at this price can we conquer the universe. We have done away with kings of the earth; let us deal now with kings of the skies. All religions are poison. They intoxicate and deaden the mind. A fight to the death must be declared upon religion. Our task is to destroy all kinds of religion, all kinds of morality."

Could anyone have said it plainer? From the first day of the Russian Revolution in 1917 until the present time there has been a ruthless program in the Soviet Union to stamp out all worship of God from among their people. Communism denies God, and says there is no need for religion. People are commanded to obey the state, which then replaces God. All allegiance is to a cold unfeeling economic and political system. The individual harnessed by the state is become a mere puppet jumping at the call of his superior officials.

"He who sits in the heavens laughs," said the psalmist, "the Lord has them in derision." Ultimately, we rest assured that God's power will bring to naught the power of any rival system or God-denying nation. May we be found so faithful to our Christ that our destiny might be to help lead the world to the feet of Jesus, who alone is the ruler and peacemaker.

PRAYER THOUGHT: *Dear Lord, may we combat the power of those godless persons who seek to destroy Thy church, by renewed efforts to win the world for Thee and Thy way.*

But according to his promise we wait for new heavens and a new earth in which righteousness dwells. 2 Peter 3:13

After four visits to Russia I am convinced that the communist system has made some real progress. People are well clothed. There are enough of the basic commodities to eat. They have provided an education for the people. The country certainly cannot be compared to some of the underprivileged nations in the world. But we remind ourselves that these people have been put to whatever use the state desires. Yet they are a dedicated people, even though their dedication is a blind one. They stoutly hold that their system is the best and that ultimately all people will be won to their way of life and thinking, and not necessarily by force. They are industrious, working long hours, and giving unselfishly of themselves to the building of a greater Russia.

In Moscow, for example, which is the showplace of the Soviet Union, and which attracts a majority of all foreign visitors, considerable changes have taken place during the last years. There is much construction work going on. On the way from Red Square to the airport alone I counted more than 120 apartment buildings in the process of construction. Some ascend into the air to a height of many stories. These are not luxury apartments like so many of those we have. Most of them consist of single rooms with communal kitchens and communal bathrooms.

However, there is a basic difference between the Soviet way of life and ours. There is something in that country that makes life seem so terribly empty. An American described this emptiness well when he said, "Here there is no hi-fi of the spirit!" Who among men wants to live without any hope of immortality, of the eternal heaven? Joy and expectation can rule in us as Christians, for we believe in God and heaven.

PRAYER THOUGHT: *We thank Thee, gracious Lord, for the richness and fullness of our lives because we have come to know Thee and to believe in the glorious future which Thou hast prepared for us.*

There is no faithfulness or kindness, and no knowledge of God in the land. Hosea 4:1

My personal description of Russia can be put in this phrase: "Darkness at noon." Here is a land that is ruled by the officials of the seven million members of the communist party. So far as I could observe on each of my several visits, there are only two classes of people—the rich and the poor. There exists no middle class as we know it in America. So long as I live I shall be able to close my eyes and vividly see those queues of people who stand patiently by the hour to buy their meager food supplies in the state-owned stores. The bulk of the diet for many consists only of potatoes and bread. Other commodities which are commonplace in the American diet are available only for a favored few. A tourist does not need to spend many hours in Russia before he is down on his knees in his hotel room thanking God that he and his family and friends are living in America.

"Darkness at noon"—this describes a godless Russia where the totalitarian state is deified. The Russian youth are taught to scoff at God and instead to worship the state. The mummified bodies of the revered leaders, Stalin and Lenin, which lie on exhibition in glass caskets, are the patron saints of the land. Great cathedrals which once heard the word of faith in God proclaimed from their pulpits are now quiet, for they have been converted into museums displaying the beautiful architecture of the land.

God is not mocked—forever. This is God's world, and He is still the Ruler. The day will come when even in the hearts of these people He will return to prove that He is Lord of lords and King of kings. Until then let us each be faithful and continually grateful to God that we have been blessed with the privilege of living in a country where there is freedom for all.

PRAYER THOUGHT: *We are grateful, heavenly Father, that we live in a land where we are free to worship Thee in the way we choose, and that we are free to lead lives of dedication to Thy Word.*

Where the Spirit of the Lord is, there is freedom. 2 Corinthians 3:17

Time dragged on wearily as I was waiting to make my first departure from Moscow back to the free world. I had seen enough, and more than enough, to make me terribly depressed. In this country my treasured faith was trampled on by most of the people. I had been observing a nation where the human soul means naked nothing, where there is no faith in immortality. I had seen the monotony of existence, the "everydayishness' of these people.

Yet I felt I had failed completely in my attempt to try to communicate what America meant to me and the abiding value of my Christian faith. It was as though a great and oppressive burden was on my shoulders which threatened to press me into the very earth. The time of the plane departure just couldn't come soon enough. When at last I landed in Copenhagen, and was again in the free world surrounded by people who understood me, many of whom worshiped the same living God as I did, it was as though this burden had rolled off my shoulders. I looked to the Lord and prayed, "Thank You, God, that I can breathe again this freedom that is mine!"

In the spiritual pilgrimage of life there are many people who are living behind iron curtains held fast by evil habits and shackled by sins and things contrary to the will of God. They go through life stooped under the burden they carry. Yet all the time they drag their ball and chains there is available for them a flight for freedom. God is the ever-waiting Pilot ready to fly us out of the land of dilemma into the land of forgiveness and beginning again. When He places His hand on our shoulders to say, "Thy sins are forgiven thee," then alone can there come into our lives a peace enabling us to go singing through life.

PRAYER THOUGHT: *Help us, dear Lord, to eliminate those things in our lives which prevent us from knowing the glorious freedom which is possible only when we have Thy saving forgiveness.*

Commit your way to the Lord; trust in him. Psalm 37:5

Standing at the airport in Moscow, I was waiting to board the plane for my first trip into barren Siberia. Never had I realized that I was embarking upon the loneliest week I have yet experienced. Presently a man from the travel agency came to inform me that I could now board the plane. It was a sharply cold evening as the group of about one hundred passengers climbed the ramp of this Russian TU 104 two-motor jet airplane.

There was provided no means of heating the plane before the motor started, so we waited shivering in our great coats, huddled silently together. No one else in the group could speak English, so already this sense of utter loneliness crept over me. After what seemed a month of waiting, a truck was attached to the nose of the plane, then very slowly it pulled the plane to the starting point of the runway. This was all designed to conserve fuel. Finally the motors started and off we flew on our thirty-two hundred mile trip to Irkutsk, Siberia. After we had been aloft for a while the stewardess served the meal consisting of a little meat steak, a few boiled potatoes, and seventeen peas. (I actually counted them!)

The discomfort of travel was not what bothered me the most on that lonely journey. Rather it was the thought that the pilot directing my flight was one who rejected any belief in immortality. What difference did it make to him if all of us should perish? Eternity meant nothing to him! Yet I realized how fortunate I was to have Christ as my pilot in whom I could have complete trust. Even soaring in the skies over a godless nation, I felt the presence of the living God at my side. This faith assured me that man's bonds with Him are everlasting.

PRAYER THOUGHT: *Almighty God, we are grateful that we may claim Thee as our pilot and guide through the journey of life, and that we can place our trust in a power far beyond that possessed by earthly creatures.*

Blessed is the nation whose God is the Lord. Psalm 33:12

Irkutsk is a city in Siberia located on the shores of Lake Baikal with a population of about 350,000 people. It is more than three thousand miles east of Moscow and is straight north of Mongolia. The warmest temperature during my stay there one winter was thirty-two degrees below zero. People have often asked me why I wanted to go there. I am then reminded of the words of Sir Edmund Hillary who, when asked why he wanted to climb mountains, would answer simply, "Because they are there!" Well, I feel much the same when asked why I would seek out this city in an enemy territory.

How would you be living if you resided in Siberia today? My guide took me to see some new housing developments and brought me to an area where they had established an aluminum factory. He said that twenty-five thousand people volunteered to leave their homes in old Russia to develop this new industrial area. I asked, "Are you sure they volunteered?"

Rather than answer me he invited me instead to visit an apartment building. It was so frozen with ice and snow that the door leading into the hallway could not be shut. Four girls lived here in a single room. There were four rooms to each section. The sixteen girl tenants shared one bathroom and one kitchen. This was living at its top best in this particular area.

Now, I do not mean to infer that just having the material things of life can bring us happiness. We are trying to get from them what is not in them to give, namely, satisfaction. However, even we in America are so prone to complain that I think we need to remind ourselves each day of the all too oft unappreciated blessings that we have. Start counting them one by one, and even two by two. Soon you will be staggered to discover how much you have for which you can be grateful.

PRAYER THOUGHT: *We are grateful, Lord, that we know the joy of living in a nation under God, where freedom is our birthright and liberty gives us opportunity to build a happy and useful life.*

"You will know the truth, and the truth will make you free."
John 8:32

Now, in the city of Irkutsk with its population of 350,000 people there is only one hotel. On registering there, I was assigned to a little dingy room and discovered that there was only one bathroom for every floor. One night I was sitting alone in my hotel room feeling as lonesome as I have ever felt in my entire life. I was huddled in my overcoat because it was bitingly cold. A tiny little radiator was struggling in vain against the cold air. On looking about me, my feeling of desolation was heightened. The plaster was cracking in the ceiling. A dim bulb was hanging on a thin electric cord extended from the ceiling. The appointments were makeshift.

Then I took out my notebook and began writing a summary of some of the day's happenings. Touching on my situation at the moment I penned these words: "I am sitting here all alone in a small hotel room in faraway Siberia. My friends and family are many, many miles from me, but I have learned a lesson tonight that I hope I will never forget. I have come to the conclusion that here is a group of wonderful people who do not know in the least what freedom means. They have never had any of the opportunities which I and my people take so for granted. I hereby resolve that wherever I go I will plead with all people I come in contact with that they give equal opportunity to everyone, regardless of race or color or creed. Together we must work with all our might for all to be free, for such has been, and of such must be, the greatness of America!"

Of course the truth that can really set us free is the truth to be found in God's Word. Jesus said, "I am the truth." This is the message that we must carry to all in our community and to the peoples of the world.

PRAYER THOUGHT: *Gracious Lord, we pray that we may bring the glorious knowledge that we are eternally free because we have Thee to all those who are yet living in the bondage of ignorance.*

"They shall all know me, from the least of them to the greatest," says the Lord. Jeremiah 31:34

Today I want to introduce you to Kim who was my guide in Siberia. His ancestry was both Korean and Russian. Earlier in his life he had been a school teacher. As such he had earned the equivalent of seventy-five dollars a month. Now as a Russian tourist guide he was earning one hundred dollars a month.

During our days together Kim and I became very close friends. At our first meeting he was very suspicious of me, but as we became better acquainted he began to place more confidence in me. Frequently he would ask questions about life outside the Iron Curtain. I don't know if I convinced him of the truth of my answers about life in America, but I tried every bit of strategy I knew to present him with a picture of life in the free world. By the time I left him, Kim would very much have liked to have had the opportunity of going with me to America.

One can hardly blame the Russian people for many of their attitudes. They know nothing except what they have been told by political propagandists. They know so precious little of the truth about the outside free world. They are taught to believe that what they have is the best that any nation has in the entire world. It is true that under communism there have been some great material gains, but likewise it is true that they have lost the one thing needful, personal freedom of belief. Human beings are considered to be of little significant value except as they contribute to the material enrichment of the state. In the Christian way of life every individual is regarded to have significance before God. Each one is important, whether he is a man of five talents or of but two or one. The worth of a man is great before the eye of God.

PRAYER THOUGHT: *We are thankful, dear Lord, that Thou art gracious and merciful to each of Thy children, and that every child of God may know the impartiality of Thy love.*

Hatred stirs up strife, but love covers all offenses. Proverbs 10:12

During my stay in Irkutsk my guide, Kim, had to order all my meals in advance, since he alone in that big city was able to speak English. A table in a small private dining room was my assigned place. One day there entered, to be seated at a nearby table, a group of eight Chinese from communist China. They had evidently come to study the glories of the system of Soviet communism.

Naturally I could not communicate with them, because I could not speak their language and they could not speak mine. Nevertheless, I smiled at them when they first entered the room; but there was no response. They just glowered back at me. Perhaps they had been pre-conditioned to react with scorn to Americans by being told that we had no respect for other nations and backgrounds. We had three meals in that dining room together. Finally after the third day of trying to show my friendship, they smiled back. By the time I left each one shook hands with me as if to say, "We appreciate your friendship, even though we cannot talk with you."

But yet I felt in a strange and wonderful way that we had talked with each other in the universal language of love. Love never fails. This is true not only on the level of international relationships, but even more is it true as we begin to love in our own homes and communities and our own friends. There is all too much resentment and hatred in the world. This is not according to God's will. It does not bring us satisfactorily to any of the goals that we naturally desire to attain. Love is the most powerful force in the world. If you will only practice it in your living, you, too, will discover what it can do for you. You will see how the dividends of your love will flow back into your own life and enrich your days, for love is contagious and will reach you again in new channels.

PRAYER THOUGHT: *Dear Jesus, we pray that we will use love as our most effective tool in implementing the goal of peace and brotherhood which is Thy will.*

"Be faithful unto death, and I will give you the crown of life."
Revelation 2:10

At the time I was in Irkutsk there were only five churches
open for worship. Four of these were Russian Orthodox
churches, and the other was a little Baptist church. Going to
the largest of the Orthodox churches, I was met by the priest
and his assistant. It was a very beautiful structure and well
furnished. No doubt these people had made great sacrifices
in order that the church doors could yet remain open in opposition to the teachings of the system under which they lived.

Soon people in the congregation learned that there was a
visitor in their midst, for dozens gathered around me. Hand-
ing me a red leather-bound book, they asked me to write a
greeting. Accordingly I brought them the good wishes of fellow Christians in America, pleading with them to be faithful
unto death, that they, too, might inherit eternal life. Under-
standably, they could not read what I had written in English,
but my atheistic guide translated my words into Russian.
When he had finished reading, tears rolled down their cheeks.
Even closer they gathered around me to express their respect
and affection for a fellow Christian.

About the only happy people one meets in Russia are those
who worship in these churches. Here is one place where they
could sing their hearts out. My, how they sang the great
hymns of faith! Imagine hearing people behind the Iron Curtain singing in trusting confidence, "Faith of our fathers, living still, we will be true to Thee till death."

We, too, have inherited a great and living faith from those
who have gone before. Are we also willing to make that same
pledge and a similar sacrifice? If we are, God's kingdom will
certainly go forward. Indeed, it cannot advance until we do
dare to commit ourselves.

PRAYER THOUGHT: *Lord, we pray that we may display a
steadfast faith in our relationship with Thee, never wavering
in that faith, even unto death.*

"Behold, I am with you and will keep you wherever you go."
Genesis 28:15

Today let us go from Irkutsk through the countryside to a
communal farm village. It is a winter day; the scenery along
the way is very beautiful. In fact it looks much like northern
Minnesota in January. Soon we have come to a village of a
few thousand people. Ours is the only automobile on the
street. There are some sleighs drawn by horses.

The village has a manager who is our host for the day.
Proudly he takes us to the community store. Here a variety
of services are offered. There is food and clothing for sale at
high prices, a barber shop, a tailor shop, and here also is to
be found the recreational center for the entire community.
The farmers all live in this village rather than on the farm
that they cultivate, but they go out each morning to a patch
of ground assigned to them, where they work. They either
walk to the location or go by sled. They are paid a set wage
for however much or little they produce. Their produce goes
into a pool until some official determines how it should be
divided.

There is a decent standard of living in this community, but
what is disturbing is the fact that there isn't a single church
open to serve the people. Here is a generation being trained
to believe that there is no God. It was not only my imagination that made me to feel that there was a loneliness that
could easily be observed as one studied their faces, a loneliness never felt anywhere else in any like degree save in communist countries that wall themselves off from God. What a
blessing it is that we know God as a loving Father and that
we can believe that He is our partner who walks with us
each day of life, shows us the way that we should go, and
brings us eternal happiness and joy.

PRAYER THOUGHT: *Dear God, we are thankful for the contentment and peace which we may feel because we have Thy
continual companionship.*

Our fellowship is with the Father and with his Son Jesus Christ. 1 John 1:3

In a little village just outside of Irkutsk I was invited to visit a typical home. Six people lived there in two small rooms plus a kitchen. A little potbellied stove, using wood as fuel, was vainly trying to heat this humble abode. One of the residents was the grandmother of the family, whose beautiful face attracted me. My atheist guide told me that she was one of the few remaining Christians in this village. As I looked at the very humble surroundings, I noticed a picture hanging on the wall. It was a beautiful painting of Christ. I looked at the picture and then at the woman. Although I could speak no Russian, nor she any English, there was real communication between us. And as I shook her hand, it felt as though I were shaking hands with a member of my own family. Indeed, we were brother and sister in the family of Christ.

These people behind the Iron Curtain cannot freely choose what they want to do. Instead, they are told what to do by some remote governing official. They certainly cannot be blamed for the fact that they know little or nothing about the Christian way of life, for what opportunity have they had to learn? In America, however, the situation is completely opposite. There is not a day but that each of us comes under some Christian influence. Every man has perfect freedom of will to determine whether or not he will live for Christ. The state does not punish him for his ultimate decision, but of course his own conscience will either accuse or excuse. Think of all we lose when we exclude ourselves from the great family of God! What a blessing it is to be a part of the Christian church, the communion of saints. Think of the deep and abiding friendships that are ours to enjoy because of the fact that we all are brothers and sisters in Christ.

PRAYER THOUGHT: *Help us, dear Lord, to keep ourselves in the companionship of other Christians, so that we may continually benefit from association with fellow believers.*

"Blessed are the peacemakers." Matthew 5:9

Today we are off to school. But it does not in the least resemble the school so many of you attend back home. In the first place, you have no choice regarding the subjects you will study. Furthermore, you will not have the beautiful classrooms to work in, nor will you have the freedom of expression granted you in your school, for this is a visit to a school behind the Iron Curtain.

Of course, it is unthinkable that you go anywhere in Russia save by previously arranged appointments. Therefore, careful preparation for your coming precedes your arrival. Everything is put in order, and the children are rehearsed for your visit. One student has been designated to bring a greeting to visitors from foreign lands. She stands up before the teacher and her classmates and brings a warm word of welcome to the guests. Then she concludes by saying, "Will you please tell the children in America how much we Russian children want peace?"

Russian people do want peace. There is a vast difference between the attitude of the common people and the policy of the Kremlin officials. Every sober-minded person around the world wants peace, because with all the powers of destruction presently available, a lack of peace means the twilight of civilization. Each one of us can play a vital part in bringing peace to the world. The place to begin is to find peace in your own heart through surrender and fellowship with the Lord. The next step is to be at peace with your fellow men, for the world begins at the doorstep of your home. Then you must with interest actively promote those things which work for world brotherhood and peace among nations. As we are willing to share Christ and His love with those about us in desperate need, we are enlisted in the finest "peace corps" of all.

PRAYER THOUGHT: *Make us more effective witnesses for Thy purpose of peace, dear Lord, by the example of our undiscriminating love toward everyone.*

"For whoever is ashamed of me, and of my words in this adulterous and sinful generation, of him will the Son of man also be ashamed, when he comes in the glory of his Father." Mark 8:38

While in Irkutsk, Siberia, I asked my communist guide to find out if there were any Protestant churches where divine services were held. He discovered that in this city of 350,000 there were only five churches open for Christian worship.

About the third day, he took me in one of the very few cars in the city to a little house. He said, "I think this is the church." Rapping on the door we were soon warmly greeted by a very friendly Baptist minister. He showed us a little chapel where people still worship Christ in this country which teaches that there is no God. Then he led me into his study. My curiosity being aroused by a motto hanging on the wall, I asked Kim, my interpreter, to translate it. These were the words which this hard-pressed pastor looked at each day as he prepared himself for service to his Lord: "You who have heard of the love of God, continue to speak." Here is a man living behind the Iron Curtain unintimidated by a Christ-hating state and fearlessly proclaiming the message of the Lord. In spite of persecution, poverty, and threat of death, he faithfully witnesses on behalf of the risen Lord as one who has not bent knee to false gods.

What about you, my friend? We live in a country where to be a Christian does not necessarily mean persecution. Yet how often we fail our Master! There are things to be done for Him that we do not do. There are moments in which we are silent when we should be speaking. Let us firmly resolve to face each succeeding challenge this day to be a witness for our Lord Jesus Christ and not miss one single opportunity to be of service. Let us thrill to stand up and be counted as those who are on the Lord's side.

PRAYER THOUGHT: *Help us, Lord, not to be cowardly in professing our love for Thee, but to stand strong and steadfast as Thy witnesses.*

"Every one then who hears these words of mine and does them will be like a wise man who built his house upon the rock." Matthew 7:24

Returning to this same Baptist minister in Irkutsk, Siberia, of yesterday's incident, we learn of another unforgettable observation about which he told me. We were talking about our mutual faith in Jesus Christ. Our entire conversation was translated through the lips of a communist guide, who professed to be an atheist. Although I could not understand the language which this pastor spoke, I felt very close to him because of our belief in the same God. I remember saying silently to myself, "Blessed is that tie which binds our hearts in Christian love."

Then I turned to him and said, "What is the future of the Christian church in Siberia?" His reply was immediate and firm in conviction: "On Christ the solid rock I stand; All other ground is sinking sand."

All of us need to be thoughtful about the foundations we build for our lives. There are other threats to the Christian faith besides communism. There exist such gods as materialism, pleasure, and power, and from these we try to draw our sense of security. Too often we forget that to pattern our lives upon these is like building upon the sand. The structure topples when the adversities descend and the storms come.

Too few of us have been willing to pay a costly price for our faith. Often I feel that the most dedicated Christians in the world are the ones who have been the most tried and persecuted. They have learned that other things in life are insignificant compared to the peace that comes into one's heart from knowing that God is, and that God cares, and that God wants us to draw from Him our strength and power for everyday living.

PRAYER THOUGHT: *Dear Lord, help us to forsake the crumbling gods which we unwisely build into our lives, and to find our strength and peace in the solid rock of Thy everlasting love.*

> Examine yourselves, to see whether you are holding to your faith. 2 Corinthians 13:5

After much difficulty with Soviet authorities, I finally was able to get permission to visit Riga, Latvia, where a few of the Lutheran churches are still open. The following experience I encountered there I shall never forget.

As a guest of the archbishop of the Latvian Lutheran Church, one Sunday morning I visited a number of these churches and was grateful to find them filled to capacity. My final visit was to the Cathedral Church. This stately edifice could accommodate 4,000 people, but it was not in use, as the people could not afford to heat the building. The congregation met in an adjoining chapel, where there was standing room only. After I had addressed the group, the archbishop took me to the balcony of the impressive cathedral where is located the second largest pipe organ in the world. An organist was on hand to play a recital on this fine instrument. I asked him if he would play one of my favorite hymns. The organ sounded forth in all its glory the melody to these familiar words: "A mighty fortress is our God, a bulwark never failing." At the top of our voices we sang, I in my language and the archbishop in his, as tears streamed down our cheeks.

In that glorious moment I felt quite sure that much the same thoughts went racing through our minds. Here we were behind the Iron Curtain, dominated by a government that teaches there is no God. But here I had discovered that in spite of this fact there still remained a magnificent minority of people who as in the prophet Elijah's day had not "done homage to Baal," but who had remained true to the faith. What about you? Is your dedication so unwavering that you would hold to your faith in God in spite of anything?

PRAYER THOUGHT: *Help us, Lord, to evaluate the true depth of our dedication to Thee and then resolve to love Thee even more, following Thy example of endless love.*

The law of the Spirit of life in Christ Jesus has set me free from
the law of sin and death. Romans 8:2

People living in Latvia still remember the freedoms they
once possessed when their land was not a satellite state of the
Soviet Union. When they were sure that one could be trusted,
and when they knew that no one else was listening, they would
open up their hearts and talk about how different life became
after the communists took over the government. They would
pleadingly say, "Can't you do something to help us out of this
dilemma? This kind of life is worse than slavery." Indeed,
one cannot help but feel sorry for those who have lost their
political and personal freedom.

And one cannot help but feel even more sorry for those who
lose their spiritual freedom. Too often we search in the wrong
places for those things we want most. Too often we think that
freedom is found in some far-off country—in the country of
sin. But soon we discover the sturdy power that sin has to
bind us, to hold us, and to lead us to our death.

Is there no way out of this spiritual slavery? Is there nobody
able to help us in our battle against evil and temptation?
Thank God, we can believe that there is a great Liberator who
comes and can cut the cords of sin entwined about us, setting
us free again. He cannot come to us, however, unless we ask
for Him. Yet, He is ever willing to answer our call. He has
asked us to call upon Him in the day of trouble, and He has
promised to deliver us. Thank God for the Great Emancipator
from sin, the One who is our advocate with the Father, pleading for us and setting over against our ugly staining sin His
perfect and holy life and His atoning death. He is our deliverer
who this day stands ready to set us free again.

PRAYER THOUGHT: *We pray, dear Savior, that we may not
fail to call upon Thee, the great liberator of all mankind, to set
us free from the bondage of our spiritual slavery and deliver
us into salvation.*

"The kingdom of the world has become the kingdom of our Lord and of his Christ, and he shall reign for ever and ever." Revelation 11:15

People in the Soviet satellite states are helpless victims in the clutch of the iron claw of communism. Christians in these countries have made great sacrifices in order to remain true to their faith. The communists use every device imaginable to influence their children to pledge allegiance to their system. They allow some few churches to be open, because they are confident that eventually the older people will die, and religion will be a lost cause, if right along in the schools the children are taught a militant atheism.

When the Russian communists took over the schools in Latvia, they asked the children, "What is the first thing you have been doing when school begins each morning?" The children replied, "We pray the Lord's Prayer." Then the teacher turned to them and said, "This prayer is wrong, because there is no father in heaven. Only Stalin is our father. You have asked your heavenly Father to give you daily bread. We will prove to you that He cannot do it." For three days they kept the children in school without giving them any food until the third day they were told to pray to Stalin for bread. When the children did so, food was brought to them. The communists said, "See, father Stalin has answered your prayers."

What could these young minds, influenced by starving stomachs, believe at that moment but that their leaders should replace their God? How subtly they work to gain the allegiance of their youth! Yet we who know God cannot help but be confident that this still is the heavenly Father's world. Even though the wrong in the world seems often so strong, God is the ruler yet. And all God's enemies will one day be conquered, for the Almighty will reign as rightful King.

PRAYER THOUGHT: *May we always remember that, no matter how powerful the forces of evil seem to be, Thou art yet more powerful, O God, and will someday rule the world with love.*

For we are not contending against flesh and blood, but against the principalities, against the powers, against the world rulers of this present darkness. Ephesians 6:12

A short time after returning from my trip to Riga, there appeared a short editorial in the daily newspaper which said that Soviet Premier Khrushchev was taking over the Cathedral Church in Riga. "No longer," he said "may it be used for religious purposes, because there are so few interested in religion. Instead, he wanted it to be used for the cultural enjoyment of all comrades in the party.

I said to myself, "You can close down the church and mute the organ that plays these great hymns of faith, but you will never be able to silence the song in the heart of Christians who will just keep on singing to the glory of God in spite of everything. For "This is my Father's world, O let me ne'er forget That though the wrong seems oft so strong, God is the ruler yet."

We need this kind of faith for what it does with our everyday living. So many forces, including communism, seek to oppose God and crowd Him out of our lives. In numberless ways each day we are faced with the temptation to take the easy way out. But no man ever finds inner peace and lasting satisfaction by compromising or selling short his faith. Every day there is the temptation to remain silent when you should be lifting up your voice in protest; to keep your hands at your side when you should be helping; and to nurse resentment when you should be loving.

God is seeking followers for His kingdom in every age. He needs brave and venturesome people in the army of which He is commander-in-chief. Following His leading, we can be confident that there is no earthly force that can defeat Him or us. As we travel along through life, we can be absolutely assured that we are on the way to victory.

PRAYER THOUGHT: *We pray, dear Lord, that we may be strong in our faith in Thee, and that we will never retreat from defending that faith.*

[There were] men of valor whose hearts God had touched. 1 Samuel 10:26

A man in Poland seized by the Nazi Gestapo lived in concentration camps for five terror-filled years. None of us native Americans can quite understand or visualize the conditions under which he and other people like him had to live when forced into these circumstances. Not only is there the horror of indescribable physical torture, but there is always the deterioration caused by mental fear of what is likely to happen next. During the years of this man's imprisonment his wife and son were killed.

Miraculously he escaped, and with the aid of friends contrived to come to America where he secured a job. The most pressing thought on his mind and heart was to help others who remained in the unspeakable kind of circumstances he had so long known. So he devoted a part of his earnings and all the time available after working hours, singlehandedly to procure sponsors so that almost 300 displaced persons could enter the United States.

How thrilling it is to find people who, having themselves known a helping hand, then turn with a heart full of love toward their fellow sufferers. Indeed, it is these people who most fully understand the needs of others and appreciate the anguish they experience. We who live in life's sunshine should be more aware of those who live in the bleak shadows. Our awareness should lead us to help them in their need, doing good even as our Lord did. No one is immune from the various troubles of life. By sharing the knowledge we have gained in enduring these trials, and by leading others to a deeper faith in God which will give them the strength to face each new day, we are again following God's command to be His witnesses.

PRAYER THOUGHT: *Teach us, Lord of love, to be ever sympathetic toward those who suffer misfortune and to extend to them the love and mercy which we have received from Thee.*

"Peace I leave with you; my peace I give to you; not as the world gives do I give to you. Let not your hearts be troubled, neither let them be afraid." John 14:27

Copenhagen is a very friendly city, and its people are most cordial. The city has many beauty spots to visit. However, the one that has always impressed me the most upon each of my visits is the Church of Our Lady which contains a number of figures sculptured by the famous artist Thorwaldsen. My first visit to this church was unforgettable. As I walked from my hotel, I observed the people along my way. Some were happy, but some seemed to have pressing burdens on their hearts. This was made obvious by the strained look on their faces. As I looked at them, I thought of just a few of the many problems I had faced in my life span, and I remembered those faltering moments when I took my eyes off from Him who is mighty to help in every time of need.

When I entered the stately church, I stood quietly in reverence at the rear of the center aisle until my eyes were adjusted to the dim cathedral light. Then the outlines of that magnificent altar scene began to sharpen. In life-size form, made from marble, Christ was standing there with hands outstretched as if He were inviting me to come forward. I advanced into the chancel of the church where I could almost hear Him say, "Come unto me, and I will give you rest."

It appeared almost as if His eyes were shut. A man by my side said, "You must kneel to see His eyes." Then as I knelt at the altar, His eyes looked down upon me. They were eyes of love, compassion, and mercy. My fears quickly subsided, for I knew once again that, if I remained in the presence of this wonderful Christ, I would have One by my side who could help me at every possible point of need. He is willing and able to help you too, for His love is large enough to embrace every individual who seeks Him.

PRAYER THOUGHT: *Dear Lord, there is great joy in the peace which comes to us when we trust Thy strength to bear us up in our times of trouble.*

Let the words of my mouth and the meditation of my heart be acceptable in thy sight, O Lord. Psalm 19:14

The setting is a service club meeting in Copenhagen. I had gone to buy a ticket at the table when I registered my attendance, but a man told me that everyone paid at the dining table. Seating myself by some new-found friends, I discovered there were many kinds of dishes on the table, several main dishes, some pastries, and fish. But everyone was given an envelope where were listed a number of items identifying the foods that were on the table. Each individual checked off what he had eaten and then placed in the envelope the correct amount of money to pay for his food. The hotel had complete trust in the integrity of these men, for by experience they had learned that on the whole they were honest and trustworthy.

Can we be trusted? Do we try to get by with things when no one is looking? Do we pretend to be somebody else? Do we attempt to put up a false front? Do we try to appear to be a person that we are not? Do we participate in shady deals?

God's eye is ever upon us. To some people this is a very terrifying fact, for they say, "We don't like to be always watched." But these are such as are afraid and ashamed of the way they are living. No one can "get by" with anything where God is concerned. We can deceive our fellow men, but we cannot deceive Him. Some day the record will be completely uncovered—the record of every man's life as he appears before the judgment seat of almighty God.

That God's eye is forever upon us is to others a very glorious truth. The heavenly Father constantly watches over His children through His indwelling in our conscience. He helps us determine our choices. He keeps us honest and faithful and true as we are in daily communication with Him.

PRAYER THOUGHT: *Almighty God, may we never fear what Thou wilt see in our lives, but only praise Thee for the constant watch which Thou dost keep over us to guard us in Thy care.*

Ascribe to the Lord the glory due his name; bring an offering, and come before him! 1 Chronicles 16:29

Copenhagen is famous for its promenades and parks. One day I passed through a park where there was a huge anchor covered with wreaths. This is a memorial to all the Danish seamen who have lost their lives while at sea. Afterwards I asked the ambassador about this memorial. He replied, "Not a day passes without someone placing a wreath at this anchor. The men who gave their lives in behalf of their country are daily remembered."

Do we remember our Lord with daily sacrifices to Him? After all, He has made the supreme sacrifice. Without His supreme self-giving, life would have been hopeless for every one of us. Moreover, He did it willingly, because He had volunteered to divest himself of the glory which is His in heaven to redeem the souls of all men for all time.

Is it nothing to you, all you who pass by? Every time we see a cross, whether it be upon a church steeple, or an altar, or worn about a neck, it should remind us of the greatest love the world has ever known. What will we do in return? Well, you ask, what sacrifices does the Lord ask of me? Above everything else He wants us, the total commitment of our life. When He has first place in our hearts, there can be no room for anger, hatred, jealousy, or pride. Is not He a God of love? When we give Him our lives we give Him all that goes with it. To each have been given talents to use. These are on loan from God and belong to Him. Each of us has been given capacities with which to make a living. An equivalent return on His investment is only fair dealing. Therefore, a part of your increment is God's due. Let us not allow a single day to pass but that we make a sacrificial gift to our Lord.

PRAYER THOUGHT: *Dear Lord, may we not forget to honor Thee for the great gift of salvation through the sacrifice of Thy Son, Jesus Christ. Help us daily to return to Thee a measure of our gratitude and service.*

Blessed be the God and Father of our Lord Jesus Christ, the Father of mercies and God of all comfort, who comforts us in all our afflictions. 2 Corinthians 1: 3, 4

In a number of localities, particularly in France, there are shrines which have been erected because they designate the fact that miracles of healing have taken place there. One day a veteran from the war who was an amputee appeared at one of these shrines. As he hobbled on a crutch up to the shrine, someone standing nearby who was merely a tourist remarked, "That silly man! Does he think God will give him back his leg?" The veteran overhearing the remark turned to him and replied, "Of course I don't expect God to give me back my leg, but I am going to pray to God to help me live without it."

God hasn't promised us that the skies overhead are always going to be blue during our days upon this earth. But He has promised us that He will give us grace to meet every trial, and that we shall have sufficient strength along the way. There can come no crippling force that will destroy us, if we keep the song of faith within our heart. With God as his strength, man is able to come through the deepest of valleys of difficulty. The longer we live, the more convinced we are that this power is available for all who keep the lines of communication open to God.

The secret is daily to live in His presence. When we do, we can face each day confidently. We can be assured that the sorrows of this present time cannot be compared with the glory which some day will be ours in heaven forever. It may be a part of God's plan in our preparation for that eternity that we endure these burdens, for then our faith can be made even more complete. God is a great God. Trusting in Him at all times must be our blueprint for life.

PRAYER THOUGHT: *Father of mercies, teach us to remain constantly near Thee in prayer, that we may receive the strength and the power which enable us to face each day with confidence.*

"I wholly followed the Lord my God." Joshua 14:8

When a certain Marshall Soult returned from a journey in Spain, he brought with him Murillo's "Virgin and Christ." When he examined the painting, he discovered that only the center of it was genuine. The border was clearly of inferior workmanship and superficial quality.

A number of years afterwards a certain Lord Overstowe, while traveling in Spain, was attracted by a painting that had a very inferior center but a superb border. There were angels and clouds, the sort of thing in which Murillo excelled. For the sake of the masterful border he bought the painting.

Later an unusual coincidence occurred. Lord Overstowe was at the sale of Soult's personal effects after his death. He purchased the painting which the deceased collector had brought from Spain. Examining carefully the two in the privacy of his gallery, he was amazed to discover that Soult's painting contained the center of the picture matching the border of the canvas he had. Detail and technique as well as tone and color corroborated his first guess. The picture now had supreme worth, because the two genuine parts were brought together.

God has meant that our total life should be dedicated to Him. Thus only can there be true harmony. You cannot have God on the edge of your life and the world at its center. There are many people who are trying to make only a partial commitment to God. They realize the importance of having Him, and yet they want also to hug the world to their hearts at the same time. This is an impossibility. God must have all of you, or He will have none of you. But remember that one of the worst bargains of the world is to gain the world and to lose the Savior.

PRAYER THOUGHT: *We pray that we will always keep Thee as the center of our life, dear Lord, for we know that if we have Thee only at the edge, the center of our life will be hollow and empty.*

"I came that they may have life, and have it abundantly." John
10:10

The following is reported to have happened during the days
of the Civil War in a suburb of Madrid, Spain. I thought of it
as I viewed the sections surrounding this proud city of Spain.
A group of soldiers was told that in the morning they would
have to make an attack on the city without any cover. Everybody knew what a dangerous assignment this could be. The
captain announced that he would soon decide which one of
the men would lead the march. He finally walked over to one
of the soldiers and said, "Sergeant X, you are the man I have
chosen." Everybody knew then that Sergeant X had a certain date with death.

The soldier went to bed that night fully dressed, his rifle
by his side, waiting for his morning assignment. During the
night, unbeknown to him and the rest of the soldiers, the attack was canceled. In the morning Sergeant X awakened. He
jumped out of bed, grabbed his rifle and said, "When does
the march begin?" The soldiers soon were told to be seated,
because the captain had something to tell them. In hushed
silence they sat as he said, "During the night the march was
canceled!" They were stunned by his words. Walking over
and pointing his finger at Sergeant X, he said, "What now
are you going to do with this gift of life?"

There is One who died upon a cross to become our Savior
from sin. By this sacrifice of His life Christ has made it possible for us to have another chance to receive abundant life.
Through Him we are given the opportunity of receiving everlasting life. The question that faces us each day should be a
challenge to all as it comes from Him who gave His life upon
the cross: What now are *you* going to do with this gift of life?

PRAYER THOUGHT: *Divine Redeemer, may we never forget
the terrible price which Thou hast paid for the gift of life which
we now may receive from Thee.*

"One must help the weak, remembering the words of the Lord
Jesus, how he said, 'It is more blessed to give than to receive.'"
Acts 20:35

Marrakech has often been called one of the most beautiful
places in the entire world. Even during the winter, flowers
bloom there in all their gorgeous colors, and the palm trees
sway in the breezes. The city itself is located on the plains
beneath the range of the beautiful Atlas Mountains which
loom up like a series of Mount Fujiyamas. This has been one
of Winston Churchill's favorite retreats when he needed to
get away from the governmental problems of England.

The city is a unique combination of natural beauty and human misery. I asked one of my friends on a visit there what
people did to make a living. He replied that one of the main
businesses was the sale of garbage in order that people might
have food to eat. Poverty and deep misery are seen at nearly
every turn. In fact, the whole country has living conditions
far below almost anything any of us in this country could
imagine.

As I was walking down a side street one day, I came upon
what happened to be the form of a human being, but it was
covered by a blanket. Here was a poor individual who had
apparently become so weak from the lack of food that she had
lain down on the dirty street to die. As I walked by, I could
hear her gasping her last breaths and quietly crying, "Allah!
Allah!"

Again I felt indicted and accused that I had not done more
to bring the living gospel to God's children, and to share my
material means with them. It is so easy for us to pass by with
the excuse that we could not possibly provide for the needs
of the entire world. Our faith tells us that even a mite in the
hands of the Lord can provide for a miracle. Lord, lay it upon
our hearts to show our concern for all people.

PRAYER THOUGHT: *Teach us, merciful Lord, to become more
sympathetic to the crying need of those of Thy children who
suffer because of our indifference and selfishness toward them.*

"What does it profit a man, to gain the whole world and forfeit his life?" Mark 8:36

When in Marrakech I was told of an incident that had taken place in that city some years ago concerning an American movie director. He had asked permission to film a certain scene for a movie in the courtyard of one of the beautiful palaces located there. Permission was granted. Then the director explained that it would be necessary to cut down one of the stately old trees in order to get cameras, spotlight, and all the other necessary movie equipment into the courtyard. The keeper of the palace objected to the plan and turned to the director saying, "No, let's cut down the wall instead." "But that will take so much time and the work of so many men," the director protested. "Yes," the keeper said, "but we have plenty of time and plenty of manpower to replace the wall. But we will never in my lifetime be able to grow another tree like this one."

This is a good lesson in so far as our sense of values is concerned. There are certain things in life that are much more important than others, but so often we get these values reversed or twisted. It is much better to lose our material possessions than to lose our soul for all eternity. Although we gain the whole world, we cannot keep it, because there comes a day when we stand alone before the throne of God with nothing but the record of our life and the state of our soul in our hands. The world constantly is trying to offer what appear to be bargains, but what in reality turn out to be expensive luxuries. It is well if we guard our lives closely and stay in the purifying presence of God, so that we may not lose all that is most important for our eternal welfare. "Nothing in my hand I bring, Simply to Thy cross I cling."

PRAYER THOUGHT: *May we always place a high value on our spiritual possessions, gracious God, and never sacrifice them to obtain the temporary pleasures of material riches.*

"Repent therefore of this wickedness of yours." Acts 8:22

A common plant called Matador, meaning murderer, grows in Brazil. Its slender stem creeps along the ground until it comes to a tree. With a powerful clinging grasp the plant entwines itself around the victim tree, growing larger and closing in ever more tightly. Up it climbs as high as the tree. Finally the plant lifts its head above the strangled treetops, now a conqueror completing its mission of death.

Like that lethal plant the evil one works slyly among the children of God. He is always offering some type of temptation that he hopes we will accept. It is our hearts that he wants to conquer. Temptations can look so innocent at first appearance. "It won't make any difference if I yield just one time," we say. Our first surrender lowers our resistance. Then it is easier to yield a second, a third, and a fourth time. Finally, before we ourselves are aware of what has happened, we are conquered and held in a lethal embrace by the power of sin.

Is there any escape from the dilemma? If man doesn't wait so long that he becomes hardened to the call of God, there is still hope. Man does not have the power to extricate himself from the trouble he is in. But there is One whose power is even greater than that of the evil one. It is God Almighty. He sent His Son into the world to break sin's chains which had entwined His children because they had failed to obey Him. He stands ready to help each one today. He will not force His way into our life. He will not violate our freedom of will by forcing us to accept His help. The key to the door of the new and free life is repentance and conviction, which is the rightabout turn of the heart from sin to God.

PRAYER THOUGHT: *Help us to live, dear Lord, so that we may never find ourselves hopelessly entangled in the vines of evil. May we through repentance keep ourselves free from its strangling hold.*

They who wait for the Lord shall renew their strength, they
shall mount up with wings like eagles. Isaiah 40:31

On the border between Argentina and Brazil there is a two-
hundred-foot high waterfall spreading its water over a very
large area. A fascinating feature of the territory of the cataract is a bird known locally as the cataract swift. It nests
on the face of the cliff behind the veil of falling waters and has
the peculiar habit of flying straight through the dashing water
hundreds of times during each day. It seems to be unafraid
of the journey ahead, no matter how swiftly the falls may
tumble over the rocky cliffs or how loudly the falling water
may roar. The reason for this calm spirit? If the bird could
speak it would answer confidently, "I have wings!"

So each Christian has wings—the wings of faith. Being a
living and acting part of a world of sin, he is not exempt from
the hardships of life. Christianity is not a guaranteed health
and accident insurance policy. In fact some Christians are
called upon to suffer more grievously than those who are not
followers of Christ.

In spite of how severe his troubles are, the Christian has the
capacity to see things through. He draws from a power beyond himself that enables him with the wings of faith to soar
over any mountain of adversity. This does not mean that God
will always lift us out of trials miraculously and set us in a
life free from evil. Indeed, often we must learn from such
times those things that will make our faith in Him more mature and ever growing. This faith gives the Christian the light
of hope in his heart as he travels life's way. His hope leads
him to dare to take the sometimes broad step of faith. God
never fails His own. One never need feel that he has to face
any situation that he fears cannot be handled when he has
behind him the resources of God.

PRAYER THOUGHT: *We pray that we may draw daily from the
resources of Thy power, almighty God, so that we can fly confidently with wings of faith through the mists of suffering and
anxiety.*

Let the peace of Christ rule in your hearts. Colossians 3:15

When flying between Buenos Aires and Santiago, we saw the famous statue of the Christ of the Andes. This is a bronze statue of the Lord, erected after the pact was made between Argentina and Chile in 1902 as a symbol of perpetual peace between the two nations. When the monument was erected on their common border in the Andes Mountains, the people said, "Sooner shall these mountains crumble into dust than Argentina and Chile break the peace which at the feet of Christ the Redeemer they have sworn to maintain." It was a thrilling sight to see this statue of our Lord high in the mountains, standing there in majestic beauty as a symbol of the one and the only way by which the whole world can find peace.

Man-made methods have utterly failed. As long as there is selfishness, hatred, greed, and pride in this world, we shall continue to live in a world of wars and rumors of war, a world of unrest and dissension among men and nations. Man does not have the capacity to rid himself of these sins. There is only One who can cause the shadowed places in life to be eliminated. He is the Prince of Peace. We can reject Him even as did the people of Jerusalem until the day comes when He is hid from our eyes. Or we can accept Him today in our daily relationships and discover the pathway to eternal peace.

Why do not you, therefore, enthrone Him in your heart and life, pledging that each day you will seek to be at peace with your fellow men, listening to His voice and following His guidance. You will then find the only way of life which can bring contentment and joy to you as an individual and to groups of men as nations. When storms threaten to swell up, let the Savior with His cross behind Him and His arm raised in benediction over the world come to you with His comforting love.

PRAYER THOUGHT: *May we daily let Thee rule in our hearts, Prince of Peace, so that our lives may be lifted out of the darkness of sin and into the light of Thy continual presence.*

"I am the resurrection and the life; he who believes in me, though he die, yet shall he live, and whoever lives and believes in me shall never die." John 11:25, 26

The Christian church has made a deep and lasting impact on East Africa. It has come not only with its Christian missions, but also through the schools and hospitals which brought doctors and nurses to man them. Perhaps the equipment is not as modern in these hospitals as in America, but many are kept spotlessly clean. The dedication of those workers was such as I had never seen anywhere else. Although they were receiving little in monetary rewards for what they were doing, yet they were among the happiest people anywhere. They truly placed service above self as long as any sufferer needed them.

A doctor took me on his rounds through one of these hospitals. We came into a room where there was a man lying in severe pain. This African had been on the operating table for many hours. He was in his little hut sleeping, when he awakened to discover that a leopard was about to spring on his child. If he had permitted it to do so, the child would have been killed. However, the African father, seeing the mortal danger his child was in, threw himself between the leopard and the child, and in so doing part of his skull was torn away.

We marvel and wonder at such accounts of parental love and human bravery. And yet sometimes we can be indifferent to the greatest deed this world has ever known. A Man once came to earth from heaven and stood between us and total death. True, He was more than man—the God-man. Yet had it not been for Him, we should all have faced the prospect of certain death and eternal separation from God. Because He offered His life, everyone of us may live forever.

PRAYER THOUGHT: *Precious Savior, may we remember the courage which Thou didst display on the Cross. Because of Thy suffering and sacrifice, we have the joy of Thy presence in this life and the glorious assurance of heaven.*

For to this end we toil and strive, because we have our hope
set on the living God, who is the Savior of all men, especially
of those who believe. 1 Timothy 4:10

The political situation was very tense in East Africa during
the early 1950's when I paid my first visit to Kenya. The
fearsome Mau Maus were on the loose. For protection women
carried pistols in their purses. Traveling was restricted to the
highways. There were roadblocks and police checks everywhere. Natives were ruthlessly routed out of their business
establishments to be unceremoniously pushed around and
frisked away, to see whether they might be carrying knives.
The Mau Mau terrorist group which was seeking independence
had very little of firearms or ammunition, but they did carry
knives with which they would slice human bodies apart limb
by limb. In fact, one night when I stayed in Arusha, they
went past the window of the room in which I was sleeping
and stealthily entering the next house cut up a family of
three, because they were known to have resisted the activities of the Mau Maus.

This particular group of people tried to get another tribe,
the Masai tribe, to join in their activities against the white
people. But the Masai refused, saying that they were Christians and as Christians they believed it was wrong to kill.
Some British authorities later said that the reason the rebel-
lion didn't reach greater strength was because of the success
of the Christian missionaries in teaching such a large portion of the population about Christ and His kingdom.

What a different world this would have been today, if we
had invested more in sending people to bring the gospel of
life to all nations! There continues to be only one way to
change the world and to bring it out of chaos into tranquility.
That is the transformation of the hearts of people everywhere
through the gospel of reconciliation.

PRAYER THOUGHT: *Help us, Lord, to accept the challenge of
our responsibility as Christians to bring the gospel of peace
and love to all nations.*

"Do not be afraid, but speak and do not be silent; for I am
with you." Acts 18:9, 10

Do we Christians dare to stand up and be counted among
the band of Christ's disciples? We could learn so much in
loyal courage from several hundreds of the Kikuyu tribesmen
in Kenya, East Africa. Christians were hated by the terrorist
Mau Maus, who reserve for such people their most savage
treatment. In spite of this fact, these Christian tribesmen
banded themselves together, becoming known as torchbearers.
They would wear a round little badge called the "badge of
courage." This identified the wearer as an enemy of the Mau
Maus. It would also mark him as a potential victim of this
terrorist group.

These tribe members did not segregate themselves from life.
Most of them were common ordinary people working in the
villages. They were subject to fierce persecution. Yet they
were free to say, "I am willing to stand up and be counted."
Such torchbearers are in a position to wield a significant and
outstanding influence in this part of the world.

Think for a moment of what would happen, if Christians
everywhere would be that willing to be marked men for God.
Too many of us try to lose ourselves in the mass anonymity of
the everyday crowds, unwilling to take our stand for Christ
when He needs us as His disciples. How dare we be so
ashamed as to hide our colors? Was Christ ashamed of our
sin? Indeed, not! Yet, how deep is our betrayal of Him! The
Christian has every reason to be proud to let the world know
that he is on the Lord's side. What a different world it will
be when all of us resolve that we are going to witness for
the Lord, no matter where in the world we may live. This
day is at hand; let us resolve to use it in the service of our
Lord.

PRAYER THOUGHT: *May we willingly offer ourselves as torchbearers of truth, kind Lord, seeking to carry high our witness
for Thee and Thy glory.*

Set the believers an example in speech and conduct, in love, in faith, in purity. 1 Timothy 4:12

Some years ago, on my first visit to Africa, the Mau Maus went on the loose. This was a native terrorist tribe, led by a man named Jomo Kenyatta. These men did not have much ammunition but they had secured some vicious knives. Searching out their enemies, they would slash their bodies apart limb by limb. Jomo Kenyatta was finally arrested and brought to trial. This was the word of his witness: "This is our country. Africa belongs to the Africans. The white man came over to us as a visitor and guest. We allowed him to stay here. He taught us there was a God. He taught us to close our eyes and pray to God. And when we closed our eyes and prayed to God, he took our land from us."

Of course, this indictment is not entirely true. Yet one cannot help but believe that the reason for much of the trouble in Africa today is due to the fact that the white man has assumed a superior attitude to the black man. It is disturbing to know that Jomo Kenyatta was raised in a Christian mission school. The reason he gave for leaving Africa and then going to Russia for indoctrination by the communists is that the lip confession of the Christians did not coincide with their living. He said, "They preached love and the equality of man, and yet they were not willing to put it into practice."

Let us honestly admit that all too frequently we are very poor examples of our Christian witness and faith. More effective than the sermon from the pulpit often is the sermon preached by the life of a person who is a friend of Christ. People are quietly aware each day as to whether your living is consistent with your profession of faith.

PRAYER THOUGHT: *Let our lives be a truthful witness of our faith in Thee, Lord, and not a deceitful pretense which may harden the hearts of those whom we strive to draw into the fellowship of faith.*

"I am the Lord your God, . . . who leads you in the way you should go." Isaiah 48:17

Upon arriving on one of my several visits to Africa, I was met in Nairobi by a missionary friend and several native Christians. The missionary had appointed himself to be my guide on a safari of several hundred miles. This trip we were to make in a jeep. Now this was the first visit that these natives had ever made to the big capital city, so they were especially attentive to everything they saw. It was as though a world of wonder had opened up to them.

On the return from Nairobi to the mission station my missionary friend was driving at an excessive speed. The more frightened I became and the more I cautioned him to slow down, the more it seemed to encourage him to drive faster. Suddenly we came to a very dangerous right-hand turn where we almost took to the ditch. After our narrow escape from accident as spontaneous as anything could be, the two native Christians began singing in the back seat, "Guide us, O Thou great Jehovah."

It was quite a lesson to all of us. We dare never put our trust in man. No matter how many things we may accomplish by our genius, we are not capable of directing life successfully along its way without the help of a Power beyond ourselves. There is only one Pilot who can safely lead us to the destination we are seeking. And while advancing on the way, we want a safe journey. He is the one sure Guide and Protector, for He never fails. He helps us conquer the difficult places, shares in our sorrow, helps bear our burdens, and finally leads us through the inevitable adversities of life to the glorious future which knows no end. In God we can trust! In Him we can rest our faith confidently, and in the sure knowledge that with Him our life is safe.

PRAYER THOUGHT: *We pray, Lord, that we will wisely choose Thy guidance for our lives, never placing our trust in the precarious power of man.*

[He] will forgive our sins and cleanse us from all unrighteousness. 1 John 1:9

Arusha is located about halfway between Cairo and Johannesburg. From this city the road to the south goes through some very interesting country on the way to Babati. My first experience traveling through this area in a jeep was a memorable one. We had driven a number of miles when suddenly we came to a place on the jungle highway where it seemed as though a house had been built covering the highway, and therefore impeding the progress of any vehicle. There were ditches on both sides which made it appear impossible for anyone to get through.

As we came to the place where we had to stop because of this obstruction, some natives opened two doors similar to garage doors. Upon their signal, we drove our car into this strange building. The missionary with whom I was riding then informed me that the car would have to be sprayed in order to eliminate the danger of our carrying with us any tsetse flies. So from the wheels to the top of our jeep the natives proceeded to do the necessary spraying job. When it was finished, the doors were opened at the other end of the building, and we continued on our journey. After another distance of miles we came upon a similar situation. Thus at various times the car was checked and sprayed as a precaution against these dreaded insects.

Wise indeed is the man who examines his own life from day to day and then honestly turns to God to be rid of the impurities which he finds in his heart. Not a day passes but that we sin and accumulate within our hearts the things which we should allow God to eliminate by His forgiving love. Only if we allow this process of renewal and restoration can we live in the assurance that we can be at peace with God.

PRAYER THOUGHT: *God of mercy, we pray daily for Thy forgiveness for the sins which corrupt and disease our souls, knowing that it is in Thy power alone to cleanse us from all unrighteousness.*

> May the Lord make you increase and abound in love to one another and to all men. 1 Thessalonians 3:12

On one of my visits to East Africa I enjoyed meeting a veteran missionary who had given the flower of his life to Africa, having been there for more than thirty years. Because of his dedicated witness and consistent perseverance, he had won the admiration and the respect of the warlike native African tribes with which he had worked. Likewise he had won the respect of the British government officials who had co-operated wholeheartedly with him in his endeavors.

In addition to being a missionary, he was a great mountain climber. Those who know him best say that he has scaled the peak of Mount Kilimanjaro at least fifty times and has been awarded a medal by the British government for his explorations.

In conversing with this adventurous missionary, one soon learns that his biggest thrill has come not from the honor which he has received from his fellow men, but rather from the assurance that God has used him to help bring thousands of His unredeemed children into the kingdom of heaven. Here is one who sincerely knows what power there is in the gospel. Here is a dedicated Christian who has willingly and unselfishly lived a life of hardship, in order that he might be used by God to bring the good news to these people.

How about you? What to you is of most importance? To win glory for self, or to give glory to God? To gain material security on earth, or to know the promise of eternal security in heaven? In an individual way, each of us meets daily opportunities to extend Christian love into the life of another. What may appear to be only an insignificant incident may be the turning point in one man's life. God taps each of us on the shoulder and says today, "Go!"

PRAYER THOUGHT: *Dear God, we pray that we will find our pleasure in working for Thy kingdom by using whatever abilities we have to bring the saving knowledge of Thee to our fellow men.*

According to the purpose of him who accomplishes all things according to the counsel of his will. Ephesians 1:11

In East Africa there are many places where no bridges have been constructed to span the rivers. Instead there is a concrete strip laid on the rocky bottom from bank to bank. Perhaps the reason for this is that most of the time the country is very dry, and therefore the government does not want to invest a lot of money in something which is used so seldom.

On one of my visits to Africa it happened to be the rainy season. It was quite an experience to cross over a stream in a jeep. The rushing muddy water obscured the concrete slab that lay along the bottom. Barefoot natives were hired to stand on either side of the slab to indicate where it was so that the car wouldn't get off the track. Many times when the natives themselves cross as the stream is flowing quickly, they burden themselves with a heavy load. If there is nothing else at hand, they carry a big rock. With the load balanced on their heads they wade into the water. The solid load helps them to keep their footing, and prevents the rushing waters from dragging them downstream to destruction.

One cannot observe this without thinking how sometimes in life those things which appear to be heavy burdens can be blessings in disguise. We cannot properly evaluate life as we look at it from the perspective of each day. Only when it has been lived completely can we see the perfect pattern. Many times the things about which we complain are those things which have led us to greater heights. All of us will make mistakes. No one is exempt from trouble. But the man who will succeed and make the most out of life is that man who is always willing to capitalize on his calamities.

PRAYER THOUGHT: *Almighty God, may we not question Thy wisdom in directing the course of our lives, but rather may we accept the afflictions that come, knowing that with Thy help, the defeat of today can become the victory of tomorrow.*

He knows the way that I take. Job 23:10

As one travels about in East Africa, especially on the mission fields, one wonders how anyone ever is able to find his way. Sometimes a jeep must travel over unmarked courses, such as river beds and open fields. There are no highways that can even begin to be compared with those here in America.

A missionary friend was telling me about the experience of one man who wanted to reach a specific destination. He tried to find a guide who knew the way. The first one he interviewed was asked, "Have you ever been to this village where I want to go?" The man replied, "No, I have been part of the way, and I have heard others talk about it." "You will not do," he was told.

Another man came and offered his services as a guide. "Have you been to this village?" he was asked. "No, but I have been almost all the way." "You will not do," he was told.

A third man came and offered to be the guide. He was asked the same question. "Have you ever been to this village where I wish to go?" "Sir," he replied, "the village to which you are going is my home." This man was hired because the traveler knew that he would lead him safely to his destination.

When we look for someone to guide us in our lives, we want one who has gone the whole way, one who knows every step of the journey. There is only one guide like this in life, and that is our Lord Jesus Christ. He stands all alone on the world's skyline. To know Him as a personal friend is one of the most meaningful experiences of life, but to trust in Him as a personal Guide and Savior is ultimately our greatest joy, for then we shall continue our fellowship with Him even into eternity.

PRAYER THOUGHT: *Dear Savior, we pray that we may choose Thee as our guide in life, so that we may trustingly journey toward Thy home and eternity.*

There are varieties of working, but it is the same God who inspires them all in every one. To each is given the manifestation of the Spirit for the common good. 1 Corinthians 12:6, 7

During some seasons of the year in East Africa, water seems almost of more value than jewels. During the rainy season there, people frugally store up water. After the first two months of the dry season have passed they begin to ration it. By later summer and early fall, before the rains come again, they are reduced to the extremity of using the same water over again four or five times. They may use it to wash their faces; then they bathe in it; then they use it to scrub the floors of their huts; and finally they reclaim as much as they can and water their gardens.

As a missionary explained this procedure to me, I was again reminded of all of the little things in life for which we should be grateful. We so glibly take so much for granted. In our own country there are so many advantages and opportunities right at our fingertips. We turn on the light switch without the least doubt but that someone is working somewhere to help the electricity come through the wires into our homes. We reach for the telephone fully confident that the operator will be on duty to place our long-distance call. We go to the department store knowing that someone will be there to show us the merchandise we want and to take care of our material needs.

We need to be reminded of the fact that life is a partnership. We are dependent upon others for the blessings we have. We are in debt to our forefathers for the freedoms and liberties they have secured for us and our children. Therefore, under the power of God, we should do whatever task is ours according to our talents and circumstances, knowing that we are partners together with our fellow men in helping to create a common good.

PRAYER THOUGHT: *We pray that ours will be lives of co-operation, gracious Lord, seeking always to labor for the benefit of others, and not just for ourselves.*

Forgiving one another, as God in Christ forgave you. Ephesians 4:32

There is a very quaint custom held by a tribe in East Africa which emphasizes peace and dramatizes it in personal action. If an individual holds a grudge against another, no matter what the reason might be, the one who is holding the grudge has the responsibility of trying to cleanse from his heart the hatred that rests there. He must visit the tribal medicine man and confess to him the ill will which he feels in his heart.

The remedy is always the same. He finds a little fruit which grows in the territory called rulani, which means, "let there be peace." Then he goes to the person against whom he holds this hatred and explains why he feels as he does. Then he crushes the fruit which he holds in his hand and scatters it all about him on the ground as he says, "As I have destroyed and thrown away these useless bits, I also promise you that I will crush and discard the resentments which I have against you. From now on let us have peace."

Many of us confess to be Christians, but still we go around bearing grudges against our fellow men or entertaining bitter thoughts about them. How often, you ask, should a Christian forgive? The answer is this: As often as you want God to forgive you. That makes the number of times limitless, for daily each of us falls short of God's glory. How often will God forgive me? you ask again. The answer is that God's love never ceases. It has no saturation point, for as often as we need His mercy there is yet a full supply. When we go astray, He is able to follow after us and call us back again into faith. Chief of sinners we are; but God sent His Son to the very depths of death that we might know eternal salvation.

PRAYER THOUGHT: *We ask Thy help, merciful God, to remove the grudges which we hold in our hearts against others, knowing that we cannot be true Christians if we refuse to forgive others as Thou hast forgiven us.*

"Not every one who says to me, 'Lord, Lord,' shall enter the
kingdom of heaven, but he who does the will of my Father
who is in heaven." Matthew 7:21

A young pastor with his wife and family who were missionaries came to a new field in the African bushland to begin
work among a people who had once been a man-eating tribe.
Of course, the missionaries needed a place to live, and so a
home was constructed for them. During the time of building
it was not unusual to see a number of the African natives
watching the construction, for they had never seen before a
house like this one. When it was finished, they were even
more curious to see the inside of the house. Missionaries actually have very little privacy, for the door of their home
must always be open. It is not unusual for members of this
Barabaig tribe to wander into the house at any time looking
about in amazement.

One of the things that fascinated them most was the fact
that this new house had two stories. All of them had lived in
little bomas or huts with the beaten down dirt of the ground
as their floor. Now before their very eyes they saw something new and different from any dwelling they had ever
imagined. As they looked at each other, pointing to the second floor, they often said, "That is the stairway to heaven."

In the life of each one of us there should be found this stairway. It is not something which man constructs, but something
which is given him without a required payment, because of
the sacrifice of Christ our Savior. Each of us can have the
Cross in our possession which then becomes the stairway to
God and to heaven through our faith which itself is also a gift
from God. However, we lose possession of this, if we neglect
our ground of salvation, and fail to live in accordance with
God's will.

PRAYER THOUGHT: *Teach us so to live, dear Father in heaven,
that we may always have access to the stairway which leads
ever upward to the glorious lands of eternity with Thee.*

Your abundance at the present time should supply their want. 2 Corinthians 8:14

We are going to a boma today located in the area inhabited by the Barabaig tribe in East Africa. A boma is a brush-secured enclosure with a gate leading to a compound consisting of a number of single room huts. The floors are of beaten dirt, and the beds are of dried cattle skins.

The Barabaig chief invited me one day to see how these people get their food. Their chief industry is raising cattle. They would never think of selling them, because their cattle herd is really their bank account on the hoof. The chief then brought into the enclosure a bull, threw a rope around its feet and felled it to the manure-littered ground. He then drew a rope tightly around the bull's neck in order to protrude a vein, whereupon he took an arrow and shoved it into the vein until it brought forth a stream of blood. One of the chief's wives quickly brought a dirty container to catch the blood. Then they sat down together on the filthy ground and mixing the blood with milk began to drink it. "This," said the chief, "is the food that we eat twice a day." Protestingly I said, "Surely you eat something besides!" He replied, "Sometimes one of our herd dies from disease. Then the whole tribe has a feast of diseased cattle meat."

It is hard for us who live in a land of luxury to believe that such primitive conditions actually exist in our world today. It is good for us to know how other people live. It will help to prod and inspire us to do more than we have done in helping further the great missionary movement and also support our government and its program of aid to the underprivileged countries in our world. This is our Father's world. Who would dare deny that this must indeed be God's will for us as well as His will for the world which He so dearly loves.

PRAYER THOUGHT: *Help us, Lord, to accept our responsibility as Christians in giving aid to those who do not have even the necessities of life.*

Never flag in zeal, be aglow with the Spirit, serve the Lord.
Romans 12:11

Seldom can one find more dedicated people than those serving on foreign mission outposts. They have made what appear to us to be tremendous sacrifices, and yet they refuse to consider them as such. They have been uprooted from their home ties, and have gone to these faraway lands, because the love of the Lord has been prodding them to share the gospel.

In East Africa one day I was sitting with several single ladies who were teaching and ministering to a group of lepers in a colony of about four hundred people. Now, these girls did not live in the vicinity, but each morning would walk several miles to get to work and the several miles home again each night through areas which would stir fear in the hearts of most of us. I asked, "Don't you find this work difficult and the environment frightening at times?" Their reply was this: "We just can't wait to get to work in the morning!"

Then I thought of the admonition of the Psalmist of old, "Serve the Lord with gladness." So many of us, when asked to do things for the Lord, are quick to find excuses, or if we do volunteer with our means and talents and time, we grumble, complain, and ask why we must always be the ones to make this contribution.

Our Lord has set for us an example. "The Son of man also came not to be served, but to serve, and to give his life a ransom for many." In the light of His sacrifice can any of us possibly do too much for Him? "The Lord loves a cheerful giver." We are called upon to answer the challenges that face us in our day. May we do it in the same spirit of true dedication as Christ had when He gave His life on the cross for the redemption of mankind.

PRAYER THOUGHT: *May we not fail to answer the challenge of Thy call to service, heavenly Father; enable us to serve Thee willingly and worthily.*

"This gospel of the kingdom will be preached throughout the whole world, as a testimony to all nations." Matthew 24:14

One of the most unusual church services I have ever participated in was in East Africa. A very good friend with whom I had shared my ministry for a year had gone there to be a missionary to a tribe of people called the Barabaigs. These primitive people had never heard of the gospel of Jesus Christ, so my friend was their first missionary. One of his initial projects was to attempt to put their language into script form.

Eagerly I waited for Sunday that I might observe the response to the service which had been announced. The invitation was passed from village to village. Since no one knew what a church service meant, it was announced that a dance would be held.

Sunday morning came and we waited under a tree which was the outdoor setting for the service. The only timepiece these people have is the sun. So over a period of almost two hours they kept wandering across the fields. The only means of transportation is to walk. They came with spears in their hands. Their bodies were dressed in cattle skins. It was indeed an unusual experience to see them seated on the ground, spears resting by their sides, listening to words which they had never before heard. One of the most inspiring parts of the service was the singing by a choir of African converts from a nearby village. Now they were in turn witnessing to their blood brothers of the love of Christ which was prompting them to serve.

May our earnest prayers today support the bringing of the message of Christ to all nations. Even as these new members of the kingdom of the redeemed bring the good news to their neighbors, so may we provide for the strengthening of the kingdom of God wherever we are.

PRAYER THOUGHT: *Lord, we pray that the comforting news of Thy gospel may reach the minds and hearts of people in every nation on earth.*

"I am coming to gather all nations and tongues; and they shall come and shall see my glory." Isaiah 66:18

A missionary in East Africa told me of a little boy who had come to him one day and asked, "Was this Jesus man you talk about a white man or a black man?" The missionary was prompted immediately to tell the boy that Jesus was a white man. But he thought again before he answered, for he could tell what was on the little boy's mind. He was sure that if he told the lad that Jesus was a white man, the boy would be very sad and perhaps would not come back to the mission station. The missionary paused for a moment, remembering that Jesus had lived in a very warm country where the people were dark skinned, but not black. So this was his answer: "Jesus wasn't a white man or a black man, but He was sort of in between the two, sort of brown." The little African boy then exclaimed in delight, "Then He belongs to both of us, doesn't He?"

Yes, He belongs to all of us. God loved the whole world. That is why He sent His Son to give His life for the welfare of all men whose faith is in Him. All of us need Him. No one is righteous of himself. No one is worthy of salvation, nor can he gain it by his own merits. God gave His life for all people with no respect to their race or the color of their skin or their circumstance of birth or their social status or their mental and physical ability. What a great God He is who can love all men.

He is so great that He belongs to each of us individually also and is concerned about the life of even one of His followers. He has a personal interest in all that we do and wants to give guidance that we might lead a useful and happy life in serving Him. What great comfort we can take from the fact that if God watches over the birds of the air, He will certainly watch over us His redeemed children.

PRAYER THOUGHT: *Loving God, we are grateful that Thou dost show impartial love to all people, paying no heed to race or color but only to the soul which lies beneath all external appearances.*

"If any one keeps my word, he will never see death." John 8:51

A missionary friend of mine who is working among some of the non-Christian people in Africa explained to me something about one of their many strange superstitions. When someone among the heathen is sick unto death, the neighbors go out into the wooded areas and cut down a certain kind of tree. Superstition has convinced them that if they put this tree in front of the door of the house where the sick person lives, it will stave off death. Think of the empty and vain hope of such false beliefs that are deep-seated in tradition.

How grateful we should be that we have joy in the great assurances which our Christian religion gives. Love makes us more than conquerors. Because of the love of Christ, we can overcome our final enemy. And what is man's final foe? Who is this enemy that makes us tremble when we must ultimately face it? Is it not death?

Two thousand years ago men cut down a tree and made it into the shape of a cross. Because of His great love for us, the Son of God died on that cross to become the Savior of the world. All of our sins were pressing upon His body that dark day, for the transgressions of mankind were responsible for His hanging from that crude frame.

If we keep this cross to the front of our life and sincerely trust in Him who died upon it, we shall have the joy of forever hearing His voice speaking to us in accents of love, "Whoever lives and believes in me shall never die." Then we shall have the sure knowledge that death has lost for us its sting. The grave will hold no fear, for death has already been swallowed up in the victory of Christ's resurrection. The greatest victory that man can ever know is to be at home with the Lord forever.

PRAYER THOUGHT: *Precious Savior, teach us to trust in Thy cross to preserve us from death and to carry us into the victory and joy of eternity in heaven with Thee.*

Who is it that overcomes the world but he who believes that Jesus is the Son of God? 1 John 5:5

A missionary told about a young African boy who was so ill he lay dying. The Christian missionary doctor was standing at his bedside. "Where are you going when you die?" the doctor asked him. The little boy replied, "I am going to heaven to be with Jesus." Then the doctor continued, "What if you should discover that Jesus has left heaven? What then?" The boy said, "I would look Him up wherever He has gone." "But suppose," said the doctor, "that Jesus had gone to be in hell?" The little boy smiled through his pain and said, "There is no hell where Jesus is."

Have you discovered this truth? All of us are called at one time or another to go through the valley of the shadow of death. But when the Lord has been our partner in life, we shall discover it to be a "going-through" kind of journey. All of us must bear burdens and face problems. But we do not have to carry them alone, for the Lord has promised to be with us in our afflictions. All of us have had moments of great disappointment. But there is One who is always what He said He would be, and He is a constant, unfailing friend. All of us have fallen into the pitfalls of sin. But there is One whose loving hand has always been there to lift us up again, to set us firmly on our feet, and to give us the power to keep going on.

Heaven begins right here on earth when we come into the right relationship with God through our Lord Jesus Christ. Neither in this world nor in the world to come will there be anything to fear, if only we walk life's way each day in fellowship with our Lord and Savior. Where He is, there are also to be found the deepest joys and the richest fruits of life. No matter who we are or what we are doing, when we live in His presence we know the joys of faith in Him.

PRAYER THOUGHT: *Dear Jesus, we are grateful that when we walk with Thee, we can be victorious over the troubles of this life, and that the light of Thy presence can remove the darkness of our despair.*

Walk in love, as Christ loved us. Ephesians 5:2

In Africa I met a little girl named Kioti, which means "nobody loves me." Rejected by her parents as being one more mouth to feed, she was set out in the bushes to die. The girl was sickly and so infected with repulsive sores that her family didn't think it worth while to save her. There were other healthy children in the family to keep from starvation.

It was there that a missionary stumbled upon her, and little Kioti was brought to her home. Doctors dressed her sores, and after a while she was nursed back to health. The missionaries dressed her in clean clothes and kept her spotlessly clean. But she was so withdrawn emotionally that it took a long time for her to come out of her shell and overcome her loneliness. They tried in every way to convince her of their love, but she did not know what the word "love" meant. One day as she looked down at her bandaged hands and clean dress, she pointed to these visible signs of tender care and asked, "Is this love?"

Love is ever so much more than lip service and sweet phrases. When the Lord said we must love as He loves us, He gave us to know that it implies doing something. Love sent Him daily on missions of mercy. Love caused Him to seek out those who were lost sinners. He defined love in concrete terms. It was doing something for those about Him who needed His help.

Every day we have the opportunity to translate love into deeds. These deeds in themselves will not save us, because salvation is not to be gained by good works. However, if we accept the love of Christ, it rises within us as a mighty spring to flow out in loving service to our fellow men. Genuinely received, it cannot be contained.

PRAYER THOUGHT: *Merciful Lord, may we go forward with renewed dedication in our ministry of love and mercy. We pray that this work may be a worthy reflection of Thy love and compassion toward us.*

"Look at the birds of the air: they neither sow nor reap nor gather into barns, and yet your heavenly Father feeds them. Are you not of more value than they?" Matthew 6:26

A great proportion of the world's population today is yet uneducated and illiterate. Many people have never been taught even to read or write. Proportionately few of them know anything about arithmetic. They are like a native herdsman who was asked one day how many cattle he had. "I don't know," replied the African. "Then how do you know when one or two of your cattle are missing?" His reply was striking and beautiful, "Not because the number would be less, but because of a face that I would miss."

So God knows each one of His children. The Lord went to great lengths in Scripture to convince us about our importance in the sight of our heavenly Father. He used expressions like, "Even the hairs of your head are all numbered." Symbolically He spoke one day about how the grass clothes the field, and all the while it is not concerned about the fact that the heavenly Father should give it strength to do this year after year. He told about the birds of the air and said that not even a sparrow, a common ordinary bird, falls to the ground without the heavenly Father's having knowledge of it. Then He concluded by saying, "Do you not know that you are of more value than these?"

If God will care for the lesser creatures, certainly He will care for you. God knows the face of every one of His children, and when we are not gathered with His family, He misses us. Our God is a personal God who because of His all-knowing and all-seeing attributes is involved in the lives of each of His children. He is then both our Father and our Friend whose love is unmatched by any other in this world.

PRAYER THOUGHT: *Heavenly Father, we are comforted by the knowledge that each one of us is important to Thee and that we are at all times surrounded by Thy loving concern and care.*

"I will lay down my life for you." John 13:37

When spending some time in Africa, I visited with a missionary friend who related to me a very interesting and dramatic incident which had happened at a thanksgiving service recently. It had become customary for the natives to bring what they could for an offering of thanksgiving at this time. Some brought money, others brought fruits and vegetables from their small plots of land, and still others gave choice pieces of their tribal handicraft.

After the service the missionary noticed that a little African girl lingered in the church. "What are you waiting for?" he asked. "I want to give something to Jesus," she replied. Then out of a small animal skin bag she drew 18 pieces of silver and placed them in the missionary's hand. "But my child," he exclaimed in complete surprise, "where did you get all this money?" Aware of the prevalence of robbery among some of the natives, he thought this is what the child had done. "Just tell me where you got this money. I promise you won't be punished." The child burst into tears, but after she had quieted her sobs she explained, "I had nothing to give to Jesus, so I sold myself for this money. Tomorrow I am going to be a slave. The reason I did it is because I wanted to give something to my Lord."

Here was a Christian who, moved by a desire to show her thanks, was willing to give her life to the Lord. Dare we do less? What a difference it would make in the strength and dynamic of the program for making Christ known around the world, if each of us began to practice the kind of stewardship that reflected sincere gratitude. Christ stands before us saying, "I gave my life for you. What have you given for me?"

PRAYER THOUGHT: *Teach us, Lord, not to withhold any part of our lives from dedication to Thee, but to give freely all that we have and all that we are to the glory of Thy kingdom.*

[We] give you in our conduct an example to imitate. 2 Thessalonians 3:9

In certain parts of Africa there is a custom that each tribal chief must form a life motto. A Christian missionary one day walking among the natives asked the leader of a certain tribe what his life motto was. The old chief slowly and thoughtfully replied, "When you pass through the jungle, be very careful to break a twig in order that the next man might find his way." What did the old man mean by this? Perhaps he was speaking of the responsibility of one toward another in helping him to walk the difficult way. Perhaps he meant that men are dependent upon one another, and that they must willingly provide for a neighbor's welfare.

It is embarrassingly true that people are concerned only about themselves and their own safety. "I must take care about myself, because no one else will," is their excuse for self-centeredness. Too few of us realize our responsibility as trail blazers for others. Whatever pathway we take, we are breaking twigs either to cast them aside or to lay them in the path. Those following us will be led into more abundant living or into lives of despair, depending upon the way that we travel. We must be very careful, because someone is always following.

The greatest trail blazer of all time was our Lord Jesus Christ. Following Him, we know that we are on the pathway that leads to eternal glory. We are commissioned to be His witnesses. We are meant to be living and faithful examples of His great life. Let us choose carefully the pathway that we take in order that those following after us might find glory in living rather than despair and unhappiness. Let us always remember that the road we take today determines our eternal destiny. Only the high road laid out by God leads to glory.

PRAYER THOUGHT: *Teach us, Lord Jesus, to direct our steps along Thy pathway and not to go astray, so that those who follow our example may also travel on the high road to eternal glory.*

"If any man would come after me, let him deny himself and take up his cross daily and follow me." Luke 9:23

To the altar of a little African church an elderly native woman came one day in order that she might worship. In Africa people do not travel by speedy jet aircraft nor by automobile nor by any other motor vehicle. When most of them travel it is by foot. This woman had spent three days walking on the jungle paths that led to this church. She was hot, dusty, weary, and hungry. To go back to her little jungle hut would mean another three days of hot, wearisome travel. A total of six days was thus required for her to be able to attend one service of worship.

The missionary pastor of the church to which this woman came later said, "When that woman knelt at the communion table I could see God reflected in her face. Later I asked her, 'Why did you make all this effort just to come to this church service?' She replied, 'Because I knew I would meet my Savior here.' "

This is the miracle of grace that happens when God comes into people's lives. This is something that is beyond human understanding. God's power is majestically at work in the lives of people everywhere. It is available for anyone who will open his heart to Him. His love is absolutely unlimited, and His power is unconquerable. Irrespective of a man's circumstances in life, he yet may know such amazing love and claim the dividends of faith.

In these days when our world is so turbulent and tottering on the brink of calamity, God is calling for dedicated men who not only are willing to make sacrifices in order to worship Him, but also have the desire to take His message into every area of life. Our highest calling is to live for Him, and if necessary to die for Him, that His love may be made known.

PRAYER THOUGHT: *Dear heavenly Father, we pray that we may have the courage resolutely to give ourselves over completely to Thee and to Thy work.*

Declare his glory among the nations, his marvelous works among all the peoples! 1 Chronicles 16:24

On the grounds of an African mission station late one evening the missionary pastor's wife went to the dispensary. She had awakened early that morning, so her day had already been long; her work had been far beyond the call of duty. It was now 11 at night. This woman, who was a registered nurse, wanted to make a final check of the patients to be sure that there were no emergencies that needed her attention. When she arrived at the dispensary she found a group of these natives gathered together with the most forlorn look on their faces that she had ever seen. This identical fear and loneliness can be seen in so many people, because they live in uncertainty of the future and in the fear of life itself. Here at this dispensary they were huddled together in the quiet, still night. Their look of utter dejection spelled out the plaintive cry, "O God, we know you are there, we know you are there, but we don't know the way!"

Think of the responsibility that rests upon the conscience of every Christian when one realizes that much of the world is as yet not won for Christ. Think of the misery and the literal hell here and now that people are suffering, because you and I have not heeded the command of our Lord to go and make disciples of all nations. They suffer not only because of their fear of the future and the uncertainty of what that might be, but they are suffering also because they intuitively are missing that glorious partnership with Christ through this life.

Look at your own blessings today. Think of the faith which you have and the love of God that surrounds you. Then resolve with complete sincerity to be a witness of Christ and to share His gospel wherever you may have the opportunity in your daily walks among men.

PRAYER THOUGHT: *Make us eager witnesses of Thy Word, dear Lord, as we spread the glory of Thy gospel everywhere among those we meet and know.*

"Do not fear, only believe." Mark 5:36

It is an inspirational experience to see what Christ can do in the lives of people. As one visits the African mission fields, one can almost point out who the Christians are by just looking at them. They seem much less burdened than do others, and there is a radiance about them which proclaims that they know the peace of God which goes beyond all human understanding.

Among these many fine Christians I would like to tell you about one in particular. The missionaries called her Aunt Jemima. She was a beautiful radiant soul, and obviously happy in her Christian life. When I visited her home in Africa, she had been a Christian for about seven years. Because a missionary had come to her dwelling and because some people in America had financially supported this missionary, she had entered into the beauty of a daily fellowship with the Lord.

One morning I returned to my bedroom in the missionary home I was visiting. As she was making the bed and tidying up things, she was softly singing as she worked. A radiant glow which only a true Christian can have was spread across her face. With a voice that seemed as beautiful as any I had ever heard she was singing these words in her native tongue: "When the roll is called up yonder I'll be there."

Life is worth while for each one of us not only because we have the presence of Christ with us each day, but also because we have the assurance that He will be with us through all eternity. How grateful we should be that we are able to hear Him daily say, "Let not your hearts be troubled." There is really nothing to worry about in the future, for He has promised, "I go to prepare a place for you. . . . I will come again and will take you to myself, that where I am you may be also."

PRAYER THOUGHT: *We thank Thee, gracious Lord, because Thou hast promised us an eternal home where we shall know the joy of everlasting companionship with Thee.*

Every man shall give as he is able, according to the blessing of
the Lord your God which he has given you. Deuteronomy 16:17

One need not be endowed with great talents to make gifts
that are significant in the sight of God. For example, the African native is unbelievably poor. For a shelter he has only a
mud hut. For furniture there is only a little reed mat. He has
no dishes at all but uses only earthen clay pots. Many natives
have no clothing except garments made from goat hides. Only
corn is in their pitiful and inadequate diet. Few indeed are
those who have machines and farming equipment. From an
economic point of view, the American would say that the African has very little to make his life comfortable or secure.

Yet it is interesting to note how the African Christian gives
instinctively to God's work. At the outstation he helps build
a church, a schoolhouse, the pastor-teacher's house, and a place
for the missionary to live when he visits the mission station.
He gives whatever little money he can earn. He also gives
grain or anything else he might possess. One native brought
a fine helmet, the pride of his life, which he had bought with
his hard-earned money, to the church. Now after hearing of
Christ's sacrifice for him, he gave that which he loved most.

Many of us are doing little or nothing today, because we feel
that what we have to give is not significant in the eyes of God.
What we forget is that God has the capacity to take the little
we might offer to Him and multiply it into something extremely
significant. A little lad has only a few fishes, but when he gives
it to the Lord five thousand people are fed. A woman has only
a fraction of a cent, but when she places it in the treasury box
the angels in heaven rejoice. Give what you have to the Master, and the greatest rewards will then flow back to you from
knowing that you are doing the Lord's work.

PRAYER THOUGHT: *It is wonderful to know, gracious Lord,
that no matter how little we are able to give to Thee, Thou
art able to make it sufficient for Thy cause.*

153

> Faith comes from what is heard, and what is heard comes by the preaching of Christ. Romans 10:17

Faith has been given many definitions. The writer to the Hebrews of New Testament days said, "Faith is the assurance of things hoped for, the conviction of things not seen." Phillips Brooks has used the five letters of the word "faith" for this definition: "Forsaking all, I take Him." A missionary in Africa, when translating the Gospel of John in Swahili, couldn't find a word to express "Believe." He took the problem to a native Christian who thought for a few moments, and then suggested, "Doesn't it mean to hear in my heart?"

What a beautiful definition that is! God is constantly trying to speak to us. Sometimes we are so engrossed in the things of the world and the traffic of life's market places that the din and roar robs us from hearing His still small voice. And then at moments of crisis we become filled with panic, because we have only our inadequate selves on whom to depend.

Each day we should set aside periods of quiet when we can be still, listen to God, and then hear in our hearts the things that He has to say to us. As His voice speaks, "My peace I leave with you," the turbulence around us is stilled.

When we come into His presence, we are attaching ourselves to His unlimited power. When we kneel to pray, we rise the stronger, declaring to the world, "If God be for me, who dare be against me?" Live each day in the full conviction that "God is for me; God is with me." If you have faith in God as much as there is life in the tiniest of seeds, Scripture promises that you will have the capacity to remove any mountain of difficulty that might ever stand athwart your way. Rest your faith on His loving promises.

PRAYER THOUGHT: *Heavenly Father, we pray that we may come to Thee in quiet and contemplation, so that we may receive in our hearts the peace of Thy presence.*

154

I shall dwell in the house of the Lord for ever. Psalm 23:6

Men around the world have basically similar longings and strivings within their hearts. Even the heathen who do not know of the living God seek to satisfy their innate desire to worship a supreme being above themselves. In various ways and customs they respond to the needs of their soul.

For example, in certain sections of Africa the natives cut a new doorway in their little bomas or huts each time a member of the family dies. Through this doorway they take the body out for burial. The reason for making this new exit is to recognize the fact that the human spirit has gone forever from the old house. It will not travel the old way again. Hence, they have developed the custom of providing a new doorway for the new journey beyond the grave.

When the beloved missionary David Livingstone died, the natives in Africa who were now his friends as well as new members of the kingdom of the redeemed of God said, "He has left the suburbs and gone to the city." When death comes we say about the deceased that he "has departed." In Africa many say the opposite, "He has arrived." As Christians, we have every reason to believe that death is not the end of life. It has lost its sting, because it has been swallowed up in victory by the resurrection of Christ. This life is like a vestibule to the real house. Our permanent residence is not upon this earth. The hymn writer tells us that we are pilgrims and strangers in this land. We travel along, preparing for that which is to come. Our permanent residence will be in God's heaven. In the Father's house is a place prepared for each of us. Some day by His mercy those who have been faithful shall establish their new residency.

PRAYER THOUGHT: *Keep us from regarding this life as our final dwelling place, dear Father, but instead lead us daily to prepare to enter Thy heavenly home where we shall live eternally.*

> If one suffers as a Christian, let him not be ashamed, but under
> that name let him glorify God. 1 Peter 4:16

A visit to a leper colony is always an unforgettable experience. These people are usually castoffs from their own family and tribe. Seeing them, one is reminded of the lepers who
ran to the Lord beseeching Him for cleansing in the long ago.
Whenever they walked down the streets, they had to call out,
"Unclean! Unclean!" As a result, no one seemed to care for
their future. Yet our Lord did. And so do the Lord's followers today.

In faraway places hospitals have been built to help cure
people of this dread disease and to rehabilitate them and put
them back to work again. A part of every dollar given to
foreign missions goes to help this cause.

Go with me today to a typical leper hospital. Here is a man
who is covered from head to foot with scaly sores. Great por-
tions of his hands and feet have been eaten away by the ancient disease. Also, he is blind. Despite these unfortunate
conditions, this leper laughs and talks with friends outside
the village church. If someone turned to the leper and asked
how anyone so afflicted could be so joyous, his reply would
be this: "Why should I be unhappy? Am I not a Christian?"

Hardly a day passes by but that we must confess that we
complain about something. How fortunate we are to know the
good news of the gospel, for then a joy unlike any other to be
found is ours. When one realizes the thrilling significance of
it all, one can say, "Why should I be unhappy? Am I not a
Christian?" That alone is sufficient, for it means for us a way
of life more abundant than any other.

PRAYER THOUGHT: *We pray, gracious Lord, that we will
never forget that because we are Christians and belong to
Thee, we need not care about our present afflictions, but only
look forward to eternity where we shall live in joy for all time.*

"Go, sell what you possess and give to the poor, and you will have treasure in heaven." Matthew 19:21

One of the many rewards of serving a group of Christians as their pastor is to see them putting their faith into positive channels of action. On a visit to Africa I was able to see the result of what even a little gift can do. Before I left America I had told the people in our community how much the American dollar was worth in helping the missionary activities across the sea. One of the Sunday school boys who had heard me decided to sell some of his toys to the neighbor boys. When I left our community, he was waiting at the airport to give me the five dollars he had earned, in order that I might bring it as his gift to some child in Africa.

When I arrived in Tanganyika I told one of the missionaries about this incident and said I would like to personalize the gift as much as I could. I wanted the little boy in America to know the far-reaching consequences of his gift. The missionary found a young African boy who was very ambitious in gaining an education. He wanted to go to school, but he didn't have a sufficient amount of money to pay for his tuition. With the five dollars that he was given he constructed a bee hive. So he raised bees and sold the honey they produced. With this money in profits he was able to go to school for a whole year. It was only a gift of five dollars, but this was enough to provide a boy with an education for an entire year.

Perhaps the greatest consequence of the gift was that the story about a little American boy who wanted to do something to help others was told around the mission field. Unselfishly he gave up what was very dear in order to be of service to others. Here was real Christianity in practice. Let us in turn seek to use our gifts so that others might be benefited.

PRAYER THOUGHT: *Heavenly Father, we pray that the example of this unselfish child might inspire us willingly to give of our abundance in order that the desperate need of others might be supplied.*

"A man's life does not consist in the abundance of his possessions." Luke 12:15

A woman who was visiting a mission field in Africa was
asking many questions about the schools, the hospitals, and
the native ways of living. She was no doubt of great wealth,
and evidently had come from a beautiful home in America.
She was one of the many who think that the *things* of life can
bring us happiness. Finally she turned to the missionary and
asked, "Where does the native live?" The missionary brought
her to a little hut. She shrieked in amazement at this type of
accommodations. "And where does he sleep?" she asked. The
missionary pointed to a dried animal skin spread out on the
floor of the hut. "And how does he eat?" The missionary
pointed to a dirty container from which he ate his food. "What
misery!" the woman exclaimed.

"But listen!" said the missionary as in the distance there
could be heard some singing. As the woman approached she
recognized the words of the native and the familiar song that
was coming from his lips, "Blessed assurance, Jesus is mine;
O what a foretaste of glory divine!"

We all should work to raise the economic standards of people throughout the world. But why do so many of us think
that true joy can be found only in the material luxuries of
life? The Lord once asked a very searching question, "What
will it profit a man, if he gains the whole world and forfeits
his life?" There are many who are surrounded by riches, but
who yet are living in hell. And there are others surrounded
by poverty who are living in heaven. It is your relationship
with God and the substance of your faith that really counts
in the end, for what you are and not what you have is what
God is concerned about.

PRAYER THOUGHT: *May we never put our trust and hope in
the emptiness of material aspirations, dear Lord, but trust
always in the fullness of Thy promise of salvation.*

"Where your treasure is, there will your heart be also." Matthew 6:21

An old African woman came to a Christian missionary one day and said, "I want you to teach me how to read. I want you to teach me to read Jesus first." "Why do you want to read the words of Jesus first?" she was asked. Her reply was, "Because I know that if I learn to read Jesus first, everything else will come out all right."

This African native had learned a wonderful lesson even in the few years she had known her Lord. "Seek first his kingdom and his righteousness," says Scripture, "and all these things shall be yours as well." Most of us are prone to follow the opposite approach. We seek the things of this life first, and spend our every waking hour in an attempt to gain them. We expend our energy in rushing to gain material wealth, and at the same time neglect our spiritual welfare.

This century has been called the century of unhappiness and the age of worry. Is it because of the fact that we lack material things? No, we have so many gadgets and conveniences that you would think we could be as happy as kings. And yet in the hearts of all of us there is a deep-seated hunger for something more. We sooner or later learn that the things of this life just do not satisfy the soul. Could not our unhappiness be caused by the fact that we have separated ourselves from the only true source of joy?

When a person puts Christ first in his life, then he knows firsthand a power that makes him a victor over all his sins and his doubts, and that puts him in contact with the only satisfying Source of supply for all his needs. Again we recall those words of our African sister who said that if Jesus is first everything else will come out all right.

PRAYER THOUGHT: *Teach us, dear Father, to spend our lives in seeking the eternal riches of spiritual things and not to waste our time in only pursuing the transitory pleasures of material possessions.*

"Thou hast led in thy steadfast love the people whom thou hast redeemed." Exodus 15:13

An African convert made this remark: "The trail ahead of me is difficult and tangled. But since I have become a Christian I have learned that there is always a Man ahead of me. So I am no longer afraid."

Each day we need to reiterate this simple faith. Jesus Christ does always go before us. He is ever in front of us. He bids us to follow Him. Though the way may be dark and seem uncharted to us, we can follow Him in confidence because He has gone this way before. There isn't a single problem that we shall have to face that was not a problem to Him in His life. There is not a single difficulty that together with Him you will not be able to surmount. The assurance of His presence is our badge of hope.

Sometimes I wonder if the faith of the new converts is not more real than the faith of us who, being reared as Christians, have had every opportunity to know the truth of the gospel. It is always an inspirational experience to attend worship services in various parts of the world and to know that we are bound together with others in Christian love.

This happened to me at a little mission station in East Africa. All about were gathered the African natives who had only recently committed their lives to the Lord. How they loved to sing these new tunes that could help them express their newly found joy! There seemed to be a confidence and a conviction in their voices that I had not heard elsewhere, as they joined together in singing, "All the way my Saviour leads me; What have I to ask beside?" This is our faith triumphant! This is our hope unending!

PRAYER THOUGHT: *We pray that we may share in the simple confidence and devotion which characterizes those who are newly committed to Thy will and way, precious Lord.*

"Every man shall give as he is able, according to the blessing of the Lord your God which he has given you." Deuteronomy 16: 17

One cannot travel in the several regions of Africa which have been influenced by the culture of the Western World without sensing the staggering sacrifices made by the missionaries who there minister daily to the needs of their fellow men. Even though these natives are of a different skin pigmentation, yet they are fellow brothers in Christ. One of the great spirits who has influenced and inspired others to yield their lives to Christ is Dr. Albert Schweitzer.

One day a newspaper man was interviewing Dr. Schweitzer in his hospital at Lambarene. He was deeply impressed with the devotion of this medical missionary who had sacrificed so many opportunities in his homeland to accept the call of Christ to plunge into the dark continent of Africa to bring what help he could. After the journalist had completed his interview, he was conversing with some friends. One of them asked this question: "What in your opinion is the most outstanding quality of the great Dr. Schweitzer?" The newspaper man's answer was significant for he said, "I believe it is Dr. Schweitzer's sincere conviction that his every task is equally important. He gives himself completely to each moment as God presents it to him. He considers his time a trust. He uses every molecule of energy God has given him in order to be helpful in everything he does."

The number of our talents varies. But to everyone God has given something unique and significant. If all of us would use our energy and talents to the very best of our ability, we would make this a different world. Today is the time to begin. To discover our talents, and to develop them to their best use by the help of God, is the challenge of this day.

PRAYER THOUGHT: *Dear Lord, we pray that we may begin now to offer our talents totally to Thy service, and that we may use every opportunity to further the work of Thy kingdom.*

"I am rich, I have prospered, and I need nothing." Revelation
3:17

A missionary in Africa told me one day about an event that
took place in one of the preaching centers of his church. He
had met an old man of the village who took great pride in
his age. He told the missionary he could easily remember
when the mission had begun its work in this area. For more
than twenty years this work for the Lord had been at his
doorstep, yet he had never become a Christian. The missionary questioned him about his life, and the man had nothing
but praise for the mission work of foreign church groups in
his country. He even rejoiced over the many people who had
heeded the message of the gospel in his home community. Yet
the last thing he said was this: "But remember, sir, the big
thing in life is still the stomach."

As the missionary reflected upon this statement, he was reminded of a man in America who had once remarked to him,
"Why should I go to church? I have all I want in life. My
needs have been satisfied with what I have been able to get
for myself." Though one of these men was comparatively rich
and the other comparatively poor, both men were worshiping
at the same altar of the multi-headed god of materialism.
Both of these men were convinced that they had found suf-
ficiency in laying ownership on the things of life.

In the final analysis, however, these are the very things that
thieves break through and steal and moths and rust destroy, as
we are reminded in the Bible. These are not the things which
give real and lasting security. God alone is the only power in
life that can give us the assurance of that security which all
men long for, which is life forever. May we see the folly of
placing our trust in products, and then realize the wisdom of
placing our trust in God our Father.

PRAYER THOUGHT: *Teach us, dear Lord in heaven, not to be
satisfied with the temporary pleasures of earth, but to look
heavenward for the enduring reward of eternal life.*

God is light and in him is no darkness at all. 1 John 1:5

The drummer was calling the lepers to worship. They had been hard at work under the broiling sun in the fields and in the cottages nearby. Many of them had been expelled from their tribes. Now they had come to a Christian institution where each day loving hands attended them. Practically all of them had been heathen when they came, but most of them became Christians before the time came for their release from the hospital. They frequently asked the nurses and the doctors, "Why are you so kind and loving to us?" which gave them a wonderful opportunity to witness of God's matchless love. They could make it clear that it was this love which impelled them to leave home and people in order to share their talents in this mission.

Finally all had gathered for worship. Some of them blinded from disease groped their way to their bench. I shall never forget their singing, "Sun of my soul, Thou Saviour dear, It is not night if Thou be near." This thought has clung to me ever since that day. The Lord is the eternal sun. Each morning afresh I am reminded that He watches over His children twenty-four hours a day.

Into our lives the shadows are bound to come. Sometimes it is pitch dark about us. We live in a world that is full of sin and evil. Temptations lurk on every hand and sin is ever more attractive. There are voices trying to persuade us to take the road of expediency, or to drift along the broad road with the willy-nilly crowd. But this darkness of the world cannot enter into the soul of one who is close to Christ the sun of righteousness, for it is never night if He is near. Isn't it true that all the darkness in the world cannot extinguish the light of even one candle? He has the power to overcome all darkness, for He alone was able to say, "I am the light of the world."

PRAYER THOUGHT: *Dear Lord, we are thankful for the unextinguishable light which shines in the lives of those who know Thee as their Savior from the darkness of the world.*

"The poor will never cease out of the land; therefore I command you, You shall open wide your hand to your brother, to the needy and to the poor, in the land." Deuteronomy 15:11

The setting again is an African church, and the congregation once more is a group of lepers. While visiting there I had the opportunity to share with them the good news of the gospel, and told them how overjoyed I was to join hands with other Christians in faraway places. One can readily sense the tie that binds hearts together in Christian love. When you learn that one who is otherwise a stranger to you is a Christian, there is an immediate bond that is stronger than any other.

After I had brought my greeting to this African congregation, a native woman was called upon to respond. She didn't come to the front of the church as others had done, but she remained in her pew as she gave her witness. These are her words: "I cannot come forward because I am blind. But I want to thank these visitors from America for coming here. I want them to go back home and thank all the people who have given of their means in order that the gospel message might be brought to me and to my friends. I once was living in darkness, but now I am a child of God. I know now what it means to be saved by the redeeming grace of Jesus Christ. I cannot tell you how wonderful it is to live this way compared to the way I lived before my conversion. I am sorry that I cannot see you today because I am blind, but I thank God that I have the faith to believe that some day I shall see you all in the house of many mansions."

Think of the outstanding dividends that we all receive from the often small investment which we make in the work of the kingdom of God. Some have called this the second blessing, as it is a benediction rebounding upon the hearts of those who first pronounced it. Let us resolve to give more than ever before that the good news might fly everywhere.

PRAYER THOUGHT: *May we be ever more generous, dear Lord, as we give of our time, our money, and ourselves to increase the circulation of the good news of salvation.*

The Lord in majesty will be for us a place of broad rivers and streams. Isaiah 33:21

Great rivers usually are tiny streamlets at their source and then grow broader and deeper as they proceed to their outlet. They usually become the widest and the deepest where they enter into the sea. However, in South Africa there are rivers that rise from among the mountain tops and are broad and deep at their beginning only to become more narrow and shallow as they advance. The thirsty sands and the burning sun lay waste the onrushing waters, until at last the mighty river is lost in the desert. The farther the water runs, the less there is that remains.

This is a significant parable of two kinds of life. The life of the worldly man is like the South African rivers. He begins with the same innate possibilities as the Christian. He has the capacity to grow spiritually day by day and to become greater within his own soul and more influential among his fellow men. But as he begins to dissipate his life in the things of the world he lays waste his capacities. He keeps selling the things of the soul for the things of the world, until at last like the prodigal son, far from home, he finds himself with nothing.

The Christian life is much like the mighty Mississippi River, which has its rise in northern Minnesota and comes forth from a very small and insignificant brook. But as it winds its way southward, it gets ever broader and broader, finally emptying itself into the open sea in an expanse so wide that it is hard to see where the river ends and the ocean begins.

Man is meant to keep growing. Scripture tells us to "grow in the grace and knowledge of our Lord and Savior Jesus Christ." As man daily communicates with God in prayer and exposes himself to the Word of God, he reaches for the perfection of the heavenly Father.

PRAYER THOUGHT: *Dear Father, even though we have but a small beginning, we pray that we may grow to be spiritually rich and full through daily communication with Thee, our source of strength and power.*

Thou art near, O Lord. Psalm 119:151

One cannot visit Africa without thinking of the great trail-blazers who endured all manner of hardships and unspeakable torments in order to bring the gospel to those who have never before heard of the Christ. The greater lights have ever inspired the lesser lights to greater consecration to the work of Christ and His kingdom.

One of these giants of the earth that so inspires us all is David Livingstone. It was his indomitable faith that sent him to Africa. Yet Livingstone did not go there alone, for he lived each day in the full knowledge that there was a real Presence by his side. And when death came, it found him on his knees talking to this Friend. Livingstone was able to endure hardship, and again and again faced without flinching the threat of death, knowing that the Lord was with him. He stoutly believed in the Bible. Like a golden thread through all the pages of his daybook is this theme, "God is with us."

It is interesting to learn that when David Livingstone died his hand was held up in such a position that it was as though it were put in the hand of God. You see, he did not go through the valley of death alone; nor do we need to do so either. There is One who has been there before, and who therefore left a lighted way for us.

It was a similar vital faith that sent Hudson Taylor to China. It was this driving faith that caused William Booth to plunge into the slums of London. It was this kind of faith that will put us at His disposal wherever we are, in order that we might witness for Christ and help our fellow men. Open your heart to Him and give Him your all.

PRAYER THOUGHT: *Gracious God, we are continually comforted and strengthened because we know that no matter where we go or in what situation we find ourselves, Thou art ever by our side.*

A faithful man will abound with blessings. Proverbs 28:20

A news item has told about an express package that reached an address in England from a South African town. The man who was to receive the box refused to pay the delivery charges. Consequently for about fourteen years that unclaimed box was used as a footstool in the express office. One day purely out of curiosity at an auction a man bid for it at a very low price. When he opened it later he was greatly astonished to find several thousand pounds of sterling in English bank notes. Because the original consignee had refused to pay the comparatively small delivery charges, he had missed receiving a small fortune.

Men are often just that shortsighted, for they deprive themselves of life's richer blessings simply because they fail to claim them. We have within our reach all of those most important things that can make life meaningful. The only price we have to pay is our life, and the Lord will take us just as we are as we come to Him. But so often we refuse to pay the price. We refuse to take time for God, to listen to His instructions, to study His Word. We refuse to take time for prayer, or to be bothered about the welfare of others, because we say we have enough to worry about ourselves. We refuse to pay a small price to receive a great gain.

Why are so many people wise in the things of the world and so ignorant in the things of the spirit? We thrill to the "big deal" which we can make in business. But the greatest thing that can ever happen is when we come into possession of the riches of eternity through faith and become joint heirs with Christ. Having this close link with our God enables us to build lives that can withstand the buffeting experiences and yet rest in His power.

PRAYER THOUGHT: *Gracious God, we pray that we may not refuse to accept the gift of eternal life which Thou hast offered to us, but that we may wisely give our lives in exchange for the riches of eternity.*

For to this you have been called, because Christ also suffered for you, leaving you an example, that you should follow in his steps. 1 Peter 2:21

One of the great medical missionaries to Africa is Albert Schweitzer. He has gained world-wide recognition. In his early twenties, he was a recognized authority in philosophy, theology, and music. He still is considered the greatest living exponent of Bach. He would likely have become world renowned, had he chosen any one of these fields of service. Yet at the age of thirty he left these fields to study medicine in order to plunge into the equatorial swamps of Lambarene, Africa, to serve as a doctor for the natives of a village almost stamped out because of disease.

People questioned him as to the reason he had given up claim of world renown in philosophy, theology, and music. "What prompted you to do this?" they asked. He has answered simply, "I came to the conclusion that God had done so much for me that I had to do something for Him. The call came to me that I should be a medical missionary, and I couldn't refuse it."

Not everyone is called to leave his particular work to become a missionary to foreign lands. There is much that can be done right where you are. But anyone who wants to live a fruitful life must always keep his heart open to the compelling call of conscience. It may call you to join in a crusade in your own community against the evil forces that are opposing the forces of righteousness. It may call you to become a better witness to your neighbor who may not be attending any church. It may call you to lend a helping hand to someone in need rather than to pass him by on the other side. Above all, it calls you to daily fellowship with God that you might be directed in the way that you should live.

PRAYER THOUGHT: *Help us, dear Lord, to accept the compelling call of conscience, that we might fulfill the purpose Thou hast planned for our lives.*

We know that in everything God works for good with those
who love him. Romans 8:28

My friend and I greatly anticipated South Africa for many
reasons. One of them admittedly was a simple desire to be
able to lie in the sun and relax after our crowded schedule of
activity at home. Therefore, it was a happy day when we arrived in Durban and saw the beautiful white sandy beaches
scalloping the ocean's edge. After a good night's rest, we went
out to spend all day in the beautiful sun. We had no idea that
it was as hot as it was. How we suffered that night, for we
awakened in our fiery discomfort early in the morning. Both
of us were red like lobsters! The next day we had to watch
the other people preparing to go to the beach from where we
sat on the porch of the hotel suffering from our burns. Envious
of them, we were irritated at our own lack of judgment.

The next morning, bitterly complaining because we had
missed this day of sun, we were surprised to read in the morning newspaper that "stingers" had raided the very beach we
would have been swimming at on the day we missed. Over
one hundred people were hospitalized, some of whom became
very seriously ill. It was then that my friend turned to me and
said, "Let's remember that sometimes misfortune can be good
fortune." We had been spared the possible chance of hos-
pitalization because our sunburn had held us away that day
from the beach.

It is good to remember that stumbling blocks can become
steppingstones. Instead of complaining about what faces us on
any particular day, let us make the best of every experience,
knowing that all things work together for good to them that
love God. Joseph said to his unscrupulous brothers, "You
meant this for evil; but God has turned it to good." God's all-
knowing love shall not fail.

PRAYER THOUGHT: *May we come to accept Thy wisdom in
directing the course of our lives, dear Lord, and not question
the reasons for our experiences nor doubt that Thy love is still
with us.*

"The Lord saves not with sword and spear." 1 Samuel 17:47

The pygmies of the African bushland are a nomadic people, for they move about from place to place. They build up and establish a little settlement, but when it becomes unbearably dirty they move on to some other place. They have little to eat, practically no clothes to wear, and they live in what we would regard as extended misery. There are few dolls or toys for the pygmy children to play with. Little infants who can barely toddle are allowed to climb trees. The sharpest knives are their playthings. When still quite young they hunt rats with bows and arrows. They also fish with handlines and at a very early age they learn to swim like fish in the running streams. The bodies of many of these people are malformed because of the lack of food or from an unbalanced diet. Many die at an early age from disease and infections.

Yet these, too, are God's children. What have we done to help these people and others in similar circumstances? As I saw missionaries compassionately minister to them, my mind conjured up the Savior standing behind them saying, "As you did it to one of the least of these my brethren, you did it to me." When astronaut Alan Shepard was unstrapped from his seat after a successful ride 115 miles up into the atmosphere in a space capsule, were you aware that every man, woman, and child had contributed $2.25 for this fifteen minute spectacular? What a different world this would be today, if we would take some of the money we spend for destruction and instead use it as God would want us to by alleviating suffering and supplying the simple needs of our fellow men. Your Christian witness will help bring this about, for it is only through the love of God that the world will be saved.

PRAYER THOUGHT: *Make us willing to spend more money to repair the ravages of disease and ignorance, merciful Lord, and less on the things of the world which can end in ultimate destruction for everyone.*

"I will follow you wherever you go." Matthew 8:19

Native Christians around the world often have a way of describing their faith that is unique and original. In the Belgian Congo, for example, a native was heard to pray like this: "Dear Lord Jesus, you be the needle and I'll be the thread. You go first and I will follow wherever you lead."

Too many of us insist on going our own way. We dislike being hampered with restrictions in life. We also rebel at being told what to do by someone else, even by one who knows the way better than we do. We see nothing glamorous in traveling a narrow way that has cramping and inflexible requirements when there is a broad way that seems so open and so appealing. Yet no traveler of the broad way has ever attained to any values that are eternal. For a season there may be the appearance of happiness and joy. Going along with the crowd, one is following the line of least resistance. One doesn't have to make the demanding decisions which the Christian does, because one just drifts along anywhere one wants to go. Yet this is a dead-end road that leads to nothingness.

Followers of the narrow way turn to the Lord and trustingly say, "You lead, and I will follow." This group does not ever have to go through life alone. No one has to be afraid of what he may need to face in the future. This does not mean that there will be no crosses to bear nor hills to climb nor dark alleys to pass through. But it does mean he will be following One who gives victory through the Cross and strength for the rough places. God will lead him all the way, even through death, the darkest valley of all, into His eternal heaven.

PRAYER THOUGHT: *Precious Lord, we pray that we will always follow Thy way, knowing that it is only by traveling with Thee on the narrow road that we shall be able to find the glory of eternity at the end of our journey.*

"Give to him who begs from you, and do not refuse him who
would borrow from you." Matthew 5:42

One of the most powerful leaders in the world today is
Gamal Abdel Nasser, the President of the United Arab Republic. At the present time this nation consists of two countries, Syria and Egypt. It is an unrealistic alliance, since they
have no common boundary. Many are certain that it has been
the hope of Nasser that he could unite all the Arab nations
into one federation which would then make them a power to
be reckoned with in the Middle East. But all these countries
suffer from illiteracy and poverty. There is grim tension
among the leaders.

It was my fortunate opportunity to visit Nasser at his home
one day. When I arrived he was in the yard playing croquet
with his children, probably trying to relieve his mind of the
affairs of state. Nasser is an attractive, intelligent young man
who, I am quite sure, has the welfare of his people at heart.
He invited me into his home and offered to answer any questions. Among other things I asked him why he had accepted
aid from the communists. His reply was this: "You have been
in my country before. You have seen that here we have a
people who are starving each day because they have no food
to eat. When I asked the free world for aid I didn't get it. I
can't hold before my starving people the slogan that they belong to the "free world," because they can't accept that. So
I had to seek aid where I could get it."

Admittedly, I was disturbed with the thought of a godless
communistic country giving aid to the underprivileged after
Christian countries had refused to do so. Perhaps there were
legitimate reasons for it. But we shall never win the battle
against godless communism until we are willing to be as dedicated to the cause of Christ as the communists are to their
ways.

PRAYER THOUGHT: *Lord, may we never turn away any who
ask for our help and compassion, but seek always to do Thy
will by offering whatever we have to those in need.*

One man gives freely, yet grows all the richer; another withholds what he should give, and only suffers want. Proverbs 11:24

The River Nile runs through the heart of the city of Cairo, Egypt. In the areas where it feeds the farming lands, the peasants stand along the river banks and throw grain into the water with long and graceful thrusts of their arms. It appears as though they are throwing away the seed into the great river. Actually the grain sinks to the bottom of the river bed. The water then recedes in the dry season, and before long little green shoots of rice plants come up through the surface. To gain the rice harvest and its yield, the seed must be thrown away.

Here is a striking lesson in stewardship. To receive, we must give. If the peasants had kept the grain without giving it to the river bottom, they would have nothing but the dead grain in their hands. By giving it away, they were making an investment that would give them in return the dividends of a crop of rice. There are many of us who say, "What I have is mine, and I am going to keep it for myself." These become dwarfed self-centered lives that do not grow. There are others who say, "What is mine, Lord, is Thine." These are the lives that keep multiplying in their worth toward God and their community.

What is in your hand? What are you doing with what you own? You can hide what you have, as did the man of the one talent, or you can invest it and bring forth greater happiness in your own life as well as in the lives of your neighbors. To live, we must give. The symbol of an unhappy life is a closed fist which keeps everything to itself, at the same time being unwilling to accept love from others. The man who is unwilling to make sacrifices of love is a man who will never receive great blessings, for it is in loving that we live as God planned.

PRAYER THOUGHT: *Teach us, gracious Lord, to share that which we have, so that our lives might be a blessing to others according to Thy will.*

> By grace you have been saved through faith; and this is not
> your own doing, it is the gift of God. Ephesians 2:8

Recently an excavation in ancient Egypt produced a great
ship that had been buried thousands of years ago. The ship
had been fitted out by those men of an earlier civilization
with every necessity for a trip to Paradise—every necessity,
that is, except the means of getting there.

In reading the Old Testament historical accounts, we are reminded of the story of those men who were going to build a
tower that would reach from earth to heaven. They probably
were very good and capable workmen, but they did not have
the knowledge or the means of getting there.

People today often make the same mistake. They try to
reach heaven in their own power. And yet the Word of God
constantly reminds us that we are not capable by our own
strength of reaching the state of perfection which would enable us to enter eternity. We do not have the cunning nor
the power to withstand even the temptations that must be
overcome, if we are to be right with God. We do not have the
self-powered capacity to lift ourselves by our own bootstraps,
and thus forgive ourselves of our own sins.

However, a way has been made available for us. Man can
be likened to a ship equipped with every necessity for a trip
to Paradise. He has a soul that can be linked with God, if only
he will allow God to reach into it. God is forgiving, so that
the past can be blotted out and forgotten. By the grace of God
man does not have to lead a perfect life in order to reach
heaven, for we all would then fall far short of attainment. God
is present in this world today to lead us on. Indeed, He is the
only one who knows the way through the valley to eternal
life because He himself has already passed through it for us.
Follow Him and know that you are loved and saved.

PRAYER THOUGHT: *Almighty God, we know that by ourselves
we are powerless to obtain the riches of eternity, but that if
we offer ourselves to Thee, Thou canst transport us through
life on earth into the radiant heights of heaven.*

> Nor height, nor depth, nor anything else in all creation, will be able to separate us from the love of God in Christ Jesus our Lord. Romans 8:39

It is impossible to describe the number of beggars one finds as one travels about the world. They ply their ancient trade everywhere. And though one would like to help them all, of course this would not be to exercise good judgment, nor would one have the necessary financial ability to place in unknown hands even a few coins. I say it is not in good judgment, because there are probably some beggars who do not deserve help, since they are too shiftless and lazy to accept jobs, even when such may be offered them. However, occasionally the heart takes over the mind, and one is forced to do what otherwise one would say is not in good judgment.

This happened to me in Egypt. I was standing by my car one day when a group of children flocked about me, begging for money. Standing a bit apart was a girl of about seven years, with no shoes and only a tattered dress covering her small, emaciated body. She had a look on her face which drew my gaze to her like a magnet. She kept pointing to her mouth and then to her stomach to indicate to me how hungry she was. Finally I couldn't bear this feeling any longer. I called her to my side to give her a few odd coins which I had in my pocket. As she received them, she smiled up at me with a look that money could not buy, and said in broken English, "I love you!"

The Lord stands before each of us today. He wants something from us. We cannot buy our eternal salvation from Him, but He wants our life—soiled though it is and nearly worthless like those few odd coins. And if we give Him that life in complete dedication, we shall hear Him say in a tone that we shall never forget, "I love you!"

PRAYER THOUGHT: *We have only our lives to offer in exchange for the never-ending flow of Thy love and grace, dear Lord. Help us to strengthen the dedication of our lives to Thy service.*

Beloved, it is a loyal thing you do when you render any service to the brethren, especially to strangers, who have testified to your love before the church. 3 John 5

It was an unforgettable experience to stand one day at sundown in the courtyard of the citadel that overlooks the city of Cairo, Egypt. Stretched before us below was this metropolis teeming with men, women, and children. Because of the standard of living there, many of them were ignorant, unclean, and sick. Since the dawn of civilization there had been cities sprawling there in all the colorful beauty of the Near East. I looked around and saw towering on the boundless waste of sand the great pyramids. They are solemn witnesses of the long pageant of human hope and despair, aspiration and defeat. It almost seemed as though they were speaking in the midst of all the surrounding misery asking the question, "Does somebody care?"

There I spoke with a number of people who had committed their lives to making the Christ of redeeming love known in that part of the world. These people had made real sacrifices in leaving their homes and families to come into this area to bring Christ to the people. I thought: If we had only shown a greater concern in the past, what a different world ours would be today! If man truly had been his brother's keeper, much of the misery even here would never have been.

The world today is in a grave situation. That situation is a call that ought to bring us to our knees in prayer. It is a summons to increase our concern, we who carry the banner of Christ. We will then resolve increasingly to support causes involved in helping others in this great family of God. Only so can we draw our precious cause of freedom back from the brink of defeat. Nothing less than this kind of costly sacrifice on our part will bring us the dawn of a new and better day.

PRAYER THOUGHT: *We pray, dear Lord, that we may not impede the progress of Thy plan for the world by our sluggishness and selfishness, but that we may bring fresh courage and speed to further the spread of Thy gospel.*

This commandment we have from him, that he who loves God should love his brother also. 1 John 4:21

Walking along with my friend from the American Embassy in Cairo one day, we noticed a large number of crippled children. It was a sight hard to bear. I finally turned to my companion and asked, "Can you tell me why there are so many crippled children in this part of the world?" The government official went on to describe the situation. Mothers take their little babies, put milk bottles on their hands and feet and then leave them there as the limbs grow, in this cruel way intentionally crippling them. In horror I asked the reason for this. My friend's reply was, "So that when the children grow up the mothers can carry them in their arms seeking sympathy from those who pass by as they beg for money." Then he continued, "They also rent their crippled children to childless neighbors, so they can go begging for money, too."

It is difficult to believe that such conditions would be tolerated anywhere in this supposedly enlightened world of the twentieth century. And yet, can we who have so much affluence place ourselves in the position of those who are so desperate that they will try anything to gain a little money and then find food for their stomachs?

The judgment is not only upon them, but upon each one of us. By our failure to do what the Lord has commanded in taking on the needs of others as our personal concerns as well, we share responsibility for the world's tragic day. It is time that we awaken out of our unconcerned sleep, and become aroused. It is time that we pray each day, "God, make me aware! Stab me awake to the needs of others and then, Lord, help me to use what I have to put into practice the gospel that I claim means so much to my life. Let me love others even as You have loved me."

PRAYER THOUGHT: *Dear Lord, if we would be in any way like Thee, we must first shake off our unconcern for the misery of others, and then serve Thee by serving them.*

"Remember not the former things, nor consider the things of old." Isaiah 43:18

Visitors to Lebanon are urged by Arab guides to visit the ruins of Baalbek. This is surely one of the show places of the Near East. Vast temples were erected here in Old Testament days in honor of the ancient heathen god Baal. Some of the magnificent columns from several of these imposing temples still stand. It is inspiring for us to see what people have built in centuries before us. Yet one cannot but sense that in all too many areas of the world people are living in the past, content to point out the glories that preceded them. They point with boastful pride to what has been done centuries ago, but have precious little to show for today.

As Christians, we are ofttimes tempted to do the same thing. We talk about the wonderful Christian homes from which we came. We speak of the devotion of our parents and other members of the family that has surrounded us. We also thank God for the blessed influences of friends. But we ourselves can never be saved without having come to possess this vital faith ourselves. It is rightly said, "God has no grandchildren."

Also, as Christians, we are tempted to live in the past as we tell God and remind ourselves of how much we have already done for Him. Sometimes we are on the brink of calling it quitting time in so far as our work for the Lord is concerned. What a serious mistake we make in thinking we have ever done enough for Him who has done so much for us. Yes, He even went to the ultimate and sacrificed His life to take away the sting of death. The longer we live, the more our faith should mean to us. The more our faith means to us, the more we shall be willing to give ourselves truly to the cause which was so dear to our Lord.

PRAYER THOUGHT: *Father in heaven, we pray that we may never be satisfied with our accomplishments of the past, but that we will strive always to strengthen our faith and devotion to Thee.*

"Be strong and of good courage, do not fear . . . for it is the Lord your God who goes with you; he will not fail you or forsake you." Deuteronomy 31:6

On my first visit to Baalbek I was accompanied by an Arab guide. As we looked through the famous ancient ruins there, he took great pride in telling me about the glories of the past. As he described the story behind the ruins of the temple, he pointed out that certain kinds of stone had been brought from other countries many miles away. When we walked over to a huge rock that stood at least three times as tall as I am, I said, "How could the workmen possibly have moved such a big stone way back in the fourth century?" His reply was, "Now it is too heavy." This statement was a satire on our modern-day capabilities, for this man was intimating in quite obvious terms that people could do things in the fourth century that they cannot do now.

As I have thought about this statement, I have been reminded of the tremendous things these early Christians did compared to some of our work today. After Christ had risen from the dead, these people who were His followers were unafraid to go out and preach the gospel to non-believers even in communities other than their own. They seemed to have more spiritual power and strength than we have today. Perhaps the reason for this is the fact that they made better use of the power that was available to them. Their lives were closely linked with God. They were men of prayer, and therefore they could be men of power.

God's strength has not diminished. We are capable today of doing what the ancients did in performing miracles in behalf of our faith, if we would consecrate our lives as totally to Him. Let us use the power of faith as did the first-century Christians.

PRAYER THOUGHT: *Almighty God, we pray that we shall use more fully the great power which we receive when our lives are totally consecrated to Thy service, so that the work of Thy church might go forth with all possible speed and diligence.*

"Come, O blessed of my Father, inherit the kingdom prepared for you from the foundation of the world." Matthew 25:34

It is always a unique pleasure to visit world leaders and to have the opportunity to get at firsthand a view of the personal opinions of those who are now influencing the history of the world. When I arrived in Beirut a message from the ambassador was at hand, informing me that the following morning I was scheduled to have an audience with the President of the Republic, General Fuad Chehab. The next morning the ambassador came to take me to the palace of the state ruler. How surprised I was as we came to the palace to see there an honor guard shooting a salute to my arrival!

Later as I recalled the incident, the thought occurred to me that all of us have a much greater privilege than this each day that we live. One doesn't need to travel to foreign lands to receive the honor of meeting our King. Every day, wherever we might live, we may go to the King of kings, the Supreme Ruler of the universe, and be received by Him. The invitations fairly leap out of nearly every page of the Bible: "Come to me." "Come, for all is now ready." "Come to me, all who labor and are heavy-laden, and I will give you rest." "Come, follow me." These are brightly glowing promises that God means us to take up.

The rulers of this day, great as they might be, are rulers only for a moment, for life passes on quickly. But the King of kings shall reign supreme forever. He shall rule not only His children in this world, but He is also ruler of the world to come. Think of all we miss in life because we neglect to come to God in prayer more frequently. His blessings are ours to claim, if we are but willing to put our hand in His and our trust in His promises. His sovereign rule is our sure hope that the foundations of life will not crumble.

PRAYER THOUGHT: *Dear God, may we earnestly accept the invitation to come to Thee through the portals of prayer and be received by Thee with blessings and loving mercy.*

A friend loves at all times. Proverbs 17:17

A European businessman who was walking along the streets of Beirut one day as a visitor to the city was approached by a refugee child dressed in ragged clothes. After having a short conversation with him, the man invited the child to walk along with him down this street. Before long they met a traveling companion of the man. The friend said quietly to him, "You aren't walking through the streets with that dirty lad, are you?" Overhearing the remark, the disappointed lad immediately started to draw away. But then he heard the gentleman say, "Why not? This lad is my friend." A great smile beamed across the lad's face as he kept walking along with his new-found friend, confident that he was wanted, and happy that someone was interested in him.

In a similar manner, the Lord turns to us and says, "I am your friend." This is an ever-faithful friendship. Though daily we commit sin and miserably fail to deserve His grace, He freely offers it to us, if we are penitent. Even though we turn aside from Him and disobey Him, yet He is ever ready to send His love into our sinful lives. Our relationship to God is an ever-lifting friendship. We stumble and fall, but the Lord is there to set us on our feet again, and send us in the direction we should go. This is an ever-growing friendship. The longer we live, the more it means to us, as we nurture it through the reading of the Word of God, through prayer, and by the use of the sacraments. Our faith in God must grow ever stronger and deeper, as our friendship develops through the experiences of life over the years. Ours is an everlasting friendship, for it continues not only through our life in this world, but through all the years of eternity as well.

PRAYER THOUGHT: *We are thankful, heavenly Friend, that Thy friendship is everlasting, so that even though we daily stumble into sin, Thou art always ready to extend Thy forgiveness and grace.*

Whatever your task, work heartily, as serving the Lord. Colossians 3:23

For a city of its size, there are perhaps more taxi drivers in Beirut than in almost any other place in the world. Most of the men who follow this occupation own their own automobiles, so their livelihood depends upon whether or not they can get business. Even at the very moment when a tourist puts his foot out of the hotel entrance groups of these men will run up shouting, "Taxi! Taxi!" Because the support of their families and all of their income depends upon capturing the business of foreign tourists, they are very eager to do so.

The thought then occurs to you about what a different world this would be, if we were as eager in our efforts to serve our King. What a wonderful message we have to share with those about us! Each one who claims to be a Christian has an obligation and also knows the privilege of sharing this message with others. We who know the Lord surely must want others to know Him as we do.

At Pentecost when the disciples of the Lord received the gift of the Holy Ghost, they couldn't wait to run out into the streets to share the message which they had heard. John Bunyan, the author of the religious classic, *The Pilgrim's Progress,* came face to face with the Lord one day. He couldn't wait to go home and tell the good news in his community. A great scientist when once asked, "What has been your greatest discovery?" replied, "The fact that Jesus Christ is my Savior and Lord." Do you have the vibrant kind of faith that compels you to be out witnessing on behalf of Him who is the Lord of life? Is your love for Him so deep that you are spilling over the joys of faith into the lives of other people? Such is our task in serving the Lord.

PRAYER THOUGHT: *May we give evidence of the depth of our faith in Thee, O Lord, by being eager and dedicated witnesses for Thy kingdom.*

"In my Father's house are many rooms; . . . I have told you
that I go to prepare a place for you." John 14:2

On my first trip to the Holy Land, I drove with a guide
from Beirut through Damascus and on to Jerusalem. It was
a very interesting journey, as about us in every direction we
saw the many places made sacred by the presence of our Lord
in this world. During that drive I thought of the story concerning a certain traveler who, longing for a stopping place,
met a native lad. The lad told him that there were tents further on where certainly there would be a place that he could
stop and be sure of finding hospitality. Then after the lad had
told the man about the stopping place, he mounted his horse
which stood waiting nearby and rode on saying, "I will go
and prepare a place for you." He then went on ahead to make
the necessary accommodations for the traveler.

This little incident casts a revealing light on the saying of
our Lord as He spoke about the mansions in His Father's
house. We are living in a tremendous world, but we cannot
long remain here. There is a future in store for everyone of
us in another world that has not yet been revealed to us. We
all have questions concerning it. Where is it? What will it
be like? Who will be there? Can we be certain now that
some day we shall walk through those eternal portals?

As we meet our Lord day by day, He turns to us and says,
"I go to prepare a place for you. There are many rooms in
my Father's mansion. One is reserved for you. Indeed, I gave
my life upon the cross that you might live with me for evermore." Let us take our Lord at His word, and believe this
promise from His very own lips. When we accept Him and
acknowledge our deep need for Him, we shall find that we
are on the road of faith which leads to God's heaven.

PRAYER THOUGHT: *Precious Savior, we are grateful that
Thou hast prepared a heavenly home for us through the sacrifice of Thy life on the Cross in order that we might be redeemed from our sins and live with Thee eternally.*

Why are you cast down, O my soul, and why are you disquieted within me? Hope in God. Psalm 43:5

My friend and I had planned to fly from Jerusalem to Cairo. The airlines agent finally informed us that the scheduled plane could not land in Jerusalem, so we would have to drive to Amman which is the capital of Jordan. It was a very gloomy day as we traveled down the road by the Dead Sea, and then on up to the capital city. One could not help but think of the kind of world Christ came into, for it was dark and dreary and gloomy then, too. The reason He came was to give the world a light that nothing could put out.

We arrived at Amman, boarded the plane, and taxied to the end of the runway. Suddenly it became very dark. A driving rainstorm descended on the area. It almost seemed impossible that the plane would be able to take off. Suddenly the aircraft lurched, sped down the runway, and ascended in the storm. Higher and higher it climbed until before long we broke through the clouds into the glorious sunlight of God's heaven.

It appears that too many people in this world are satisfied with low-level living. They plod along in the same ruts day after day. They are discouraged by the stresses and the strains of life. They are surrounded by the clouds of fear and anxiety and hopelessness. All the time there is the possibility by God's help to lift life to a higher level where the glory can suffuse our living and also where His presence can lead us on.

Life's storms come to all. No one who lives can escape them. But we can each rise above them. And when you do, you discover that there is power for truly great living, greater power than ever you dreamed existed.

PRAYER THOUGHT: *Help us, dear God, to lift our lives out of the depths of anxiety and hopelessness by trusting in Thee to aid us, and grant us the peace of such trust.*

Happy the people to whom such blessings fall! Happy the people whose God is the Lord! Psalm 144:15

An American family brought back from across the seas a young boy. He was a refugee, because both of his parents had been killed. One day the man of the house took his newly arrived foster son downtown to a variety store. He gave him a quarter telling him to buy anything he wanted. The man remained outside the store wondering what the boy would choose.

We can well imagine that the youngster, unaccustomed to seeing such a heaped-up variety of things, was excitedly walking up and down the aisles of the store looking at candy, gum, toy cars, and other bright objects designed to attract a boy's fancy. "What should I buy?" he asked himself. In a moment he found the answer. Wreathed in a smile the boy walked out of the store proudly holding in his hand a miniature American flag. One could easily read what was in his mind and heart. He was grateful to be living in a country where freedom and love surrounded him in his new home.

We take this land of ours so for granted! We don't begin to realize how we are living in the lap of luxury. One does not need to travel very far to learn how bountifully God has blessed us. Ought we not continue to remember, however, that these are gifts from God? We in no way hold sole ownership over them. They are ours only for a time. There comes a day when all men must give an account of their stewardship according to the opportunity which has been theirs. How grateful we should be for the accident of our birth in this goodly land and for the many opportunities we have each day in a great country where we can live our lives out in freedom and worship God according to the leading of our own consciences.

PRAYER THOUGHT: *Gracious God, we pray that we may not be ungrateful for the many blessings which are ours because we know Thee as our God, and for the freedom which we have because we live in this land of liberty.*

> Thy kingdom is an everlasting kingdom, and thy dominion endures throughout all generations. Psalm 145:13

As I was traveling by plane to Jerusalem, I tried to recall in my thoughts the many places where I had recently spent some time. I had been to lands where Napoleon's armies had marched in his mad selfish attempt to conquer the whole territory of Europe. I had traveled the continents the Caesars had subdued in pursuit of their goal to conquer the lands of the Mediterranean world. I had seen the heart-rending destruction caused by the most recent dictators of Europe in their unsatisfied hunger for the complete conquest of the continent. Then I was struck by the fact that every one of these empires, ruled and molded by their powerful dictators, is dead and in ruins. No man-made empire could survive the test of the years.

Now, in Jerusalem, I thought of that empire which had its humble beginning through the birth of a little Babe in a stable manger in the quiet city of Bethlehem. His spiritual empire still remains. I thought of this Babe grown into manhood who came into the world to bear our griefs and sins and carry our sorrows. I thought of Him as the light of the world who takes all darkness out of living, who reconciles us with the heavenly Father, who stands as our advocate before the judgment throne of God to say, "Forgive them, for they know not what they do." I thought of the power of His life, who lifted us up out of certain death into eternal life by His nail-pierced hands and death on the cross. I thought of the miracle of salvation that came to us from the Lord of lords and King of kings by His resurrection from the grave. In this little corner of the world there lived One who some day will reign supreme over all the world. His kingdom of love shall endure until time is counted no more.

PRAYER THOUGHT: *Almighty God, we are grateful that we do not have to put our trust in the fleeting power of earthly empires, but that we can look for the coming of a King and a kingdom that will endure throughout the ages.*

"Did not I weep for him whose day was hard? Was not my soul grieved for the poor?" Job 30:25

Standing by a sheep gate in Jerusalem one day, my roving eyes discovered a rocky pool in the main line of traffic. My guide pointed to it, saying that it was the pool of Bethesda. His remark made me recall the incident in Scripture which tells us how in Jesus' day there gathered around this pool a multitude of the sick of that day—the invalids, the blind, the lame, and the paralyzed, all of whom were thought to be incurable.

One man in particular had been ill for thirty-eight years. Although hundreds of people likely passed by him each day, no one had stopped to help him or to show any concern. That is, no one had bothered to help until Jesus came along. Stopping at his pallet, the Lord looked on him and said, "Do you want to be healed?" Now, the people had the belief that if one could be the first to step down into the pool, once the waters were disturbed, one would get well. So the man turned to Jesus and said, "Sir, I have no man to put me into the pool when the water is troubled. Therefore, I do not even have a chance to be healed." The Lord turned to him and said, "Rise, take up your pallet, and walk." At once the man was healed.

These two lessons among others I would have you learn: The Lord has so much love in His heart for you that He will not pass you by, no matter what your need might be. He cares. He is your very best Friend. To Him you are significant, for you are a somebody rather than a nobody.

The second lesson comes out of the question: What about you? Do you pass by closing your eyes lest you get involved where there is human need? Or is your heart so overflowing with love that you can't help being your brother's keeper.

PRAYER THOUGHT: *Fill our hearts and minds continually with Thy love, dear Lord, and teach us to show this love in turn to our brothers.*

"Who is on the Lord's side?" Exodus 32:26

Above the Jaffa gate in Jerusalem there is a small plateau located high on the hillside. This is known as the "terrace of indecision." When it rains, the water falls on the little terrace forming a pool. It is so level there that the water does not know which way to run. It can fall off the eastern side, or it can run off the western side. If it decides to go to the west, it travels down through the beautiful valley of roses, and then on to the plains of Sharon. If it goes to the east, it runs down barren slopes into the Jordan River, and then on to the Dead Sea. This water cannot stay where it is. It must make the choice to go one way or another.

So it is with life. Every man decides which way his soul shall go. The choice is before us every day to travel into the valley of roses with the Lord, or to walk away from Him and on to the region of the Dead Sea. No man can remain neutral in this world of conflicting interests, political philosophies and systems of thought and culture. We are either for Christ, or we are against Him. There is no neutral ground. Life does not stand still. It moves in one direction or another. But the life that moves onward toward God and His will is the life that has significance and meaning. This is the only life that can ever be eternal, for it is rooted in the abiding things of God.

Choose you this day the way that you will go. The broad way offered by the world leads to destruction but, foreboding as it may seem, the narrow way leads to life eternal. Make this your day of decision that you will join other Christians on this journey of commitment and trust in the great God of heaven and Ruler of the universe.

PRAYER THOUGHT: *Help us, gracious Lord, to choose the road which leads onward and upward into salvation, where we can at last be at home with Thee throughout all eternity.*

188

Then Jesus was led up by the Spirit into the wilderness to be tempted by the devil. Matthew 4:1

Approaching Jericho by air, a friend sitting next to me said, "Look, there is the Mount of Temptation." It was a great rocky barren and precipitous hill. One could readily imagine that if one stood on top of it, one could look out far into the distant horizon.

We thought of the day when the Lord stood on a promontory with the evil one at His side, being tempted, even as we can be tempted today. The evil one said to the hungry Jesus, even as he pointed to the boulder-strewn ground which we were now viewing below us, "If you are the Son of God, why don't you turn these stones into bread?" Jesus had fasted forty days and forty nights in the wilderness. In His humanity He was as susceptible as anyone of us would be to the temptation to use His divine power only for self-preservation. But He turned to the devil with unfaltering voice and said, "Man shall not live by bread alone."

The second time the devil turned to Him and said, "If you are the Son of God, why don't you jump down from this pinnacle, and prove that you are the Son of God by not being killed?" The devil wanted the Lord to induce faith by something sensational, when the Lord well knew that only by the giving of His life on the cross could He ultimately save man.

The third time the devil said to the Lord, "All these I will give you, if you will fall down and worship me." This was the devil's biggest lie, for these things did not belong to him in the first place. Again the Lord resisted. Rebuked and defeated, the devil departed.

We, too, are tempted in like manner. No one lives who isn't tempted. The more dedicated we are to the Lord, the more eager is the evil one to conquer us. Stand firm in the Lord!

PRAYER THOUGHT: *Help us, dear Lord, to stand fast in the faith when the power of evil threatens to overcome us. We pray that we may be victorious over temptation as Thou didst triumph over the devil.*

Through love be servants of one another. Galatians 5:13

There is a road which leads from Jerusalem to Jericho. Each time I have traveled upon it I have thought again about the story of the good Samaritan. The road travels downward all the way. It leads through very rugged country and winds around barren sun-baked hills with their deep gullies. One can easily understand how it was an ideal hiding place for bandits who would swoop down upon frightened travelers and rob them of their goods on this roadway in the long ago.

About half of the distance between Jerusalem and Jericho, which is located by the Dead Sea, there is a place called the Good Samaritan Inn. Just before coming to it, there is a location which I visualized as just the perfect spot from which the bandits could leap out upon the traveler those many years ago. I thought of the wayfarer who lay beaten and dying. I saw two people pass by on the other side. They no doubt felt sorry for him, but they didn't take time to help him. A third man, one of another race, came by. Seeing the robbed man, he not only felt sorry for him, but he halted in his journey to help him. He bound up his wounds, put him on the back of his beast of burden, and took him to this little inn where he left him and paid for the stranger's lodging.

That man came home late for dinner that night, but I am sure that when he entered the house, his family saw a different look on his face. Perhaps he spoke words similar to these, "I helped someone today. I know I have never had a more wonderful feeling in all my life!" After the Master had told this story, He said to His disciples, as He still says to us today, "Go and do likewise." Give of yourself to the task of loving those who are crying for love. May we not pass by daily opportunities to be true disciples of our loving God.

PRAYER THOUGHT: *Let us not be indifferent and hardened, but merciful as Thou art merciful, O Lord, when we see the needs of others.*

"Today salvation has come to this house, ... For the Son of man came to seek and to save the lost." Luke 19:9, 10

Jesus, in passing through Jericho, made an occasion to be remembered for all time. As I passed that same way one day centuries later, I thought of a citizen of that ancient day named Zacchaeus. A very rich man, he held the title of chief tax collector for his city. He wanted to see Jesus, because he had heard so much about this traveling teacher. But he was at a disadvantage when Jesus came, because there was a large crowd, and he was a man of small stature. So he ran out ahead, and finding a sycamore tree climbed it, because he knew that Jesus would pass that way. When Jesus came to the place where Zacchaeus was in the tree, He looked up and said to him, "Zacchaeus, make haste and come down; for I must stay at your house today." Immediately Zacchaeus hurried down and received Him joyfully as a guest in his home. When the leaders of the church saw it, they all murmured, "He has gone in to be the guest of a man who is a sinner."

Think of the miracle that happened in Jericho that day. Zacchaeus looked at himself as he stood in the presence of Him who is the light of the world and, abhorring himself as he was, penitently promised to repay all those he had defrauded. Jesus said to him, "Today salvation has come to this house . . . for the Son of man has come to seek and to save the lost."

Here indeed is hope for every one of us. If we are earnest seekers, the Lord is not at all hard to find. Indeed, He is always willing to come and to abide with us. In His presence we too shall discover all the wrong we have done, just as Zacchaeus saw his sins exposed in the light of the Master's presence. In His purity we realize the evil state of our hearts. May we resolve to seek His forgiveness, and then turn to live as His worthy followers.

PRAYER THOUGHT: *Lord of mercy, we are grateful that we can seek Thy forgiveness and that if we do, Thou wilt enter our hearts and change an empty life into a life full of Thy love and grace.*

Let each of you look not only to his own interests, but also to the interests of others. Philippians 2:4

Thousands upon thousands of Arab refugees who have been uprooted from their homes, and have no other place to go, have been living in Jordan in recent years. Many of them have been forced to move underground to live in caves with their cattle. One day when I went into one of these underground homes, I discovered thirty-two people living together in one cave. I saw a little babe who had no bed but the hard stone floor. Of course, the children have no cribs in which to sleep. Others by the thousands have lived for years under tattered and torn tents.

Whose responsibility is it that these people are suffering and living under such dreadful conditions? Such a time as this is a test of the depth of the godliness that is in each one of us. If our righteousness is only a veneer, we can pass off the needs of these people and others like them with easy-flowing excuses like these: "There must be someone nearer who can help them." "We haven't paid for our new car yet." "We must save for a rainy day." But the man in whose soul God is enthroned proves his faith by his selfless, loving deeds and by his willingness not only to pray for these people, but to give them the help they so desperately need.

Not only across the seas, but in our own communities, there are those whom we must not pass by. The prayer of every Christian should be, "God, let me be aware. Let me be aware first of all, of the great love and mercy which have come to me in Christ and for all the gifts that still come from Thy hand. Let me daily count the blessings which flow into my life from Thee. Then, God, let me be aware of the needs of others, and enable me to help them. Soften my heart, Lord, so that I shall see what needs to be done and be led to do it in a spirit of love."

PRAYER THOUGHT: *Lord, let us not shrug off the responsibility of caring for others. Make us more willing to shoulder the burdens of our brethren in Christ.*

"You will seek me and find me; when you seek me with all your heart." Jeremiah 29:13

An American was traveling in the Holy Land. Before reaching the Holy City with its sacred places, he read the Gospels extensively, preparing himself to walk reverently where Jesus had walked. It was his hope and prayer that his journey to the most sacred spot on the globe would suffice to make the Master more real to him. It was in a spirit of great anticipation, therefore, that he arrived in Jerusalem. He walked about the city, was guided to various historic shrines, but still the Master seemed afar off. The places of which the visitor had read did not bring the Lord near to him.

Then one day in Jerusalem another visitor made it possible for him to find that for which he was seeking. This traveler was a poor man who had reached the Holy Land by much sacrifice. He, too, was a Christian and wanted to visit the homeland of our Lord, so that his faith might be renewed and that he might be inspired to give even more of himself to kingdom work.

On seeing the rows of miserable beggars near the Wailing Wall, this traveler was greatly moved. Allowing his sympathy to dominate his more practical nature, he went into the marketplace early in the morning and bought as many rings of bread as he could carry in his arms. These he distributed among the hungry and the needy. Some of them kissed his feet in gratitude as he fed them. The first traveler wrote that day in his diary that he had found the Master again.

It is said of the Lord that He always went about doing good. He has commanded us to follow His example. If we then obey His command, we shall know His presence, for has He not promised, "If with all your heart you truly seek me, you will surely ever find me"?

PRAYER THOUGHT: *Gracious God, help us to be rid of the tendency to look at every opportunity with regard to personal gain, for it can keep us from knowing the joy of true self-sacrifice and service.*

The wilderness and the dry land shall be glad, the desert shall
rejoice and blossom. Isaiah 35:1

Much of the soil in the Holy Land is sandy and rocky. There
is very little vegetation because of the dry soil and hot winds
which almost choke the plants before they take root. When
vegetation does appear, one wonders how these little plants
can possibly survive.

One day as I observed cacti growing out of this burning
sand, I thought of the life and hope that comes to men in times
of grief and desolation. There were also beautiful flowers
sprouting forth from several of the cactus plants. Just as in
this barren desolation of the Holy Land, these beautiful flowers spring forth, so in man's state of desolation and despair
there comes his only hope, the Rose of Sharon, which is our
Lord Jesus Christ.

The little cactus flower can change ugliness to beauty. The
words of Jesus and His presence in our life can change futility
into hope. Only as He enters into the hearts of men can
there come the peace which satisfies the soul.

How foolish it is for men to try to get along without the
Creator! Yet there are many who try to live apart from Him.
They wonder why their winnowing years are mere stretches
of monotonous existence. Life here is so "daily," complained
one such person. Others wonder why they lack the luster of
vibrant living and why everything seems to turn to dust and
ashes. "Why," they ask, "must I go so lonely and attached to
nothingness?"

Is it not because they have refused the Lord of life to come
into their desolation to change the barren places into places of
beauty? This God has the power to do; this He promises to
do, if we will but open our hearts, and allow Him to take
over.

PRAYER THOUGHT: *Make our lives blossom with the beauty
of Thy presence, gracious Lord, changing the barren wastes
into flourishing gardens of devotion to Thee.*

We know that in everything God works for good with those who love him. Romans 8:28

For several hours I had been walking along the streets of the ancient city of Jerusalem. Making my exit out a gate, I walked a distance down the road, until around the bend I saw clearly the Mount of Olives. This has always been one of the favorite holy places for tourists to see, as it always has been mine also. I love to stand on its eminence overlooking the Holy City and think of that time when Jesus gave the Great Commission to go into the world and make disciples of all men and nations, adding the great promise that He would be with us always, even to the end of the age, so that man would never have to walk alone. But before one can get to the top of the Mount of Olives, just ahead on the lower slopes of the Mount is the Garden of Gethsemane, nestled on the low rise of a foothill. As I walked in this holy place I thought to myself, "One cannot reach the heights without going through the valleys."

There are many people in life who complain about their hardships. They wonder if God has run out on them when trouble comes. Why doesn't He help me? they ask. God never intended that life should be a sweet slumber on a bed of roses. He himself had to go through the Garden of Gethsemane before He had His Easter. Can we who follow Him expect less? Then often we forget that some of our defeats when looked at closer may be considered to be more like times of triumph and victory. Even as the storms strengthen the trees of the forest, so these storms of life can be a victorious experience for everyone of us, for we can come through with the help of God. With His help, we can never be defeated, no matter how severe the difficulty might be. In that promise we can live and know with all certainty that the Lord is faithful and will never forsake His children.

PRAYER THOUGHT: *We should not ask for an easy life as one of Thy children, dear Lord, but only for Thy help which will enable us to weather whatever storms we meet on the sea of life.*

"I have said this to you, that in me you may have peace." John
16: 33

As I stood on the height of the Mount of Olives, I was overwhelmed with the thought that here it was that our Lord spent
one of the strangest days of His life. Here He probably dis-
patched His disciples into the city to fetch a donkey upon
which to make His last entry into Jerusalem. After they had
done as He commanded, the procession began. The Lord
paused on the brow of the hill, and turning to the people who
lined the roadway said to them, "Would that even today you
knew the things that make for peace, but now they are hid
from your eyes." They had been close enough to touch Him
during the three years He ministered to them. And yet, His
message hadn't penetrated their hearts. Like so many of us,
they had sought for peace where there is no peace. This deeply
grieved our Lord.

As the procession advanced on its way, the crowd grew
wild with ecstacy as they tore off their outer garments and
spread palm branches in His pathway. Some of the multitude
called out, "Who is this?" The world still asks that question.
The only true answer was given on Good Friday by a hard-
hearted centurion of the Roman army. Watching this Man die,
he too asked, "Who is this?" His own reply is worth remembering, "Truly this man was a son of God!"

If Jesus had not been the Son of God He would never have
been able to offer this great new hope for the world. For who
but God can redeem the world? This same God Almighty
stands before the door of your heart this day and every day,
asking the simple question, "Do you want to know the things
that belong to peace?" If you do, there is only this one prayer
to pray: "Come into my heart, Lord Jesus, come in to stay."

PRAYER THOUGHT: *Help us to come to Thee, dear Lord,*
where we may receive the peace which goes far beyond all
human understanding, and which will dwell in our hearts
forever.

He who has a bountiful eye will be blessed, for he shares his bread with the poor. Proverbs 22:9

On top of the Mount of Olives outside the city of Jerusalem there is located a beautiful church on the grounds of the Augusta Victoria Hospital. It is built in a most masterful and lovely mode of architecture. All who pass by marvel at the structural style.

As I entered the church, what a surprise it was for me to find that all the pews had been removed. Instead, stacked from the floor almost to the ceiling, were bundles and packages of relief clothing and other goods that had come to this place from America as well as from other parts of the world. Barely visible was the inscription high above the altar which read, "Inasmuch as ye have done it unto these, my brethren, ye have done it unto me." Standing there in reverence and praying, I participated in one of the most inspirational worship experiences that has ever been mine to know. One is inspired by what the friends of Christ around the world, who are grateful to Him for His great love, are enabled to do toward alleviating the sufferings and want of others.

But we shall have to admit that so far our sharing has been only token giving. How the world desperately needs more of what we can share! We have so much. In comparison, others have so little. However, these men of other lands too are God's children, for they belong to Him. They are not responsible for the accident of the place of their birth. From across the seas they are now crying to us who had the good fortune of being born in a free land, "Come and help us." By helping them we are helping our Lord, for He has told us that we all are our brother's keepers. We are all children of the heavenly Father. The world today is in desperate need. God's children are calling for help. Will you not be one to answer?

PRAYER THOUGHT: *Merciful Lord, help us to show Thy mercy to those who call to us. May we be generous as we answer their needs in all ways possible.*

"All authority in heaven and on earth has been given to me."
Matthew 28: 8

Standing on the summit of the Mount of Olives I thought of the last commission which the Lord gave to His disciples. Will His holy feet touch the mount again on His return with glory? Someone has summed up the message He left in His last conversation before ascending to the Father in the theme of "The Four Alls."

"All authority in heaven and on earth has been given me," said the Lord. No one else can dare make this claim, because to no one else has all power been given. Here is the only One who speaks with divine authority. Here is One who made the world and who now still holds the world in His hands. Here is One upon whom we can surely depend and build our hopes for eternity.

"Go therefore and make disciples of all nations," is His command. This message is not meant for a privileged few, but it is meant for all people. We who know the good news of the gospel of Christ have been challenged with the command to be the witnesses that shall bring that life-saving message around the face of the globe.

"Teaching them to observe all that I have commanded you," continued the Lord. He came to earth to teach us how to live and how to die. He left behind Him the Word which is our blueprint for living. No one need lose the way along the course of his life, if he follows the instructions given by the One who now is the conqueror of life.

"Lo, I am with you always, to the close of the age." What a wonderful promise! We can always be in companionship with Him who has all power. We can joyfully and confidently go through life singing, "If God is for us, who is against us?" Man need never walk alone.

PRAYER THOUGHT: *Dear Lord, we are grateful for Thy promise that we need never be without Thy companionship in this life, for Thou art all-powerful and able to give us victory in every conflict.*

> God is faithful, and he will not let you be tempted beyond your strength, but with the temptation will also provide the way of escape, that you may be able to endure it. 1 Corinthians 10:13

On the top of the Mount of Olives is located not only a hospital, but also a relief center. Goods come here from all parts of Europe and America to be packaged and given to the needy Arab refugees who number into the hundreds of thousands and are settled in the small area of Jordan. Every type of clothing one can imagine is sent. These must be hung on racks according to size. The United Nations staff working there provides lists of the refugees in the various villages, the number of individuals in each family, and the ages of the children. In this way an attempt is made to fit the clothing to the prospective needy in some degree.

A great number of people are employed in this relief agency. Most of them, as well as those whom they are helping, have very little in the way of material possessions. Therefore, they are tempted to steal some of the useful clothing which has come from faraway places and which cannot be purchased in stores in this land. As we watched them working, my friend standing beside me whispered, "They need a strong eye." Indeed, someone must constantly supervise and watch them, so that they will not take what does not belong to them.

In relation to our own lives it can also be said that the strong eye of the Lord is always upon us. No matter where we are or what we are doing, He knows everything. He is aware of our thoughts, and has an insight into our motives. There is nothing that we can hide from His knowledge. How grateful we can be that He is with us to give us the added strength to resist the temptations which daily surround us. He is present in life and would love us into goodness, giving us every blessing that His love can bestow.

PRAYER THOUGHT: *We thank Thee, Almighty God, that we can have always with us Thy strength and guidance to guard us from succumbing to worldly enticements.*

> As therefore you received Christ Jesus the Lord, so live in him.
> Colossians 2:6

Walking the streets of Jerusalem one day, I casually engaged in conversation with a man who readily admitted that he was a professing communist. Before long he emphatically tried to show me how democracy had failed. He pointed to the thousands of Arabs who had suffered through the recent years because of lack of clothing and food and places to live. Instantly I reminded him of the fact that we in the United States had given much aid through both our government and church-sponsored programs of economic and technical assistance. He replied, "The little aid you have given is like putting roses on the casket of a man you have just murdered." Yet he turned to me and said, "To be perfectly honest with you, the only force in the world we are really afraid of today is Christianity. It alone has the power to defeat us, but we need not really be afraid as long as Christians fail to practice it daily."

There are too many people today sitting back and saying, "Let the church be the church. Let it be a preaching station and that alone. Let it stay out of the realm of our daily life." This, however, is not the message of Jesus Christ. His gospel was directed to all with whom He came in contact. No one in need ever crossed His pathway but that He stopped to offer help. No one was turned away empty. No one was too insignificant or unworthy to make a claim upon the love of Christ. Unless we are willing to follow in His steps and sacrifice in a much larger measure than we have in the past, we shall find ourselves in great difficulty. The Lord's way is the only way of deliverance from the tightly encircling inroads of atheistic systems of thought and control.

PRAYER THOUGHT: *We pray, dear Lord, that we may renew and again strengthen our dedication to Thee, so that we may become a meaningful force in the fight to win souls for Thy church.*

"Serve him with a whole heart and with a willing mind." 1 Chronicles 28:9

The story is told of an Arab beggar who sat at the gate of a rich man's house. The wealthy owner was very kind to this poor man, as each day he would give him gifts of food, clothing, and whatever else he needed. In return the beggar was required to do nothing.

However, one day the rich man wanted to send a certain message some distance away. All of his servants were busy. So he wrote out the message on a piece of paper, took it to the beggar, and asked if he would deliver it for him. The beggar proudly lifted himself from his comfortable position and said, "I solicit alms, but I do not run errands!"

Many of God's children are like that. Each day God showers His blessings upon us. We do not deserve the least of His mercies or love. He gives us richly each day our daily bread and other necessities and even comforts of life. He surrounds us with family and loved ones. He plants in our hearts the hope of everlasting life. He stands by our side to guard us against the tempter. He is in our heart constantly to be our Savior from sin. He is the light of the world to lead us on through the unknown way.

Then comes the day that He wants us to go on an errand for Him. Perhaps He comes to us and tells us that there is someone He wants us to talk to about His love, someone who desperately needs our help, someone we may be able to win for His kingdom. What then is your answer? Do you say, "Lord, I solicit your blessings, but I do not run errands"? We can never gain salvation by our own deeds, but the least we can do in grateful love is to listen to Him when He speaks to us, and to obey Him when He commands us to go on a mission of love for Him.

PRAYER THOUGHT: *May we never be ungrateful, Lord, for the blessings which Thou hast bestowed upon us. May we increase the glory and greatness of Thy kingdom by unquestioning obedience to Thy command.*

Do not neglect to do good and to share what you have, for such sacrifices are pleasing to God. Hebrews 13:16

One day while in Jordan I talked with a father who along with his family had endured some very trying circumstances. They had lost everything they owned of material things, and were on the verge of starvation. Then came the day when all they had left was a little crust of bread which he hid away high on the shelf. "Early one morning," he continued, "'I heard someone stumbling around. I went to investigate and caught my daughter munching on this last crust. In my anger I beat her until I had drawn blood." Imagine a father beating his own child because she was starving to death! Then he looked at me with piercing eyes and said, "And you, Mr. American, have you ever known the fierce gnawing pangs of hunger?" I had to reply with a negative answer.

Many Americans throw more waste food in their garbage cans each day than some people across the seas have to live on. Indeed the Scriptures tell us that man shall not live by bread alone; but bread is important. All of God's children require the basic necessities of life.

According to studies conducted by well-known economists there is sufficient land in the world to produce enough food for all of God's people. The heart of the world's problem lies in the adequate distribution of this food. America is engaged in a program to bring technical assistance to the underprivileged countries of the world. We as Christians must support an expanded program of this kind. I have visited areas where our technicians have taught the people who now produce seven times as much food as before. This was done simply by displacing primitive methods with modern tools and know-how. Our concern must be for bread everywhere.

PRAYER THOUGHT: *Make us more aware, heavenly Father, that in Thy family we cannot live only for ourselves, but that we must consider also the welfare of those who suffer from poverty and disease because of ignorance and lack of assistance.*

"I am the vine, you are the branches. He who abides in me, and I in him, he it is that bears much fruit, for apart from me you can do nothing." John 15:5

In many areas of the Holy Land the countryside is covered with vineyards. Jesus used the vine to convey lessons, even as He used many other things about Him to reveal basic spiritual truths. He frequently pointed up what He said with illustrations, using picture language that even the most unlettered in His audiences could understand. Now, in order to have a productive vineyard, there are certain things which are necessary. In the first place, there must be a healthy stalk. Again, an expert vinedresser is needed in order to keep the vineyard flourishing. In the third place, each graft must make a healthy living contact if there is to be produced a worthwhile fruit. If these three conditions are provided, good fruit will be the result.

The Lord once made this analogy: "I am the vine, you are the branches." He indicated that when we cut off our connection with Him, we wither away and die, because we have lost our connection with life itself. If this condition persists, we are in sore trouble. Ultimately it will mean spiritual death, for there can be no life where there is no contact with God.

On the other hand, if the branch remains connected with the vine or if the individual remains close to the power of Jesus Christ, then he will be able to produce fruit. His will be a healthy spiritual life that will not only reach out a hand to receive, but will also reach out a hand to give. Other people will see the fruits of the Spirit, some of which are love, gentleness, consideration, kindness, and forgiveness. Such living is real and abundant living. The Lord offers this way of life to each one of us today. Now He holds before us the key to a life that is rooted in the love of Almighty God.

PRAYER THOUGHT: *Dear Lord, we pray that as Thy branches we may remain close to our source of strength, and that our fruit may be a witness to our spiritual contact with Thee.*

> In him we have redemption through his blood, the forgiveness of our trespasses, according to the riches of his grace. Ephesians 1:7

An Arab definition of a friend is this: "A friend is one to whom you can pour out all the wheat, chaff, and grain together, knowing that the gentlest of hands will take it and sift it, keep what is worth keeping, and then with a breath of kindness blow the rest away."

God is that kind of friend. It is our privilege to turn to Him each day and confide in Him regarding everything in our life. We need not be afraid of Him, nor can we hide anything from Him, for He knows what is in the innermost place of our hearts. He knows not only every act, but also every thought. Yet there is no one who is as longsuffering and willing to forgive as is God. Not only is He willing to forgive, but also ready to forget. God is able.

Look at God as He goes about in the person of Jesus. His arms of love are outstretched to those in the gutters of life, if they will only recognize their wrong and seek the help He is able to give them. His love reached for one of His disciples, Peter, after he had shamefully denied the Lord. And it would have reached Judas too, had he only repented of his sin; for is God not able "to save to the uttermost"?

On the cross His hand of love reached the soul of the penitent thief who asked to be remembered. He gave him the promise that already that day he would be with Him in Paradise. For His enemies who surrounded the cross and led Him to the most cruel death that history has ever recorded, He prayed, "Father, forgive them for they know not what they do." Knowing that His great love will forgive us, let us trust also that He will direct us in the way that we should go and give us the light of His guidance.

PRAYER THOUGHT: *Merciful Lord, we are thankful that because we have Thee as our heavenly friend, we are assured of Thy never-ending forgiveness, if only we come to Thee repenting of our sins and shortcomings.*

I know, O Lord, that the way of man is not in himself, that it
is not in man who walks to direct his steps. Jeremiah 10:23

Just west of the Dead Sea there is a mountain peak known
as the Masada. Its fame comes from the fact that it was the
last stronghold to fall after the Romans had captured Jerusalem.

Some years ago a certain man and his friend left their quarters on the banks of the Dead Sea and made their way toward
Masada, hoping to climb it. They found themselves at the
steep east side of the mountain. The ascent looked so difficult
they wondered if they should attempt such a climb. But having come this far, they did not want to turn back.

They finally succeeded in struggling to the top. On returning to Jerusalem they learned that the ancient historian, Josephus, had once written that it was impossible to climb the
Masada, especially on the east side, "simply because it takes
away the courage of everybody by reason of the fear that it
puts into the soul." But not having read Josephus before, they
attempted the climb, and all unaware that this climb was impossible, they had succeeded.

God wisely has hidden from us the things of the future. If
we had to face the full sweep of life all at once, it would un-
nerve us and probably prove impossible to handle. But God
is the only One who knows what is ahead. He knows exactly
what is going to happen because of His all-knowing and all-
seeing power. He is well equipped to help us handle every
situation. The secret of real living is to put our trust in Him
and then to live each day as it comes along, knowing that His
grace will ever be sufficient for us. He stands at our side to
upbuild and support our faith. This is the day which the Lord
has made. Let us rejoice and be glad in it and live today to
the fullest extent of its possibilities.

PRAYER THOUGHT: *Almighty God, we are grateful that Thou
dost not reveal the future to us, but that with Thy wisdom and
power, we may meet each day and each adventure with sufficient knowledge and understanding.*

"The eternal God is your dwelling place, and underneath are the everlasting arms." Deuteronomy 33:27

While walking along the shores of the Dead Sea a tourist stumbled, lost his balance, and fell into the water. He could not swim. Afraid that he might sink and drown and struggling for his life, he began to fight the water, flinging his hands about vigorously. Finally he was exhausted, his strength completely drained. Then to his utter amazement, he found that the water bore him up. Try as he might, he could not sink. The water of the Dead Sea was so heavy with salt that even when he lay motionless he remained afloat on the surface.

This is a parable of life. Many struggle and try to keep going by their own strength. We try to do things to gain merits in the sight of God. Before long we exhaust our own resources. We become desperate. Our fears, anxieties, and worries pile up within us. We are sure we are going to break down under the heavy load. We come to the point where we are afraid to face life. We live in dreaded fear of what is going to happen next. When at last we give up our own feeble efforts, and relax in the arms of the everlasting God, we discover that He is there all the while to bear us up and keep us from succumbing.

Someone has suggested the motto: "Let go, and let God." Let God take over your life. He is your Father Almighty. Knowing all your needs, He is capable of helping you to solve whatever problems you might face each day. Man is not meant to live in this world unattached, alone, and dependent upon his own strength. Man is meant to be God's child and to receive of His limitless strength which enables him to live each day abundantly. Let go of your selfish desires, and then let God put faith in your heart.

PRAYER THOUGHT: *Dear Lord, we so foolishly look to ourselves for an answer when trouble comes into our lives. Help us to seek Thee first, that we may always know the strength which comes to us when we place ourselves in Thy care.*

This slight momentary affliction is preparing for us an eternal
weight of glory beyond all comparison. 2 Corinthians 4:17

It was at the intersection outside of Jericho that Jesus turned
to His disciples and said, "Behold we go up to Jerusalem."
Since the city of Jericho is eight hundred feet below sea level,
turning south to go to Jerusalem meant great physical strain
as it meant journeying to a high level. It was also a mental
and spiritual ascent which meant agony for the Lord, because
He knew that He would have to suffer and die.

The road to Jerusalem leads sharply upwards for twenty
miles. Even today the highway is called the "ascent of blood."
The caves on each side of the road serve as cover for robbers
who come from their hideouts to plunder travelers. Many
times they leave them stripped and half-dead, as was the fate
of the man in the story of the good Samaritan. I thought of
all this when the Inn of the Samaritan was pointed out to me
on this barren stretch of road.

When Jesus said, "Behold we go up to Jerusalem," and then
added that the Son of Man would have to die on the cross, He
wasn't holding a very pleasant prospect for His disciples. He
knew full well the desertion of His friends, the filling up of the
bitter cup of suffering and woe that His enemies would put to
His lips.

The north fork of that intersection turned northward to the
happy scenes of His home and blue Galilee and friends. But
Jesus has never promised that our lives would be free from
crosses and mountain climbing. In fact He has said, "If any
man would come after me, let him . . . take up his cross and
follow me." The climb of the Lord is always upward. Life
then is more beautiful every day when we live in fellowship
with Him.

PRAYER THOUGHT: *Teach us, dear God, willingly to accept
the steep and rough road to salvation, so that we may at last
behold the wondrous beauty awaiting Thy children in eternity.*

I have gone astray like a lost sheep. Psalm 119:176

In a mountain grazing spot deep in the Holy Land three native shepherds brought their flocks to the same water pool where the sheep drank together. After the flock's thirst was satisfied, one shepherd called out, "Men-ah" which is the Arabic word for "follow me." His sheep turned obediently and came to him following him up the hillside. The next shepherd did the same thing, and his sheep went away with him. This man didn't even bother to count his flock.

An American tourist who was standing nearby said to the remaining shepherd, "Give me your cloak and staff. Let us see if they will follow me as soon as they follow you." So he put on the shepherd's clothes and called out, "Men-ah," but not a sheep would move. They did not know the voice of the stranger. "Will your flock never follow anyone but you?" asked the man. The shepherd replied, "Yes, sometimes a sheep gets sick and then it will follow anyone."

Is this not also true with the flock of Christ? His sheep know His voice and follow after Him. But when we get sick with sin, and temptation fastens its hold on our lives diverting us away from His pathway, we are likely to follow the alluring voices of the world. And when we do this we forget that we will be induced to follow down pathways that lead to destruction.

It is possible, however, for us to remain spiritually healthy. But in order to do so, we must constantly live in the spirit of prayer and remain in close communication with God. When He speaks to us, we must be willing to listen and to answer. When He commands us to do something for Him, we must act. When He sets forth a program for our lives, we must be willing to recognize it and with His help attempt to fulfill it.

PRAYER THOUGHT: *We pray, dear Lord, that our faith may be so strong that we can resist the call of unworthy masters and follow only the divine path which Thou hast set before us.*

Here there cannot be Greek and Jew, circumcised and uncir-
cumcised, barbarian, Scythian, slave, free man, but Christ is
all, and in all. Colossians 3:11

It was in answer to His disciples' request, "Lord, teach us
how to pray," that our Lord gave to us the perfect prayer. It
begins with this phrase: "Our Father who art in heaven."
Whenever we express our needs in the words of the Lord's
Prayer, we should think very carefully. God belongs not only
to us, but also to all people irrespective of nationality, race, or
creed.

Situated on the Mount of Olives is a church called the
Church of the Lord's Prayer. On an inside wall, on a tablet,
the prayer is inscribed in various languages. A young lad may
stand there reading it in German, another may read the English version, and still another from the local community may
read the prayer in Arabic. Racial and religious differences are
swept aside, as they stand before the same God, praying the
same prayer in three different languages.

If we offer this prayer sincerely, we cannot in word or in
thought deny the brotherhood of man. Too often a selfish mo-
tive has crept into our thinking. We think more than enough
of ourselves, but are prone to forget the needs, the hopes, and
aspirations of our fellow men.

The world is very small today. Indeed, it doesn't take an airplane many hours to fly around it. The whole world belongs to
God, so the problems of our brothers and sisters in the far
corners of the world are also our problems. Let us be challenged to close ranks with all men everywhere and so earnestly
follow the ways of tolerance that anyone will know at a glance
that we are sincere when we pray, "Our Father who art in
heaven . . . . thy kingdom come, thy will be done, on earth as
it is in heaven."

PRAYER THOUGHT: *Dear Lord, help us to realize that we are
not separated by distance and time from our fellow men, but
only by selfishness and indifference to Thy will, and that also
we may cross this barrier because of Thy enabling love in our
lives.*

209

I am continually with thee; thou dost hold my right hand. Thou dost guide me with thy counsel, and afterward thou wilt receive me to glory. Psalm 73:23, 24

Nearly every river in the world winds at some point as it flows into a larger body of water. It may run along a straight course for a few miles, but soon it is curving and bending again.

As I stood on the banks of the River Jordan one day and watched it wind its crooked course, my point was perfectly illustrated. From the air it would look like a huge twisting serpent. This river by survey is about two hundred miles long. But if it were to move in a straight line, it would cover only about sixty-five miles. How do rivers get that way? Often they follow the lines of least resistance. They are always hunting for the easiest way. When the stream comes to a mountain, a low hill or a barrier of any kind it flows around it. Therefore it has made its crooked course.

There are people, too, whose lives become twisted and crooked. They choose to follow the lines of least resistance. They are persuaded by majority opinion. These individuals are those who follow the crowd. They think it is much easier to do what everyone else is doing than to risk being called a non-conformist. They think it is easier to yield to temptation than to stand up for Christ.

These are days in which man is everywhere tempted. Many have forgotten the great faith of their fathers. Likewise they no longer remember the sacrifices which Christians in years gone by have been willing to make for their faith. They too often gamble away their lives forgetting that they are in danger of selling their souls for nothing.

Wise is the man who stays close to the Lord in prayer to receive directions from Him as to how to live. He is the only true guide who has gone all the way before. He is the Good Shepherd who takes care of His sheep.

PRAYER THOUGHT: *Gracious Lord, teach us to place our lives in Thy loving care and to accept the wisdom of Thy direction in the way we should go.*

"For everyone who exalts himself will be humbled, and he who humbles himself will be exalted." Luke 14:11

The city of Bethlehem is only a few miles from Jerusalem. A little village located in the hills, it is surrounded by the plains where the shepherds tended their flocks when the Lord was born. Over the place of the birth of Jesus there stands today a building known as the Church of the Nativity. The door through which you must go to enter this church is very low. As you approach it, the guides warn you in these words, "Stoop low if you would enter." Immediately one thinks of the Bible verse, "He who humbles himself will be exalted." We must stoop low to enter into the glories of an abundant life.

Two men went up to the Temple one day to pray. The prayer of the one was nothing but a recital to God of all the great things he had done. He had kept the Commandments. He had tithed. He had given to the poor. He was grateful he was not like other men. Undoubtedly this prayer never reached heaven. The second man then prayed, "Lord, be merciful to me, a sinner." The angels sang when they heard this prayer, because another sinner had repented and had in humility confessed his sinfulness.

Stand with me in front of the bronze star of Bethlehem on the pavement of the lower level of the Church of the Nativity. We read these words: "'Here Jesus of Nazareth was born.'" The words of Scripture come to mind, "And his name shall be called Jesus, for he shall save his people from their sins." Let us resolve to cast away all pride and self-righteousness. There is no hope in any man-devised way to save himself. But God's way is sure. It is through faith in our Lord Jesus Christ as our Savior that our sins are forgiven and that we have the hope of eternal life.

PRAYER THOUGHT: *Teach us, dear Lord, to rid ourselves of the pride and self-righteousness which sometimes appear to be insurmountable obstacles on the road to salvation.*

I have become all things to all men, that I might by all means save some. I do it all for the sake of the gospel, that I may share in its blessings. 1 Corinthians 9:22, 23

After touring the ancient village of Bethlehem, I went out to the shepherds' fields one night, accompanied by a friend from Jerusalem. As I let my mind reconstruct the lowly coming of our Lord into the world, I thought also of the great legacy which He left with us. "Peace I leave with you," He said. Yet anything but peace was in the hearts of the people here about me. Instead there was bitterness due to grinding poverty and hopeless distress.

In the stillness of the night I heard a low moan come from the olive trees. Turning to my friend I said, "What's that?" He replied, "Probably it is an unattended Arab mother giving birth to her child." Before long I heard the moan turn into an hysterical cry. Apprehensively I said, "What's that?" He answered, "Probably the little one is dying in her very arms."

Think of the emotional stress in the lives of people with things akin to this happening around our world today! It is easy to understand why communism has made such devastating inroads into these countries during these last years. Isn't it in part because of our failure to nourish their hopes and extend timely help so desperately needed?

Many of these people are like drowning men who grasp for a last hold on something. They might not even know the simple ABC's of communism, but it is something untried. How could it be worse than what they know today? By our indifference to these people, and our failure to come to their side with help, we are cultivating the ground in which communism will surely flourish. We must aid them, because God commands us to love.

PRAYER THOUGHT: *Dear Lord, may we realize more fully that our failure to fulfill our responsibility as Christians in bringing aid to distressed souls encourages them to accept whatever assistance they can find, no matter what source offers it.*

"For this I was born, and for this I have come into the world, to bear witness to the truth." John 18:37

As I stood in faraway Bethlehem, I naturally thought of one of the greatest events in the history of mankind, which took place there. The world at that time was in deep darkness and gloom. How excited the angels in heaven must have been as God prepared to send His Son to earth to be the Savior of the world. Then the event happened! The slender finger of a brightly shining star pointed to a humble manger. Shepherds in a nearby field saw the light. The angelic choir sang out, "Peace on earth good will toward men." Little could anyone realize on that night the peace that would ultimately come into the hearts of men throughout all generations because of the birth and the life of the Babe who made a cry in Bethlehem's stable. This coming of Christ was to change the lives of men everywhere down through all ages.

As I stood in the church which memorializes the scene of the Nativity, a divine service was in progress. I couldn't understand the words they were saying, because the service was in their own language. But the thought occurred to me that here were people oceans away from my home worshiping the same God that I worship in my church and in my heart. He is the same God of peoples everywhere in the world, regardless of skin color or geography or background. He is a God that cannot be contained in one place. We can never leave Him behind, however far we may travel. "He is going before you to Galilee," said the resurrection angel to the disciples. Christ is out there to meet us, however far we may roam. He is the only God who can bring peace to the hearts of men and give strength and satisfaction for everyday living. He is with us this day and every day that we live.

PRAYER THOUGHT: *We thank Thee, Lord, for Thy continuing presence with us and with all mankind, and for the gift of salvation which was made manifest by the coming to earth of Thy Son, our Savior.*

"Truly, I say to you, as you did it to one of the least of these my brethren, you did it to me." Matthew 25:40

There is a stone nearby the star of Bethlehem marking the spot where it is traditionally believed that Jesus was born. This stone through the years has been worn smooth by the kisses of pilgrims who have come here from all parts of the world to express their love and adoration for the Savior. As I watched some of them give this outward exhibition of love for Him, the thought occurred to me: How much better would it not be, if we would give real evidence of such love in our daily relationships with our fellow men.

Very close to the place where that impressive church housing the stone stands, I saw evidence of dire human need which I cannot blot out of memory. Near the field where the shepherds had stood gazing in awe at Bethlehem's brilliant star was a cave housing several hundred refugees. Little children stood around in ragged dirty clothing which had been originally sent by sympathetic people from America and other countries. A little boy had a castoff bathrobe cut down to his size. He must have worn it every day, because the garment was nearly threadbare. This was the only clothing he had to cover his body week after week. Inside the cave I watched a mother prepare the family meal for the day. It was a single pot of porridge. This was the only kind of food they could afford. It constituted the only nourishment they would receive for the entire day. As little as twenty dollars in American money provides the clothing, food, and the little housing by which these people keep body and soul together for a long year. Again we hear the clear echo of the words of Christ, "Inasmuch as you have helped these, you have helped me."

PRAYER THOUGHT: *Gracious God, teach us to be aware of the tremendous need of those around us, and of the endless possibilities which are open to us in which to do Thy will.*

Blessed is he who considers the poor! Psalm 41:1

On the road from Bethlehem to Jerusalem I stopped at a tent city. There, huddled together under tattered bits of canvas, were twenty thousand Arab refugees—twenty thousand of God's children.

Wherever I looked along a muddy pathway that they called a street, I saw human suffering and need. People were desperately seeking clothing, food, and—more than that—love. Little children with bloated stomachs and spindly legs were victims of disease. Most of them had less to eat in one day than the scraps we throw in our garbage cans. Rickets caused by malnutrition is very common. People are slowly and painfully starving.

The only clothing that one of these unfortunates whom I stopped to visit with had to wear was a dirty piece of burlap wrapped around his hips. When I returned to my car, he said in a voice heavy with hopelessness, "Why don't you Americans drop a bomb on us and end our suffering quickly rather than letting us stay here day after day dying by degrees!"

The story of suffering repeated itself in Jerusalem where I visited a hospital located on the Mount of Olives. As I walked down the corridor, I heard whimpering. Pausing to look in one of the rooms, we found here emaciated bodies of babies almost too weak to cry. They were mere bundles of bones, victims of malnutrition. A little milk and gruel would have made all the difference in their condition. They just hadn't had enough to eat.

Thank God, there are still people in the church with a desire to share, because they yet have a sympathetic heart. May more of us give evidence of our willingness to divide what we have with our less fortunate brothers throughout the world.

PRAYER THOUGHT: *Dear God, may we give evidence of our love for Thee by striving to alleviate the suffering and misery which is all around us.*

215

"Seek first his kingdom and his righteousness, and all these things shall be yours as well." Matthew 6:33

Close by the village of Bethlehem lies the ancient community of Bethany. Here is where Mary and Martha and Lazarus had lived. It was the place where Jesus often slipped away from the crowded Jerusalem to find rest. He felt so very much at home here. On arriving there one day, He found Martha upset and very excited. She was out in the kitchen bustling with preparations to set food before their favored guest, but in the meantime Mary sat at His feet relaxedly listening to the words of wisdom Jesus had to speak. At last Martha emerged from the kitchen, hot and flushed with anger, asking Jesus to rebuke Mary for her thoughtlessness. Jesus turned to Martha and said, "Martha, why are you burdened by so many things? Mary has chosen the one thing needful."

The Lord never criticized a person for commendable zeal, but He frequently reminded His children that first things should be put first. Emphatically He declared, "Seek first his kingdom and his righteousness, and all these things shall be yours as well." There are too many people who seek the things of this life, giving first rate loyalties to second rate causes. *Things* are not of eternal consequence. To a certain extent they may be needful to our comfort and health. But the Lord cannot feel at home in your life, unless you put things in their proper perspective.

The Lord today is still looking about for Bethanys where He may be guest. The question of the day is this: As He comes to your heart and life, do you make Him feel at home? Or are you too busy with the things of the world even to hear the knock at the door of your heart? If you make room for Him, life will take on a new depth of meaning and the dimension of eternity in the presence of the living God.

PRAYER THOUGHT: *Dear Lord, we pray that we may never crowd Thee out of our lives by allowing the things of the world to become more important to us than the things of eternity.*

Whatever you do, in word or deed, do everything in the name
of the Lord Jesus. Colossians 3:17

Palm branches, broken bread and a cup, the fragile reed and
a tattered robe of royal purple, the spiny crown of thorns, a
handful of nails, and then a cross. These are some of the symbols of the week of our Savior's passion. The Palm branches,
however, were signs of a jubilant celebration. The people of
the city apparently were in a joyful mood at the time of the
entry of Jesus into Jerusalem. The people cried, "Hosanna!
Blessed be he who comes in the name of the Lord." One day
as I walked up to the crest of a boulder-strewn hill that overlooked this city of sacred memories, I thought back on this
long ago. As I walked the gravelly pathway, I tried to think
of what may have been in the minds of the mob who lined the
dusty roadway leading to the gates of the city, each person
hoping to get to meet Jesus. Perhaps their outward display of
what passes for popular devotion was only spontaneous mob
psychology. Apparently they had the planned intention of
making Him their king, but it was only a flash enthusiasm,
born of the moment, for making Him their king for that day.

I ask you a question so personal as to turn your life inside
out. How about it? How unswervingly are you devoted to
Him who is indeed the Savior of mankind? Do you call upon
Him only in times of great need, making Him to be your king
for a brief day? Or are you unshakingly His and devoted
therefore to His cause? If He is to give you what your life
needs you, too, must bring forth the royal diadem and crown
Him Lord of all, which means that you will make Him Lord
over every area of your life. Walking with the Savior Christ,
you can know the enabling power to be victorious.

PRAYER THOUGHT: *Teach us, King of kings, to be loyal subjects of Thine in every aspect of our lives so that we might be
truly devoted to the cause of Thy kingdom.*

"Could you not watch with me one hour?" Matthew 26:40

On the night in which He was betrayed, Jesus, feeling the need of prayer, sought a quiet spot in the Garden of Gethsemane. He brought with Him the eleven disciples. Judas had absented himself from the group already because of his treacherous heart. Before they crossed over the brook Kidron, he had slipped off to sell the information about the Master's whereabouts to Jesus' enemies.

Jesus took the lead toward the garden. Eight of the disciples remained at the outer gate of the garden. Then He took three of them, Peter, James, and John, and going a little deeper in among the olive trees, Jesus asked them to watch and pray. He himself left them when He went a few paces farther. But there in the Garden of Gethsemane the three disciples fell asleep. Standing in that setting many hundreds of years later, I could yet almost hear the voice of the Master as He said, "Could you not watch with me one hour?"

It is easy for us to criticize the actions of other people. However, it would be much better and more profitable for us, if we would turn the searchlight of God's Word upon our own lives. How faithful are we to Christ? Do we bypass the opportunities that come our way to help Him and to be His hands and feet in the work which He wants done? He requires very little of us in comparison to what He has done for us. So often we are asked to do something for the church and its program of speaking to the spiritual needs of men. We say we haven't the time, because we are too busy with other things. If ever you are tempted to make such excuses again, go back in your thoughts to the Garden of Gethsemane and hear the Master say—this time to you, "Could you not watch with me one hour?"

PRAYER THOUGHT: *May we not fail to answer the call of service for Thee and Thy church, dear Savior, but eagerly may we accept any opportunity to return thanks for Thy great gift of salvation.*

218

Pilate . . . took water and washed his hands before the crowd, saying, "I am innocent of this man's blood." Matthew 27:24

What was once the judgment hall of Pilate has had to be excavated through the debris of the centuries, until the authentic pavement of Gabbatha has been laid bare. Built over it is a nunnery surrounded by beautiful gardens. As one stands on the worn cobblestones at this place, one is reminded of the fact that Pilate has long since been gone and that Christ is alive for evermore.

A trial unlike any other took place there many years ago. Jesus was brought into this hall along with a notorious criminal named Barabbas. Pilate was trying to avoid making a decision that he shrank from, since it violated his sense of Roman justice, and opened him to unpopularity and violent hatreds. He therefore asked, "Whom do you want me to release? Barabbas or Jesus?" Pilate was worried. His wife had sent a message earlier, "Have nothing to do with that righteous man, for I have suffered much over him today in a dream."

"Which of the two do you want me to release?" again said the frightened voice of Pilate. "Barabbas!" came the hoarse voice of the mob. "Then what shall I do with Jesus who is called Christ?" cried out Pilate. They all shouted, "Let him be crucified!" "So when Pilate saw that he was gaining nothing, but rather that a riot was beginning, he took water and washed his hands before the crowd saying, 'I am innocent of this man's blood; see to it yourselves.'"

But not any one of us is innocent of the shed blood of Christ. By our sins we all have joined that angry mob saying, "Let Him be crucified!" Yet, there is good news, for by His death He redeemed us and caused the judgment hall to be transformed into a garden. What would be our deserved death sentence was changed by Christ into victory over death.

PRAYER THOUGHT: *Precious Savior, we thank Thee that even though we must also bear responsibility for Thy crucifixion, Thou dost still love us and hast redeemed us from our sins.*

"It is the Lord your God who has fought for you." Joshua 23:3

Walking along the Via Dolorosa, that narrow street in Jerusalem where it is believed that Jesus marched on His way to the hill of Calvary, one cannot but be filled with deep emotion. For it is on such a walk that one thinks of the significant sacrifice Christ made that all might be delivered from sin, death, and the devil. As I walked along this route thinking of the events that took place in this city nearly two thousand years ago, I was filled with deep emotion. Here had been enacted the greatest rescue that has ever occurred in the history of the world. It was at Calvary that the world witnessed its most titanic battle in which the fate of all mankind to the last day of the world hung in the balance. It was a battle between God and the devil and all of his followers.

Christ was victorious. That means that the cross is no longer a symbol of defeat. It is now the sign of victory. Christ has won decisively the battle for the souls of His children. He has rescued them from the eternal despair of hell, which is the abiding place of the devil and his angels. In real fact then, all man needs to do is to accept this free salvation offered to him.

"Behold I stand at the door and knock," said the Lord, "If any man hears my voice . . ." This is the deciding condition. Are you listening to God? Daily He calls you to repentance. Daily He offers you forgiveness. Daily He holds out in His hands to you the gift of the assurance of everlasting life. This day you can claim this victory He has won over death for the eternal salvation of the faithful.

PRAYER THOUGHT: *Gracious God, we thank Thee for the victory which is ours because Thou didst battle against the devil for our souls, and we pray that we might willingly accept the gift of salvation which Thou hast won for us.*

He was despised and rejected by men; a man of sorrows, and acquainted with grief. Isaiah 53:3

As one walks the narrow street to Calvary with its stations of the cross, one is led into a little chapel which memorializes the flogging of our Lord. There on the wall hang three paintings in the chancel of this little chapel. One of these paintings depicts Pilate washing his hands, thereby trying to get rid of the guilt that he thinks might be attached to him because of his part in the judgment and sentencing to death of Jesus.

Another shows Barabbas, the notorious criminal and man of blood, as a released man walking free. However, one's attention does not remain long with either of these two paintings. Rather soon one's eyes are focused intently upon the third picture. It portrays the pained face of our Lord, with the piercing crown of thorns crushed upon His brow. "He was despised and rejected by men; a man of sorrows, and acquainted with grief." As a lamb He was led to slaughter. But He became the lamb of God who takes away the sin of all the world.

Because of what Jesus did for each one of us children of God, there is an open door that leads straight to God's forgiveness and love, an open door that eventually leads men to eternity. It was because of God's unbounding love for each one of us that He allowed His Son to suffer and even to die in order that we might be blessed in possessing the hope and the certain promise of everlasting life. No amount of suffering that we may have to bear in this life could begin to compare with what our Lord endured in order that we might be kept from dwelling forever with the devil. Each day by our living we should indicate to God how thankful we are to Him for saving our soul and redeeming our life from otherwise certain destruction.

PRAYER THOUGHT: *Dear God, we are ever grateful that because of Thy matchless love for us Thou wast willing that Thy dear Son should suffer death on the cross in order that our souls might be redeemed from the clutches of sin.*

Who for the joy that was set before him endured the cross.
Hebrews 12:2

One of the choice places for meditation in Jerusalem is Gordon's Calvary which is a skull-shaped hill outside the city wall. At the foot of this ugly precipice is to be found a tomb hewn from the rock with its huge stone yet standing there. Here benches have been set in a lovely garden for one to sit and meditate.

Now, Scripture does not say that in the place where the Lord was crucified there was a desert. But it does say that by this holy place there was a garden. The ugliest of deeds ever performed by man to another man was done in a lovely spot. Near the cross, a symbol of death, was a garden, a symbol of the promise of the perennial unconquerable life of the world.

It would be well if we kept in mind the fact that the garden and the cross sprang from the same soil. Joys and griefs often have the same origin. Nothing is more wonderful than to dwell in the love of Christ. It was a love that made Him bear our sins upon the cross.

But the end of the story is not the cross. God is able to effect glorious results from these things which otherwise seem so tragic. Around the cross there is always a garden. To the Lord's crucifiers the cross was a symbol of shame, defeat, and death. When they placed the Lord upon it, they mocked Him. They put a crown of thorns upon His head, a scepter in His hand, and in derision hung a sign above His head which read, "This is the King of the Jews." Little did they know that Christ was going to change this cross into a symbol of deathless glory. There are crosses that come into our lives, but there is a garden by the cross. It gives us the promise that because of Christ there lies a better day beyond the darkness.

PRAYER THOUGHT: *Help us, our Redeemer, to remember that even as Thy cross of trial and death stood in the midst of a garden, so also when our lives are filled with defeat there is yet a more beautiful day of hope ahead.*

He died for all, that those who live might live no longer for themselves but for him who for their sake died and was raised. 2 Corinthians 5:15

The scene is Calvary. It is a big, rocky ledge outside the wall overlooking the city of Jerusalem. As I stood at that holy place one day, I recalled some of the events that happened there some two thousand years before. The betrayal of the Lord for thirty pieces of silver, the outspoken denial of Peter, the false witnesses gathered in the crowd, the trumped-up trial, the loud anger, and the bitter hatred of the mob; all these things took place near the very location where I was standing. I thought of Christ, carrying on His back that heavy rugged cross up a narrow street. I thought of Him, climbing the hill, and finally breaking down in complete physical exhaustion. I visualized the soldiers as they laid the cross upon the ground, and nailed His body upon it. I could imagine the earth shaking as they dropped it with a thud into the hole which had been dug for it. I could almost envision Him there dying for you, for me, and for all people.

Filled with emotion I quietly prayed, "Thank you, Lord, for saving my soul. Thank you, Lord, for making me whole. Thank you, Lord, for giving to me Thy great salvation, so rich and free." At that very solemn moment, as though He were by my side, I could hear His voice distinctly say to me, "Now, my child, go out and prove by your living that your life has been worth saving."

The challenge of the Cross faces us each day that we live. There would be no hope for the future, nor any purpose for us to continue on, were it not for the fact that Jesus Christ is our Savior from sin. God has sent His Son to face the death penalty that we should rightfully pay because of our evil doing. He says: "This have I done for you. What will you do for Me?"

PRAYER THOUGHT: *Dear Lord, we know that our lives are not worthy of Thy great suffering and sacrifice for us, but we pray that Thy love will surround us and forgive us our unfaithfulness.*

223

Cast your burden on the Lord, and he will sustain you. Psalm 55:22

The Cross is a steppingstone to victory and joy. As I stood at the hill of Calvary outside the city wall, I said to myself, "You've sinned every day of your life. You're the one who should be carrying the cross. Such a death is what you've deserved. The nails should have been pounded into your hands, for they have been at so many tasks other than what the Lord has wanted them to be busy with." And in that moment my heart felt as heavy as lead for the sins I had committed.

Eternal death would stare me in the face and would have been my fate and yours, too, if our Savior had not voluntarily come to take that place of guilty sinners. We should have nothing to look forward to, except the eternal darkness of separation from His presence, if God had not defeated once and for all time the devil and the awful power of sin.

But God gained the victory. The Cross is now become the steppingstone to joy. Moreover, it teaches us a lesson. The crosses that we must bear today can be steppingstones, too. They need not lead to despair and defeat; instead, they can lead to victory. Out of the difficulties and trials of life we should seek a meaning. God can use absolutely anything to His advantage. But of one thing we can always be certain, and that is that the full weight of that which is on our back can be shifted to stronger shoulders. It will not be too heavy for God's Son, and He will bear it away. And so we can manage to exchange joy for despair and peace for a disturbed conscience. God's power and strength is with us each day to sustain and help us.

PRAYER THOUGHT: *Teach us, Almighty God, to accept the purpose of every cross which we must carry, so that through this understanding we might also accept patiently the greater cause for which we suffer.*

Fear not, for I am with you, be not dismayed, for I am your God; I will strengthen you, I will help you, I will uphold you with my victorious right hand. Isaiah 41:10

As I stood in Jerusalem at the place of the Garden of Joseph of Arimathea, I couldn't help but recall the first Easter morn. I tried to visualize the holy women on their way to the tomb. They worried about who was going to roll away the stone from the entrance of the tomb! They must have forgotten for a moment about the power of God. I thought of how much they had missed on that beautiful day because of the fact that they were worried. They missed the beauty of the day. They missed hearing the singing of the birds. They missed seeing the beauty of the flowers that surrounded them, as they walked heavy-hearted to the tomb. When they arrived at their destination, they discovered that all their worrying was in vain, for God had rolled away the stone. Man cannot defeat God, nor is there any power stronger in the world than His.

As I stood there, I began thinking about how much we miss in life because we worry. We are concerned about things that have already happened. Yet there is really nothing we can do about it, for yesterday is gone. It has already been lived. The best we can do is to capitalize upon our calamities and use them to build stronger lives for the future. We worry about things that will inevitably happen. There is nothing we can do about these. At the same time by worrying we dissipate our strength. But most of all I think we worry about things that will never happen.

It seemed that I could hear my Master say that day, "Why are you worried, O you of little faith? I am with you and I will help you carry the load. My strength is sufficient for anything that will come in life's pathway." His promises are not vain sayings, for those who love Him have trusted His Word and know that what He says can be relied upon in any situation.

PRAYER THOUGHT: *Make us more ready to lean on Thy strength, dear Lord, so that we may know the unencumbered life which comes when we trust only in Thee.*

"Fear not, I am the first and the last, and the living one; I died,
and behold I am alive for evermore." Revelation 1:17, 18

When visiting the garden tomb of the Lord, I recalled the
very vivid description which I had read earlier of a man who
had attended an Easter service in this very place. He had
looked forward to the experience very much. Now the night
before had seemed endless. Finally when the service began
early in the morning, it was so dark the minister had to read
from the Bible with the aid of a flashlight. Then with dramatic
suddenness the sun burst over the horizon, banishing the darkness and lighting the sky. The man exclaimed to himself, "You
can't hold back the dawn!"

Christianity is primarily the religion of the dawn, although
it recognizes the past with all its sins and failures. It also proclaims that there is a living Savior. It addresses itself primarily to the future and to the potential of man. To as many as
receive Him is given the "power to become" is the promise of
Scripture.

It has been my experience to visit many shrines around the
world where all manner of gods are worshiped. There are gods
of all descriptions, all sizes and shapes, who are given homage
for all kinds of reasons. But the only place I have ever gone
where there is an empty tomb is at Jerusalem. The Christ who
there conquered death for all men and rose to everlasting life
is the only one in the history of the world that death could not
hold under its power. It was because they had faith in a Christ
who could conquer death that the disciples became such dedicated apostles of the truth. We too can live in the assurance
that, even though periods of darkness come into our lives, we
can't hold back the dawn. The ever-abiding hope of our partnership with the great and Almighty God is that His love surrounds us each day, even now and on into eternity.

PRAYER THOUGHT: *Lord, because we know that Thou art
ever victorious over death, we can never be afraid of the dark
valleys through which we must go, for we are confident that
we shall see the dawn of eternal day.*

He presented himself alive after his passion by many proofs, appearing to them during forty days, and speaking of the kingdom of God. Acts 1:3

Jesus' disciples were heartbroken, as they beheld their Master stretched out upon the cross. Some of them fled from the grim scene and, fearing for their safety, hid behind barred doors. Others of them, not belonging to the inner circle, wandered with freedom about the streets. All were in a state of shock. They had no desire to return as yet to their homes.

On the Sunday after Good Friday two of them decided to return home to Emmaus. One day I walked that same road, my mind reverting to that thrilling experience which was theirs. As they were walking, One whom they thought to be a stranger joined them. He politely inquired as to why they were so evidently sad. They related all the bad things that had happened on Good Friday. The stranger tried to explain why these things had to occur. He volunteered that some day perhaps they would discover glory even in this gruesome event which seemed at the time all loss. When He was about to leave, they persuaded Him to join them for supper at the inn.

As they were sitting at a table, they recognized their Master in the characteristic thanks He gave in the breaking of the bread. This was Jesus! Their Friend whom they had thought lost was alive again. Jesus was risen from the dead! Now they had every reason to believe that with God anything was possible. Their hearts glowed as they walked with Him.

That joy can be ours every day. That inner glow of companionship with One who is able to set us on the way of hope again can be ours as we walk with God. His presence affords us comfort and yet challenges us to go out and work for Him.

PRAYER THOUGHT: *Precious Savior, may we ever walk with Thee and be strengthened in the companionship of Thy presence and in the knowledge of Thy resurrection and victory.*

Whatever is born of God overcomes the world; and this is the victory that overcomes the world, our faith. 1 John 5:4

Before Jesus ascended into heaven, He told His disciples that they should wait in Jerusalem and that there they should continue praying in faith, expecting something to happen. One day, as I sat by myself in the Holy City, I tried to imagine their feelings. What must these disciples have been thinking, I pondered silently. Perhaps this thought went through their minds as they waited without direction for those ten days: "God has forgotten all about us. He isn't going to send anybody to comfort us like He said He would." Not so, I concluded, but they did what the Lord had commanded, they "waited." They had faith. They trusted that something great was going to happen and that God would keep His promise.

Finally, on the Day of Pentecost the Holy Spirit descended into their midst and entered their hearts. Peter preached a sermon fully inspired of God and the other disciples became supercharged with the deathless dynamic of the Holy Ghost. Their entire lives were changed by that dramatic event, as they went out into all parts of the world unafraid of death, that they might be witnesses for the Christ to whom they had now rededicated their lives.

So here again each of us can learn a lesson. We do so need more patience with God, for He will bring into our lives what is best for us in His own good time. We need to spend more time in our personal devotional and prayer life. We need to have more faith when we pray that our prayers will be heard and answered according to God's desire. God is not limited in His ability to help us regardless of our need. We need to have our faith strengthened in a great God who alone has the right to say, "Great is thy faith; be it done unto you as you will."

PRAYER THOUGHT: *Almighty God, increase our faith and trust in Thy power and wisdom, so that we might know the victory over the battles of life, the victory that comes to those who fully trust in Thee.*

228

Having gifts that differ according to the grace given to us, let us use them. Romans 12:6

As I walked along those pathways where Jesus may have walked, I thought of how each person has special significance in the sight of God. Jesus told the story of the talents to point out that some people have many and some only a few. The number is not the important thing. It is what we do with our talents and how faithful we have been in using them that God is interested in.

At that time I was reminded of the fable of the three trees that grew in the days of Christ. One said, "When I grow to be a big tree I will be cut down and made into lumber. That lumber will be used to build a big hotel where kings will lodge." The second tree said, "When I grow up I want to be cut down and made into lumber to build a big ship that will cross the ocean." The third tree said, "When I grow up I want to remain in the forest and point men to God."

None of the three trees got its wish. The first tree grew up and was cut down, but the lumber was used to build a little manger. The tree complained and complained, until one night the Son of God and the Son of Man was born there. Then it was at peace.

The second tree was cut down and made into lumber to build a boat to sail on the Sea of Galilee. It complained and complained, until one day the Son of God and the Son of Man stood on its deck and spoke wonderful words of life. Then it was at peace.

The third tree was cut down and made into a cross. The tree complained and complained, until one day the Son of God and the Son of Man died upon that cross. Then it, too, was at peace.

Whatever your lot in life, God can use you! Let us be willing to let Him use us according to His will.

PRAYER THOUGHT: *Dear Lord, use each of us in the way Thou hast prepared us to serve Thee.*

If any one has the world's goods and sees his brother in need, yet closes his heart against him, how does God's love abide in him? 1 John 3:17

On my visits to the Holy Land, I have often thought of the lessons that came from the unusual geography of this River Jordan which, beginning high in the mountains, keeps the blue waters of the Sea of Galilee full and then descends through the valley until it empties into the Dead Sea. I stood by the Sea of Galilee one day where the Jordan River makes its entrance and could almost imagine it saying, "Welcome, River Jordan, you have given life to the trees, the grass, and the flowers along the way. I am very happy to receive you." Around the Sea of Galilee there are blooming flowers, happy children, and birds singing. Because it is a fresh water lake, it abounds in fish life.

Another day I stood at the place where the Jordan River runs out of the Sea of Galilee. Again I almost heard it speak, "You are too good to keep, so I must pass you on." The River Jordan continues on its way, finally flowing into a second body of water. There I stood another day and imagined I heard this sea say, "Welcome, River Jordan, now you are mine. I will keep you for myself." Around this sea there are no flowers blooming, nor happy children, nor birds singing, for its waters are heavy with salt and bromides. It is called the Dead Sea. It receives without ever giving.

This is a parable of life. No man can truly remain alive spiritually, unless he is not only willing to receive, but also to share. Nothing that we have is really our own. Everything has been given to us as a trust. Some day each of us will be called to give an account of our stewardship. What we keep for ourselves, we lose. It is only what we give away that we save. We can't take our possessions with us when we go to heaven, but we can send our spiritual riches on before we get there. It is more blessed to give than to receive.

PRAYER THOUGHT: *Gracious Lord, help us to be an example of Thy generosity as we share Thy gifts to us with others.*

230

Until the Spirit is poured upon us from on high, and the wilderness becomes a fruitful field. Isaiah 32:15

My first visit to the state of Israel was in 1949. The country was then celebrating its first anniversary of independence, so the people were in a festive mood for they now had a land which they could call their own. I had anticipated touring the countryside, and soon was given the opportunity to do so. Traveling to the south of Tel Aviv in the Negev area, I passed through Beersheba. The one restaurant open in the town had no screens on the windows, and flies were positively numberless. As I viewed the vast areas of sandy dune surrounding this city and in the land further south, I couldn't understand how anything could rise and prosper on this dry, parched earth in the years to come.

Since that time I have revisited the country on several occasions. Unbelievable miracles have happened there. The desert has been made to bloom. It is impossible to describe the changes that have taken place. They have been innumerable and fantastic. The waters of a little river have been channeled into irrigation ditches, and as a result this sandy land produces crops in great abundance. The arid parched ground has been changed into a garden.

It is possible for this to happen in life, too. Many lives are precisely like the seared desert. But let God come in, and He brings the waters of life which can transform your dull, monotonous living into a fruitful and luxuriant garden. Soon will be discovered the sturdy perennial blooming there—faith, which is our trust in God. Bright-faced hope is there, too— hope which brings the joy of living. And above all, there is that love which never fails, and which transmits to you a power that will never leave you.

PRAYER THOUGHT: *We pray, gracious God, that we may receive the water of life which can transform the desert of our lives into a luxuriant garden of trust and faith in Thee.*

"If you seek him, he will be found by you." 1 Chronicles 28:9

During one of my first visits to Israel, I was very conscious of the fact that the people were struggling hard to maintain an economic balance in their country. They were willing to make great sacrifices in order to keep this homeland where they could be free from persecution. A very strict rationing program had been put into practice; consequently I didn't want to ask for things which the people themselves could not afford to have.

My lodging reservations had been made in a beautiful hotel in Tel Aviv overlooking the sea. It was January, and the weather outdoors was desperately cold. For two days when in my room I had to sit with my overcoat on, since there was no heat. I thought this was one aspect of the rationing program. Finally, after I had suffered from the cold, I went to the manager of the hotel and asked him if there was any possibility of getting a heater. He seemed surprised to learn that my room was cold. Going with me to my room he showed me in one corner a thermostat which had been set low. He turned it up, and within a short time I was comfortable.

I remember then pondering these thoughts which came to mind. Here I had been suffering when right at my fingertips there was a control which would have given me what I needed. A stretch of the hand and my chill misery could be exchanged for warm comfort. I thought then about people living without God and His power and strength and love, when all of these are available only for the asking. "We have not because we ask not." But when we ask for the unlimited resources of God at our disposal, we can soon discover that in many strange and inconceivable ways living turns wonderful again, because we are linked with the only true Source of life and its meaning.

PRAYER THOUGHT: *Dear Lord, may we never forget we have easy access to Thy strength and comfort simply by bringing our need to Thee.*

I would rather be a doorkeeper in the house of my God than dwell in the tents of wickedness. Psalm 84:10

Into the newborn state of Israel have come several millions of people from many, many lands. One of the greatest problems of this new country is to integrate all these people coming from various cultural and national backgrounds into a common way of life. The highly educated Jews among them came from Europe, with their university training and academic degrees. On the other hand, the Yemenite Jews came from an illiterate impoverished people.

One day a leader of the country told me of some of the problems that face this new state. He cited the following situation as only one of many examples. A group of Yemenites had pitched their tents which they had made from cattle skins. This was their customary way of living in their former home. The government decided to help them with a housing program. The plan was to pay people salaries as they built their own houses. They were not pretentious buildings, but at least the structures were better than the cattle skin tents. When the houses were completed, instead of moving their families into them, the Yemenites put their cattle in the houses, while they themselves continued to live in their tents of cattle skins.

In a spiritual sense, we often do that very thing. We live in misery, when alongside us is a home of happiness and hope that we could be living in. God has made possible for each one of us a more abundant life. The longer we live, the richer it can become. Finally, He has prepared for us the house in His heaven. Every man decides which way his soul shall go. A beautiful home has been prepared for us. Let us make certain that we are traveling on the road that leads to its open door, where God will be waiting to receive the faithful.

PRAYER THOUGHT: *Teach us, dear God, to choose wisely the shelter of Thy love, that we may enjoy the blessings of a rich and abundant life through Thy grace.*

We know that if the earthly tent we live in is destroyed, we
have a building from God, a house not made with hands, eternal in the heavens. 2 Corinthians 5:1

Hundreds of thousands of people have in recent years
flocked from all parts of the world to the new state of Israel.
Many of them are refugees, expelled from countries where
they were unwanted. They had been living all their lives under the threat of death. One day I visited a community where
many of them have settled, near the Negev. They were building a communal village on this sandy desert stretch of Israel's
land.

A young man in his early twenties was hard at work, industriously absorbed in his task and singing as he worked. Walking to him I said, "How can you be so happy under such
circumstances? In your lifetime you will probably never get
rich. The best you can hope for is to maintain a marginal type
of living, and you'll have to work hard even for that. How
then can you be so happy?"

He looked at me, pointed to the stony ground, and said, "This
is mine! This is mine!" At last he had found a place where he
could lay his head down at night without fearing that the axe
of the persecutors would be upon it by morning. For this security he was willing to pay a stiff price.

All of us seek that kind of security in a spiritual sense. We
want a homeland where we can be free from sickness, suffering, and death. These are life's crosses which are so difficult
to understand and perplexing to bear. Happy is the man whose
faith is so secure that he can look through the thin veil that
separates us from the golden shore, and live with eternity in
his heart, saying, "This is mine! This is mine, not because I
can gain it with my own strength, but mine because Christ my
Savior died for me, and has gone before to prepare a place.
There I shall know the victory of everlasting life."

PRAYER THOUGHT: *Gracious Lord, we pray that we may so
live that we shall come to know the everlasting shelter and
security of an eternal home with Thee.*

All these blessings shall come upon you and overtake you, if
you obey the voice of the Lord your God. Deuteronomy 28:2

Nazareth is the town where the Lord spent most of the
years of His brief earthly life. Today Arabs make up most of
its population. The simple dwellings and shops fronting to the
narrow streets make one feel that one has stepped back two
thousand years to the little village in whose dusty streets Jesus played as a lad.

One day I walked up one of these narrow pathways and
seeing one of those open carpenter shops and a father and son
working, I pinched myself to be sure it wasn't a dream. Suddenly I came upon a synagogue which was the little church
that Jesus had come back to for a Sabbath's worship after He
had been away from Nazareth on His preaching mission. On
invitation, He went up in front to read the sacred Scriptures.
It was the ancient prophet's outline of what He was to be to
those who one day would put their trust in Him.

He said, "He has anointed me to preach good news to the
poor." By this He did not mean just those who were poor
from an economic standpoint, but He also spoke to those who
were poor in spirit, and to those who recognized their inade-
quacies. His message was to those who were bankrupt in
soul, and who reached for a power beyond themselves.

He had come to proclaim release to the captives, to set at
liberty those who had been imprisoned by the evil one, and
were victims of their own mistakes and wrong choices. He
had come to give recovery of sight to the spiritually blind who
had lost their way in this world which has so many confusing
highways. He had come to make men whole again. He had
come not only for the men of His own day but also for us living today.

PRAYER THOUGHT: *We renew our thanks to Thee, O Lord, for*
the blessings we have because we know Thee; and we pray
that we may not become indifferent in our awareness of these
manifestations of Thy grace.

> Being found in human form he humbled himself and became
> obedient unto death, even death on a cross. Philippians 2:8

Every time I return to Nazareth, I wonder about the so-called "silent years" of the Lord of which we know so little. Yet through all these years He was preparing for His great mission. When an infant, His parents fled with Him into Egypt, for Herod was going to destroy all the boy babies two years old and under, because he had heard prophesied that a claimant to his throne had been born, and so his reign was threatened. At the age of twelve, Jesus in the Temple astounded the elders by His ability to comprehend their teachings.

How He spent the remaining thirty years is a mystery. We know that He worked with His father, Joseph, at a carpenter's bench in Nazareth which is a picturesque little town, located about midway between the city of Haifa and the Sea of Galilee. Although part of this village has modern, wide streets, there are still many narrow passageways typical of the streets of many centuries ago when Jesus lived and walked there.

The place which memorializes the early years of the Master is a crude little room with stone walls and floor. This is where He once lived as a child. There were no chairs, as the family would sit crouched on the floor. The table upon which they ate was only a stone slab. The place where they kept their food was merely an opening in one of the stone walls. The simplicity of the surroundings reminds one of the humility of the Savior who humbled himself even unto death on a cross. He did not spend His life in a rich man's house, but in the humble circumstances of the poor and the common man. Though He was King of kings, and some day shall rule over all the world, He gave His life for all the people of His kingdom.

PRAYER THOUGHT: *We are everlastingly grateful, precious Savior, that Thou didst humble Thyself for our sakes, even to Thy sacrifice and suffering on the cross.*

"You are the light of the world. . . . Let your light . . . shine before men." Matthew 5:14, 16

My guide in the Holy Land turned to me on one of our excursions and said, "Yonder is the Mount of Beatitudes." I could almost visualize Jesus with the crowd about Him, as He sat down and taught them basic spiritual truths saying, "Blessed are the poor in spirit, for theirs is the kingdom of heaven. Blessed are the meek, . . . Blessed are those who hunger and thirst for righteousness, . . . Blessed are the merciful, . . . Blessed are the peacemakers, . . . Rejoice and be glad, for your reward is great in heaven." He continued by saying, "You are the light of the world. A city set on a hill cannot be hid. . . . Let your light so shine before men."

There is so much darkness in the world today. The reason for this is not because of what God has failed to do. There is darkness in the hearts of men and on the face of the earth, because we who are the followers of Jesus Christ have failed to obey His explicit commands. We know the truth that sets men free. We know Him who is the light of the world that can cause all human darkness to vanish. And yet we have failed to bring this Light to the still unlighted corners of the earth. The darkness of disobedience hovers around our shoulders.

On that day when He preached the famous sermon from this mount, Jesus also said, "Ask, and it will be given you." What a wonderful promise of the love that God is always ready to send into our lives. Should not this compel us to go out and give something of our lives in return for what God has bountifully showered upon our lives? Above all other gifts, He has led us out of death into life. Now we have a story to tell to the nations—a story of mercy and love and hope for all men.

PRAYER THOUGHT: *May we bring the light of our witness into the dark corners of the earth, precious Savior, so that the story of Thy love and mercy may brighten and give hope to the lives of others.*

> This, the first of his signs, Jesus did at Cana in Galilee, and manifested his glory. John 2:11

Cana is located about midway between the villages of Nazareth and Tiberias. As you walk along the village streets, there comes into your recollection the fact that it was here the Master passed with His disciples so many years ago. You are close to the place of one of the happiest experiences of His ministry. I asked my guide, "Where is the place of the well where was drawn the water which Jesus turned into wine?" He led me down a narrow side street. Some of the walls were tumbling down. But still on top of these ruins were beautiful flowers blooming. There was yet hope in the midst of despair, flowers in the midst of destruction.

It is not long before you come upon the church which memorializes the place of that miracle. Your attention is immediately focused upon a beautiful statue of Christ located in a niche below the steeple. It is not of Christ on the cross. Rather it is the victorious Master. In one hand He holds a scepter. In the other hand He holds the world with the cross upon it. The crown of thorns has been exchanged for a crown of triumph. There I found myself breaking forth with the familiar musical strains, "And He shall reign forever and ever. . . . King of kings and Lord of lords."

Jesus had brought happiness to that home, when He found the house full of people, and the refreshments to serve the wedding guests running low. The Lord immediately stepped into that situation and demonstrated His tremendous power and thoughtful concern. For two thousand years He has been stepping into the lives of men everywhere to bring order out of chaos and to light candles of hope in darkened places. Even when situations of life have seemed utterly hopeless, He has lifted men and set them on a new road. This He can yet do for men this day.

PRAYER THOUGHT: *Dear Lord, we are ever in grateful awe of Thy power to change chaos into conquest, to bring light from darkness, and to transform our despair into delight.*

Through many tribulations we must enter the kingdom of God.
Acts 14:22

Leaving the city of Cana, one travels west until one comes
to the brow of a hill. Below lies the beautiful Sea of Galilee.
Snow-capped mountains loom in the distant background. In
the immediate distance are the borders of a foreign country.
The Sea of Galilee is seven hundred feet below sea level, and
is much smaller than several of the lakes in the state of Minnesota.

The city of Tiberias is located right on the shore of the lake.
Thousands of refugees from all parts of the world have come
to make this area their home. Many of these places are merely
small huts made from tin or whatever other materials may be
found. The only playgrounds little children have is a dirty
patch of hard baked mud in front of their hut. Here they min-
gle with a few animals belonging to the family, perhaps their
only possession.

Throughout the country of Israel refugees have been coming
in large numbers during the past several years in order to establish homes. Many of these people were unwanted in their
former homelands. Many of their loved ones had been killed
in cruel persecutions not because they had committed any
wrong, but only because they had been born into a certain religious faith. Now after gruelling trials they had arrived here
to establish and settle a new homeland.

To me this contemporary situation became almost a parable.
In this life we shall have many trials and persecutions, for we
are pilgrims and strangers, and can tarry only during our life's
brief day. But one blessed day we shall have a new homeland,
fashioned not after this world, but fashioned by the hands of
the Almighty. This city shall be called the City of God. We
who have been redeemed by Christ shall dwell there forever.

PRAYER THOUGHT: *Though we must endure earthly trials
and tribulations, we can yet be joyful, dear Lord, because we
know that this life is only a temporary pilgrimage on the journey to our eternal homeland with Thee.*

239

Thanks be to God, who in Christ always leads us in triumph.
2 Corinthians 2:14

Come along with me today to the shores of blue Galilee in far-off Israel. As I stood there not long ago, I thought of the many events in the life of the Lord associated with this particular area. One devoutly wishes that He could have been there to speak. My thoughts went to the Scripture story of the disciples who had been out fishing all night without luck. They were a very discouraged group when they wearily rowed back to shore in their empty boats. But the surprise of their life was waiting for them. One whom they did not recognize at first, but took for a stranger, stood in the morning mist on the shore and then called out to them. Immediately they recognized His voice. Said astonished Peter, "It is the Lord!"

Suppose you had been with this group in the boat early that morning. Suppose you had a day or two previously seen Jesus expire on the cross. Suppose you had seen His limp bloodless and lifeless body let down and then placed in the tomb. Try then to imagine your amazement upon seeing Him alive again. There He stood as real as life, with the telltale nail-pierced hands and wounded feet. He was indeed the master over death!

All of us can have days and nights of empty fruitless living. We toil but without getting anywhere at all. Then we become discouraged and are ready to throw in the sponge. The Presence is always there to shore us up and give us encouragement to keep on trying. And the miracle of a Christ-centered life is simply this, that when we do, we have learned the secret by the help of God of wresting victory out of the jaws of what appeared to be certain defeat. The Son of God is more than a match for all the powers of evil.

PRAYER THOUGHT: *Teach us, dear Savior, to look to Thee for strength to overcome the problems which sometimes threaten to overwhelm us, so that we may be victorious in life as Thou hast been victorious over death.*

The Lord is faithful; he will strengthen you and guard you from evil. 2 Thessalonians 3:3

One day, as I stood by the Sea of Galilee, the waters were especially rough. It is not a large body of water, but it is of considerable depth below sea level. The lake is subject to violent storms because of the difference in temperature of the shore land and that of the mountains above it. Winds descend on the center and then are swift on the opposite shores.

The disciples, many years before, had been out in a little boat upon this lake with their Lord. Jesus was asleep in the boat when a great storm arose like the one I was then witnessing. The wind roared violently, and the waves lashed over the sides of the boat, but the Lord kept on sleeping. The disciples turned to the Master, awakened Him, and anxiously said, "Have you no concern for us, Lord? We are afraid that we are going to perish!"

Jesus turned to them and replied, "Why are you afraid, O men of little faith?" Then the master of the sea very calmly spoke these words: "Peace! Be still!" The waves subsided; the winds quieted; it was calm once again.

There are many times in life when within our hearts and souls violent storms arise as suddenly as did this storm on the Sea of Galilee. We ask the question, "Where is God now? Why has He left me alone?" As always He is nearer than the breath we breathe. The One who is ruler of the waves of the Sea of Galilee is ruler over the storms of life. If in these times of need you simply call upon Him you will hear Him say, "Peace! Be still!" Soon the waves of anxiety and fear and worry will subside. It is wonderful to walk each day with the Lord and to know that you are in the presence of One who has the power to overcome any force of evil that might confront you.

PRAYER THOUGHT: *We are grateful, dear Lord, for the calming power of Thy love and strength as we call upon Thee in our unnumbered times of distress and confusion.*

"Behold, the Lamb of God, who takes away the sin of the world!" John 1:29

The River Jordan runs out of the Sea of Galilee and moves on to the south. As I saw this beautiful river wind its way along, I thought of the time that Jesus came from Galilee to the Jordan to be baptized by John. After the baptism the Spirit of God descended and, lo, a voice from heaven was heard to say, "This is my beloved Son with whom I am well pleased."

John had announced the purpose of Jesus' coming into the world when he said, "Behold, the Lamb of God, who takes away the sin of the world!" Here was one who knew His mission. He was to be despised and rejected by all those about Him. Even His own family would think Him mad and misunderstand Him. Yet He steadfastly set His face toward the goal of becoming that Lamb of God who takes away the sin of the world.

As I stood by the banks of the River Jordan on a beautiful day the thought occurred to me that life was made beautiful only because of the coming of Christ into the world. How drab and hopeless life would be without Him! How sad and futile would be our existence here, if there were no future. How helpless is man unless he is connected with the power that alone can release him from sin's bondage.

Each day the Savior comes to us offering forgiveness. We need not carry our burdens alone. If we are penitent, we shall hear our heavenly Father say from heaven, "Behold, the Lamb of God, who takes away the sin of the world!" Then our faith should accept in confidence the truth that we are forgiven, and that our record of sin has been wiped clean. "Though your sins are like scarlet, they shall be white as snow," said our God.

PRAYER THOUGHT: *Lord of mercy, we realize how hopeless life is without Thy love and forgiveness and we are grateful that Thou, as the Lamb of God, can take away the burdens of our sin.*

Be kind to one another, tenderhearted. Ephesians 4:32

Galilee is a most beautiful part of the Holy Land, located in the new state of Israel. In its season it is a countryside of rolling hills, blooming flowers, blossoming grain, shepherds and sheep. It is one of the few places in the area that yet remains as of old. Much of it is untouched by the commercialism which one finds so distasteful in other parts of the land made holy by Christ. I am reminded of a friend's comment: "I was so glad that beautiful blue Galilee was so big that it couldn't be roofed over by a shrine but had to be left just as it is!"

One day, while traveling through the places where Jesus had worked, I ended the journey at Tiberias on the Sea of Galilee. Deciding to go for a swim in this beautiful fresh water lake, I found the experience invigorating. Some children nearby were also enjoying the water. After my swim, when I walked back to the car, these children followed me and surrounding me asked questions about my life. "What are you doing here?" they asked. "Where do you come from?" Through my interpreter I told them I was a visitor, and that my home was in the United States of America. A little freckled-faced boy standing by my side, with eyes full of awe and wonder, looked up at me and pleaded, "Please sir, please sir, take me back with you to America!"

His parents had been victims of religious persecution in the country where they had previously lived. Now the state of Israel was caring for this orphaned boy. My desire was to take him back home with me, but of course that was impossible. However, it became my vow that I would urge people to bring the love, affection, and material help of America to underprivileged boys throughout the world. Surely this is what the Master would want us to do.

PRAYER THOUGHT: *Gracious Lord, fill our hearts with a sense of brotherhood that will move us to extend the hand of friendship and the embrace of love toward Thy children.*

"Master, we toiled all night and took nothing! But at your word I will let down the nets." Luke 5:5

Standing on the gravelly beach of the beautiful Sea of Galilee, I was reminded of an incident that had taken place there years before. I visualized two boats floating on the lake. It was morning. The fishermen had gone from their boats, and were washing their nets. This practice is still observed there even to this day. The Lord got into one of the boats which belonged to Simon, and asked him to row it out a little way from the land. Then using the boat as a pulpit, He turned to Simon and said, "Put out into the deep and let down your nets for a catch." With a bit of reluctance Simon replied, "Master, we toiled all night long and took nothing. But at your word I will let down the nets." When they had done this, they had caught so many fish their nets began to break, and they had to call for another boat to help them.

The key to this entire incident is Simon's willingness to say in substance, "Lord, at your word I will do exactly what you have commanded me." He even went against good fisherman sense which years of experience had given him. In daily living we, too, need to take the Lord at His word. When He bids us do something, we should do it in confidence that, even though it seems impossible, He will yet give us the power to accomplish what He asks. We need to have our faith increased in a God who never fails His children. When He tells us to trust in Him, we should be courageous enough to believe Him. In trying out His promises, we discover that all things He has said are true. Launch out in faith, for the Lord always abides by His word and is loving even at those times when we in no way deserve a claim on His mercy.

PRAYER THOUGHT: *Teach us, gracious Lord, confidently to perform whatever tasks Thou hast set before us, knowing that Thou art able to guide us into victory.*

244

"Whoever humbles himself like this child, he is the greatest in
the kingdom of heaven." Matthew 18:4

Standing in the ruins of Capernaum, I recalled the day when
some of the disciples came to Jesus saying, "Who is the greatest in the kingdom of heaven?" Just then Jesus called to Him
a little child and put him in their midst. Then the Master said,
"Truly, I say unto you, unless you turn and become like children, you will never enter the kingdom of heaven. Whoever
humbles himself like this child, he is the greatest in the kingdom of heaven."

Now the ancient city of Capernaum is no more. All that remains are a few ruins and tumbled piles of stones, marking
the graveyard of a once prosperous city by the sea. Jesus
himself prophesied the ruin of this city. Here must have lived
a community of people who depended upon their own greatness and who did not recognize the need of a power beyond
themselves. Because it laid a foundation on shifting sands,
this city was ultimately destroyed.

Our Lord has come with a different message. His evaluation
of greatness is that it does not consist of possessing an abundance of material things. A person is great in His sight who has
the faith of a little child. Now, a child is humble, he is dependent, he is loving, and he is trusting. Why is it that we who
are supposed to be mature men are so determined to outgrow
this quality? People who go through life singing are always
those who have maintained the simple and unquestioning faith
of a child. This is not to say that such people are childish in
their ways and actions. They are only childlike in the depth
of their trust. If any of us qualify for this group, it is as we
continue to grow in our faith, keeping at the center of our
spiritual life that sincere and unashamed dependency upon
God. That faith is the very lifeline of our spiritual welfare.

PRAYER THOUGHT: *Dear God and Father, we pray that we
will have faith in Thee like that of a little child, for it is in this
simple trust that we can know the greatest blessings of Thy
love.*

His righteousness endures for ever. Psalm 111:3

Badness is short lived and passing; it does not endure. But goodness is solid; it outlasts even the stars. So says the Word of God. In traveling about, this fact is made clear. In the Bible we read about the city of Capernaum. Visiting the site of this ancient city in the Holy Land, all one finds there are the heaped ruins of a few buildings. Yet He who predicted Capernaum's doom, namely, Jesus Christ, remains the same yesterday, today, and forever.

If you were to seek Nineveh's site where the prophet Jonah preached before the days of Christ on earth, you would not find one stone piled upon the other. That once great city has now been utterly obliterated. Yet the God who called upon the people there through His prophet Jonah to repent is the same God today as He was in that ancient time.

Silence and desolation reign over the darkened, rubble-lined streets of Pompeii. Here once rang out the people's merry laughter and songs as if to say, "Let us be merry, for tomorrow we die." Yet the God who allowed the worldly ways of these pleasure-mad, sinful people to come into judgment remains the same in our own day.

The conditions that were true then are true today. Repent or perish! This is the ultimatum that faces us. Our soul is our most valuable possession. At the last Supper Jesus said solemnly, "My body given . . . My blood shed." Each of us is literally saying something closely akin to this. Either you give yourself to good, or you give your life to evil. Each individual pays the price for the way he chooses. The price of evil is destruction and death. The reward of good and the free gift of God, however, are everlasting life and true joy.

PRAYER THOUGHT: *Almighty and everlasting God, help us to choose the enduring way of salvation, and not to put our trust in things evil that will only one day fall into ruin and rubble.*

"Whoever drinks of the water that I shall give him will never
thirst: the water that I shall give him will become in him a
spring of water welling up to eternal life." John 4:14

Teheran is a city with many very interesting sights. It has
an elevation of nearly four thousand feet. Nowhere in the East
can one find more beautiful walled gardens and sparkling
pools, winding pathways and lovely blooming flowers. But
in the midst of all this beauty there is a city of unbelievable
poverty and filth. The Moslems believe that any running water
is pure. The water supply for this city comes down from the
snow-capped mountains nearby and flows into "jubes" where
it gets dirtier as it continues on its way through the streets.
It is not an uncommon sight to find people washing their clothes
in this water, bathing in it, washing their teeth or cleaning
their dishes. All these several things can be done in the same
jube within a stretch of fifty feet.

It is indeed sad to know that there are still people after these
nearly two thousand years since the coming of Christ who yet
do not realize that only He has the power to give the pure
water of life that can allay our deep thirst. He said, "Whoso-
ever drinks of the water that I shall give him will never thirst."
Those who drink of the impure waters of the jube are destined to be disease-cursed and to die. Those who come to
Christ and drink become spiritually strong.

Man is destined to be eternal because of the grace and mercy
of Christ. In ourselves we would all surely die. But men must
know and accept Him in order that they might have eternal
life. It is, therefore, our responsibility to carry the message
to all the world, because we have been blessed with hearing
of Him and His love. Because this is still a mission unfulfilled,
there remain great areas throughout the world. Let us hear
His voice and then act to fulfill His will.

PRAYER THOUGHT: *Merciful Lord, may we answer Thy call
to witness with greater zeal and dedication, so that every soul
in every land may one day drink only of the pure water of life
which flows from Thee.*

"We will obey the voice of the Lord our God." Jeremiah 42:6

It is a very interesting experience to visit the bazaars of the city of Teheran. Along the streets are seated coppersmiths and potters, busily working at their trades. There are many shops whose main business is to sell leather sandals and cartridge belts. Many varieties of spices are on display and for sale. There are stalls filled with fruits and vegetables, protected by old ragged awnings. Occasionally one can pass by a tea house where sweets are sold. And above the roar and confusion of the bazaar rings the cry of the hucksters, peddling their trinkets, trying to get the attention of some prospective buyer.

It can be rightly said that we live in the very midst of competing forces. About us at every turn are people and philosophies which in a sense are shouting for us to accept what they have to offer. As we seek to find a way out of our dilemma, and a pattern for more fruitful living, some say that we should try the voice of achievement. Some say we should listen to the voice of prestige or pleasure. Some political systems offer the alternative of power in the sight of one's fellow men. Some economic systems cry out with the allure of money and possessions.

Yet, in the midst of all the confused hustle and bustle, there is the still small voice of God seeking our allegiance. The choices we have for living are about as numerous and confusing as those one has while shopping at a bazaar. There is, however, only one good bargain in life and that is, after listening to the voice of Christ, to accept His way, whatever the cost might be. Turning a deaf ear to the passing importance of all else, men can find an all-sufficient love and storehouse of goodness in the merciful heart of God.

PRAYER THOUGHT: *God of love, we pray that as the voices of the world clamor for our attention we may steadfastly keep our ears tuned to Thy still, small voice and let it guide and guard us with love and mercy.*

Bear one another's burdens, and so fulfil the law of Christ. Galatians 6:2

India is a country with outstanding potential. But it is also a land of great heartache, of great extremes. One cannot forget the fact that half of the children there die before they are ten years of age, and that over half the population can neither read nor write. As you walk up and down the village streets, you see all about you this appalling human need and unmitigated suffering. Many of the children have little clothing to wear, if any at all. They run around the streets with swollen eyes and diseased and infected bodies. Many are left to care for themselves during the day. Both parents must work hard from sunup to sundown, in order to earn a bare living. I found mothers working in dimly lighted and poorly ventilated factories. They work as many years as they can, until overtaken by blindness. Forty-hour weeks are unheard of. Their only work bench is a dirt-packed floor. For all their efforts many of them receive as little as twenty-five cents a day computed in American money.

We who live in a land of affluence forget about those patient people in faraway lands. We have not sensed the heavy responsibility that rests on our shoulders to improve the lives of our brothers. The conditions of these people existing in other parts of the world under such meager circumstances must become our concern. These people are also a part of God's family, and therefore are our brothers and sisters. If we claim to be sons of God and co-laborers together with Christ, their problems are our problems also, and must be shared by us all. What a new life of hope it would give them to discover that somebody cares and is willing to go out of his way to help them! Will you not resolve to be that somebody?

PRAYER THOUGHT: *Enable us to answer the call for help which comes from fellow members of Thy family, Lord, and willingly to supply their need with our abundance.*

The Lord will keep you from all evil; he will keep your life. The Lord will keep your going out and your coming in from this time forth and for evermore. Psalm 121: 7, 8

India is a country where there is much sickness and intense suffering. There are also far too few facilities to take care of all these people who are in need. However, one day I happened to come upon a very unusual situation. In this poor country I discovered a private home that had been turned into a hospital. This was unusual because of many reasons, one of which is the fact that it was one of the cleanest places I had yet found in this part of the country. The story of the beginning of this hospital caught my imagination.

A young lady had lost her husband in death. Naturally she grieved the passing of her loved one. Yet she resolved that she was going to do something for humanity which would take her mind off her grief. She went out into the streets to find people who needed help. She didn't have to look very far before she saw people in need. Gathering twenty-one lonely people into her home, she lovingly cared for them. These people were the patients that I saw one day as I entered the hospital. They were all so happy. In these circumstances it was difficult for me to understand the reason. I turned to the woman and asked the question, "How do you account for the fact that these people are so happy?" She replied, "That is easy to understand, for now they know they belong to somebody."

Every man has that longing and desire. Jesus came into the world to tell each one of us that we belong to somebody, that we belong to Him. Jesus said it by His life. He never passed by anyone in need of His help. All were His children. He was concerned about each soul. He proclaimed His love by His death. He died that all of us might be restored into the father-son relationship that had been broken by man's sin. Indeed, today each one of us can triumphantly say, "I belong to God!"

PRAYER THOUGHT: *Heavenly Father, we are grateful for the assurance we have as Thy children of receiving the everlasting security of Thy love.*

He has distributed freely, he has given to the poor; his righteousness endures for ever. Psalm 112:9

Some years ago on my first visit to India, I had my first
opportunity for an audience with Prime Minister Nehru. Mr.
Khrushchev and Mr. Bulganin, who were then both leaders
of the Soviet Union, had just visited India. Thousands of people had come out in great crowds along the streets to welcome
them. I asked Nehru, "Does this mean that your country is
turning toward communism?" He replied, "No, they would
turn out to welcome any of the great rulers of the world. If
the President of your country would ever come, I can assure
you that he would receive the greatest welcome of all."

On a more recent visit to India, I followed by only a few
weeks the visit of Dwight D. Eisenhower, who was then President of the United States. No one else in the history of India
has ever received the genuine welcome that he did. Along the
parade route there were gathered hundreds of thousands of
people. One Indian mother had carried her child for many
miles that she might be present. As President Eisenhower
passed by, she held her boy high and said, "Look, there is the
king of America! There is the man who sent us food when
we were hungry, and sent teachers to our schools to help us
learn things."

What a blessing we could be to the world, if we would simply be willing to share more than we have done with those
less fortunate than ourselves. Then we would really be praying that God's kingdom might come and that His will might
be done on earth. In our hands He has placed His goods. He
has made us His stewards. Now our task is to share His wealth
with our kingdom brothers and sisters.

PRAYER THOUGHT: *Teach us, gracious Lord, to share willingly
the abundance of what we have with the multitudes of people
in this world who suffer from lack of both material and spiritual possessions.*

> The Lord God has given me the tongue of those who are taught, that I may know how to sustain with a word him that is weary.
> Isaiah 50:4

Some countries of the world acknowledge almost as many gods as they claim population. Heathen idols face you wherever you turn. Some primitive people in their superstition and ignorance even worship sticks and stones, streams and rivers. Others give of their pitifully meager income to build beautiful temples in which to house images of their gods. They have utter faith in these gods, even though lifeless statues can do nothing to help those who worship before them.

In India one day I observed a native woman carrying a little child in her arms approach one of these temples. She completely prostrated herself and then lifted the little one before the idol. The child was sick and deformed from disease. In her despair the woman prayed thus: "Grant that my child may be perfect and fair and strong like other children." When she turned to go on her way again, a man approached her and asked, "Friend, to whom have you prayed?" Her reply came thoughtfully, "I don't know, but surely there must be someone somewhere to hear a mother's cry and to keep a mother's heart from breaking."

The living God has not promised that He will grant every crippled child or diseased man perfect health. But He has promised to give strength for each day which will keep our hearts from breaking. This is the faith that is ours today. How can we help but to be challenged by the fact that there are many around the world who do not know about this living God, who are yet shooting arrows of their prayers into the abysmal dark, praying to helpless idols. They have not been told that there is a living God, able to strengthen them and bring the desperately needed help. It is now our responsibility to bring the gospel to all who reside in lands of darkness today.

PRAYER THOUGHT: *Dear Lord, may we never falter as we carry the comforting torch which is knowledge of Thee to those who now pray to powerless statues for help in their desperate need.*

He who gives to the poor will not want, but he who hides his eyes will get many a curse. Proverbs 28:27

The sacred cow still roams the streets of old Delhi. In many places they are given priority. Cars stop to wait for them to cross the streets. Along the street markets the sellers of food will allow them to eat from their stock, without any attempt to drive them away.

In many parts of the world, grocery stores are not the same as they are in America. A man's produce, such as cabbage, carrots, or cauliflower which he may want to sell will be situated in a little mound of mud on the side of a street. One day I noticed a cow munching at a little store with its slender stocks, where the shopkeeper allowed the animal to eat as much as she wanted. The cow then dropped a half-eaten head of cabbage on the street. A little Indian child, too weak to walk, crawled along the street until with a quick motion it grabbed the leaf and stuffed it into its hunger-bloated stomach.

At the sight I asked myself, "God, why do your children have to suffer so?" Then I could hear Him say to me, "You are partly to blame." I readily admit to this, and so must we all. We have been selfish in wanting things ourselves, and unwilling to share them with others. Such selfishness has resulted in trouble. America is intensely disliked in many areas of the universe where people are jealous of us. We have so much, and they have so little. Yet, unless we are willing to share in order to improve their standards of living, we stand in danger one day of losing all we have. There are many in the world who need the dedicated support of every Christian who believes in the directives of the gospel of Jesus Christ and is willing to put these into practice in his daily living.

PRAYER THOUGHT: *May we never close our eyes or our hearts to the desperate need which is all around us. We pray, gracious Lord, that we may always seek to share every blessing with those who call to us from the depths of suffering.*

The light shines in the darkness, and the darkness has not overcome it. John 1:5

Sometimes, when I find that I am threatened by feelings of fear or worry, I remember the occasion in the southern region of India when I once saw a certain cable. The large bucket that was hanging from it was being pulled out of a blinding misty fog. It so happened that we were standing on a hill where we could see that the whole valley below was enveloped in an ocean of mist as far as our eyes could view. A cable running from an iron ore mine to a railroad loading place on the plain below was swinging overhead. Out of the mist it came into view, and back into the mist it disappeared again. Suddenly, out of that fog, came a huge aerial bucket suspended from the cable. It could not see where it was going, and yet this thing without a soul lumbered on, confident that the cable would hold it and bring it to its destination.

There is a lesson here for life that we need to learn. If we are on God's side, we can be sure of the direction of our life. We may not be able to see all that lies ahead of us, but we have every confidence that the God who takes us through the days of sunlight will take us through the shadows of life, too.

The beauty of such a confident trust can be the possession only of those who love the living God. Daily our prayer should be, "Lead, kindly Light, amid the encircling gloom, Lead Thou me on." We have never been asked to go into the uncharted tomorrow alone. But we have been promised that there shall be by our side One who knows the way. With this assurance our fears vanish, for we realize that in the final analysis, when life is laid bare, we need nothing else but this partnership with the Almighty God.

PRAYER THOUGHT: *Lord of light, we are grateful that when we must travel through the dark shadows of our lives, Thy light is always ahead to guide us into the brighter hopes of tomorrow.*

You became an example to all the believers. 1 Thessalonians 1:7

Touring the mission fields in India was a unique and inspiring experience. Here one finds again the same dedication and zeal for Christ as is evidenced by Christian workers all over the world. These people are willing to live in conditions of grave hardship without recognizing it as such because of the deep satisfactions they receive from knowing that they are leading the heathen to the living God. Such joy can come only from serving the Lord. They take you into the native villages where they have labored many long hours every day for years, and show you the difference even in the appearance between the Christians and the non-Christians. By the radiant glow on the faces of these converts, one can tell that they have been released from their fear of bondage and from the superstitions of their heathen religions, and now have been led to the living God.

A visitor one day asked the youth of a confirmation class in India what it was to be a Christian. One of the little Indian boys volunteered the answer, "It is to live like our missionary."

As Christians, wherever we live, we are given the challenge to set an example for those who follow after us. Parents cannot expect their children to do what they themselves refuse to do. Each day there are people who cross our path who are looking to us who wear the Christian badge in our hearts and who are noticing how we react to certain situations. They listen to the language we speak. They watch the things we do, and are aware of what we fail to do. They look to us for help in forming opinions and attitudes to certain moral and social questions. Therefore, each of us must resolve to be a careful person, for there are so many around who follow us.

PRAYER THOUGHT: *Gracious God, we pray that we may always be given the strength and faith to walk as worthy examples of the great witness we must bear to Thy love and grace.*

Show yourself in all respects a model of good deeds. Titus 2:7

In India I heard an interesting story about a Moslem trader which has now come to be used by many even here in America, because it tells such a universal truth. One day this Indian came to a European friend of his and asked for a copy of the Bible. "Why do you want a copy of the Bible?" asked the friend, "you can't even read it." "That is right," said the Moslem, "but still I want a Bible. This is my reason. When a European trader comes to do business with me, I take the Bible, put it in his hands and then watch him. If he opens it and reads it, I know I can trust him. If he throws it aside, I will not do business with him."

At some time in his life a Christian must have been an outstanding influence upon this Moslem. For he had learned the lesson that those who truly believe in the Word of God can be trusted, for they will try to live upright and godly lives. This thought places a great responsibility upon each one of us. Are we true to the faith that we profess? Are we patterning our living upon the things we have been taught from God's holy Word? Are we being faithful to God's best plans for us? Are we following the way of the Master?

There are people who may be observing us each day to see whether we are putting into practice the message of the gospel. We are tempted so often to compromise and think that it makes no difference if just once in a while we go the way the world beckons us. But at that one time of weakness or carelessness someone might be influenced by our disloyal act and consequently be led astray. Let us each day resolve to show our colors. If we are truly Christian, let us prove our creed by our living. Let God shine forth in all that we do and are.

PRAYER THOUGHT: *May we never prove disloyal to our faith in Thee, dear God and Father, but live every day as wholly sincere and dedicated children of Thine.*

If God so loved us, we also ought to love one another. 1 John 4:11

An Indian worker comes home. He is exhausted after the heavy labor of the day. His dwelling is characteristically dirty, squalid, and cramped. Sometimes he has to share with others the one room which is his. Or perhaps he lives in a shack with holes in the walls and broken tiles on the roof. Even after his hard day of labor, his pocket is nearly empty of any money.

In the home besides his wife are several children, usually undernourished, dirty, and sometimes in ill-health. The wife, who also works besides trying to perform her normal functions as a housewife and mother, is also tired at the end of the day. It takes real effort to make any kind of happiness shine in such conditions, for life seems to be futile and hardly worth the effort to keep on working.

Living standards in India as well as in many other areas of the world certainly must be improved and, if at all possible, with great speed. Unless this is soon achieved, the present democratic government will be swept aside, and there will be another victory for the world of communism. To the man whose family is starving the promise of bread to appease his hunger is all he wants. He will listen to the one who gives it to him, no matter who he may be.

However, the nation of India must do more than feed her people more adequately, if democracy is to survive and grow strong there. These millions of Indians must be inspired with a dynamic new faith in the future and the hope of a better life. Is it too impossible to think that the church must take the lead in helping to provide this new life? It must be inspired by a gospel of love which will cause us who have more to share than ever with those not so fortunate as ourselves.

PRAYER THOUGHT: *Teach us to shoulder our responsibility as Christians, God of mercy, by showing Thy love and compassion toward those who suffer from lack of the necessities of life and from ignorance of Thy saving gospel.*

> Make me to know thy ways, O Lord; teach me thy paths. Lead me in thy truth, and teach me, for thou art the God of my salvation. Psalm 25:4, 5

On a recent visit to India, our guide on the way to the Taj Mahal was a Sikh. He was a very well-mannered gentleman who with ease could be engaged in a most interesting conversation. When we asked him why Sikhs wore beards, he said that this was just one mark of their faith, and that there were many others. These men let their hair and beard grow long as a sign of strength and virility. They wear a wooden comb in their long hair. The thin iron bracelet on their right arm is a reminder to them that they must think twice before doing anything rash or wrong. Moreover, they always carry an iron handled knife on their body for protection.

The iron bracelet on the right arm especially intrigued me. This serves as a constant reminder that they must not do anything that would violate their conscience. In a world in which sin is so rampant we all need sharp reminders of the fact that in yielding to sin we destine ourselves to doom. God has placed within everyone of us an inner voice which is called the voice of conscience. If we keep our lives in tune with God, He speaks clearly through this voice to let us know what we should do and what we should not do.

Yet how men vainly prefer their own desires to heeding the will of God. Such preference spells trouble, for it plainly means disobedience to God. Let us resolve to communicate daily in prayer with Him, so that we might discover and know for certain what is His will for our life and that we might have His daily presence with us to guide us. "Speak Lord, for Thy servant hears," should be our daily request of the Almighty. In seeking His help, may we listen and follow His guidance.

PRAYER THOUGHT: *We pray that we may daily communicate with Thee through prayer, Lord, and always listen to Thy voice coming to us through our consciences, guiding and guarding us as we go through life.*

Do not enter the path of the wicked, and do not walk in the way of evil men. Avoid it; do not go on it; turn away from it and pass on. Proverbs 4:14

The road to Agra where the matchless Taj Mahal is located is thronged with traffic both day and night. Upon this highway travel buses crammed with people, in fact, sometimes they are as much as hanging out the door. Others are walking, some are being drawn in bullock carts, and others are riding along on bicycles. There are many little towns which one must pass through whose streets literally swarm with pedestrians. Very frequently on the side of the road one will see this sign printed in English: "Don't take risks." One can understand the reason why this is placed so frequently along the side of the road, because there are so many chances for accidents along the way.

This is a good motto for the highway of life as well. Don't take risks. Don't risk the chance of losing the way to eternity by mere carelessness in your manner of living. God has given us many warnings and words of caution in His Word. He has told us that whatever we sow, we shall also reap, for the harvest is according to the seed, and especially according to the care which that seed has received. Why risk the sowing of bad habits when you can only then finally expect to reap destruction? Where is that man so blind to his own good as to risk separating himself from the Lord, only to find himself finally lost in darkness?

Later when I stepped into the hotel at Agra I saw another sign: "Watch your step." Foolishly I disregarded it and as a result fell and received an injury. Spiritually speaking, we must watch our step, too, for often we foolishly follow our own immature judgment. There is, however, no danger at all, if only we will follow in the steps of our Lord.

PRAYER THOUGHT: *Teach us, gracious Lord, to observe the signs warning us against the hazards of yielding to temptation, for we must be cautious as we travel through life in order that we do not stray from the pathway to salvation.*

Happy is he who trusts in the Lord. Proverbs 16:20

On the way to the Taj Mahal, India's addition to the seven wonders of the world, one sees many interesting sights. One may observe how people live in their villages, how they till the soil, and how they bring their farm products to market. The highways are crowded not with automobiles, but with bicycles and bullocks. These are all slow-moving means of transportation, which make it necessary to spend hours getting to the city to market farm goods.

Enroute to the city the farmer must be alert to steer his animal, because the landmarks are unfamiliar to the plodding beast of burden. But once he has delivered his goods, he starts back home with the empty cart. As you pass him on the highway, you observe a very curious sight, for there is no one in the driver's seat, and the animal is plodding along alone. If you look carefully, you will find the owner of the cart fast asleep in the rear of the box. When I asked my guide about this incident he said, "The animal knows his way home, and he will take his owner right through the gate to his little hut. The owner has such confidence in his animal taking him in the right direction that he can now comfortably relax after a hard day's work."

Man can trust an animal, but how difficult it is for many people to have this same confidence in the living God! Our Lord knows your way home. Instead of worrying and fretting about the petty incidents of each day, and being anxiously concerned for the future, why not relax in the presence of the Almighty with utter confidence that God our Lord and Shepherd has traveled that way before and is willing to direct us in the way we should go. If we follow close to Him, we shall stay out of trouble, and will find the road to victory.

PRAYER THOUGHT: *Teach us, Lord, to seek Thee first when we are distressed, so that we shall not stumble along on a lonely road which leads only to confusion and despair.*

Do you not know that you are God's temple and that God's
Spirit dwells in you? 1 Corinthians 3:16

One should not travel in India without visiting the Taj
Mahal, a famous marble mausoleum located just outside the
city of Agra. It is set down in a beautifully landscaped garden.
Built during the years between 1630 and 1648 by Emperor
Shah Jahan, it was a memorial to his favorite wife, Mumtaz
Mahall, who died in 1629. The structure is an octagonal building seventy feet high with sides measuring 130 feet. It is surmounted by a dome, giving an additional height of 120 feet. At
the four corners of the platform, centered by the mausoleum,
are minarets standing 133 feet high. The building is constructed entirely of white marble, and its graceful beauty is
enhanced by its reflection in a pool. The interior decorations
are magnificent, including twelve different kinds of stone. The
mosaics and inlaid work are of unsurpassed beauty.

On my first visit to the Taj Mahal I arranged to arrive there
in the middle of the night, in order to see it at sunrise. It was
a magnificent sight to observe the sun of God's heaven casting
a pinkish hue on the white marble. As I sat there in awe, the
thought occurred to me that so often man will spare no expense to build monuments to himself and those dear to him.
But are we willing to make sacrifices to build monuments in
flesh and blood to the greater glory of God? Buildings of mor-
tar, brick, stone, and marble will one day crumble and fall, but
temples in the hearts of men will last forever.

Moreover, life can be of unsurpassed beauty when we allow
the King of kings to come into the throne room of our soul and
reign there for ever and ever. When this happens men will
see in us the unsurpassed beauty of God as He is mirrored in
our lives. Indeed, we are created as temples of the living God.

PRAYER THOUGHT: *Come into our hearts this day, dear Lord,
and there establish Thy reign, working out Thy will in our lives
and guiding us along the pathway that leads to eternity.*

Declare these things; exhort and reprove with all authority.
Titus 2:15

At the Taj Mahal in India there is a piece of marble sixteen feet across and about eight or ten feet high at the very center of this magnificently beautiful structure. As one visits this great wonder of the world, one observes that a Mohammedan guard stands on the marble parapet. As you walk up, he shouts out loudly that only Allah is great, and that Mohammed is his prophet. This statement echoes and re-echoes as people stop to listen.

What a difference there would be in the world today, if all Christians would figuratively raise their voices and shout to all the world, "Jesus must reign as King of kings and Lord of lords!" All too long now men have been worshiping false gods, such as systems of thought, economic gain, political power, or even man-made idols who are pitifully lifeless, and thus cannot give the help we so often desperately need. For too long our voices of witness and praise have remained mute, and we have failed to communicate our Christian faith to people about us.

The early disciples could not wait to go and tell to others the things about the Lord that they had seen and heard. Today, sad to say, many of us cannot wait to gossip and to bear false witness against our neighbors. Yet how we hesitate and make excuses when it comes to speaking out the good news of the gospel to our fellow men. The Lord has given us the program by which the world can be spared from destruction. We have not even really begun to put this program of love into practice. Until we do, we shall still be in trouble. Each day, even by our very living, let us resolve to let the world know that we are indeed followers of the King of kings, so that others might be led to accept His way also. Only He is great, and only to Him should go our allegiance.

PRAYER THOUGHT: *Teach us, King of kings, to witness eagerly to the truth of Thy gospel, so that the work of Thy kingdom might go forward in glory.*

There are varieties of service, but the same Lord. 1 Corinthians 12:5

Many have been impressed and inspired by Dr. Frank Laubach's work among the illiterates in many places of our world. He is known to many of us as a great student of prayer, for he has written many a life-changing treatise on this subject. He is also a man who diligently follows the motto which hung over a living-room door in my home reading, "Ora et Labora" meaning "Pray and Work." This man has touched for good thousands of lives and has wielded a tremendous influence across the world.

When traveling in India, I saw at firsthand some of the results of his work there and the changes which had come into people's lives. I talked to a minister one day who related an experience which had been his. Dr. Laubach came for a visit to his home. They engaged in conversation about spiritual matters for about an hour, although on looking back upon the occasion now it seemed to have lasted only about five minutes. Then upon taking leave from the pastor, Dr. Laubach said, "Let's have a word of prayer." Bowing his head, he began as follows: "Lord, I can see you standing in this very room, and you are smiling." The presence of Jesus is just that real to this great man of God.

The Lord is standing near, and He is always smiling on those who are lovingly engaged in His work. Let's nail an old heresy: One need not be a preacher to serve Him. Every area of our everyday life is important, and Christ needs diligent workers everywhere. He wants to walk in your shoes, be you a businessman, housewife, student, farmer, schoolteacher, lawyer, or whatever profession is yours. All have been commissioned to serve Him.

PRAYER THOUGHT: *Precious Lord, may we never forget that every work which is done in Thy name is valuable, and that we can serve Thee wherever we are in life.*

> I appeal to you therefore, brethren, by the mercies of God, to present your bodies as a living sacrifice, holy and acceptable to God, which is your spiritual worship. Romans 12:1

An Indian mother was very devoted to her favorite heathen god. She had two children both of whom she loved dearly. One was sickly, and the other was in robust health. She fervently believed that her heathen god demanded a great sacrifice from her. Deciding to give her most precious possession, she took her healthy child and threw it into the river as a personal sacrifice to this dumb idol. When asked why she didn't choose the sickly child to be thrown into the river, the woman replied, "Do you think I would give anything but my best to my god?"

Now, what about our giving as Christians? Do we give the remains or the first fruits? Do we give the very best that we have? Do we put God first in our program of stewardship? Or do we take care of our own needs and luxuries before deciding what shall be His share of our possessions?

It isn't the amount that one gives, but the amount in proportion to what one has been given, that is the real test of dedicated stewardship. All that we have belongs to God, even our very lives. We are simply caretakers of our possessions for but these few brief years in this swiftly passing life. Some day we will be called upon to give an account of how faithfully we have taken care of that which has been given us.

What God wants above everything else is the commitment of our life to Him. Once we have given Him that, it will naturally follow that we shall also be willing to give Him our talents and our means. The challenge that should ring in our ears each day is this: "Son, go work for me today in my vineyard." May our lives be a fit answer to that challenge.

PRAYER THOUGHT: *We pray that we may not deny Thee the only gift which is really ours to give, O God, but that we may willingly offer ourselves for Thy work and give to Thee through service the best that is within us.*

The god of this world has blinded the minds of the unbelievers, to keep them from seeing the light of the gospel of the glory of Christ. 2 Corinthians 4:4

We are all starkly aware of the fact that the communists are at work in every country of the world. They are especially active in areas where people are undernourished, sick, and lonely. There are masses in the world today who, like drowning men, are grasping for the last hold to something that might keep them from death. Because they are hopeless, they are willing to try anything that might provide for them a better life. When the communists make great promises, they naïvely believe these empty promises. Indeed, anything sounds better than the depraved state of living in which they now exist.

Once converted to the cause, these people become as dedicated as any group ever. A missionary in India told me that he knew a few young men who have pledged their lives to the system of communism who now are giving as much as 55 per cent and more of their meager incomes to their cause. Perhaps this is one of the several reasons why this communistic plague is spreading all over the world today. Could it be true that the communists are more zealous and willing to sacrifice for their godless way of life than Christians are ready to do for the Lord's work?

Most of us are aware of the dangers of the communist system, although even in such a claim we must admit that the communists are seeking every way quietly to undermine the governments that now stand firm. We cannot be too cautious! Yet we are unwilling to do much to combat it. As followers of the sovereign God, we are possessors of the only good news that can possibly save this world from destruction. We must proclaim it. We have a story to tell to the nations. Let us tell it with enthusiasm today.

PRAYER THOUGHT: *Help us, Lord of love, eagerly to spread our knowledge of Thee throughout the nations of this world, so that ungodly forces might be overwhelmed through the devotion of Thy children.*

He who contributes, in liberality. Romans 12:8

Those who follow the Hindu religious teachings must bring their thankofferings to their local priest. The ceremony goes like this: They fall to their knees, close their eyes, and then place the offering in the open hand of the priest. When asked the reason why they do this they reply, "We close our eyes because we are ashamed to bring so little, and we fall on our knees because then this act humbles us."

A gift does not need to be large in order to be significant. It is great or small in proportion to the amount of other things we possess. One of the greatest of all examples of Christian stewardship is the woman who came into the Temple one day and gave "all that she had." It wasn't very much, just a fraction of a cent, but it caused the treasury bell to ring and Christ to give her a commendation that keeps ringing down the centuries.

There was another who came to the Lord whom the evangelists called a rich young ruler. He had been greatly blessed, but was unwilling to pay the price of discipleship—to dedicate all he had to the service of the Lord. As a result he failed to commit his life to the Lord. Scripture says that he went away sorrowful.

Are we giving to God in proportion as He has given to us? Are we giving Him not only our money, but our time and our abilities, and even our very lives? How much time do we spend working and doing things for Him in comparison to the time we spend to satisfy our physical needs? No matter how much we give Him, we ought to close our eyes and drop to our knees because we bring so little, and are therefore humbled as we think of how He gave His life for us upon the cross.

PRAYER THOUGHT: *Dear God in heaven, we humbly present our offering as a small return for the matchless gift of salvation which we receive from Thee because Thy Son gave His life on a cross for our eternal redemption.*

I know, O Lord, that the way of man is not in himself, that it is not in man who walks to direct his steps. Jeremiah 10:23

A group of illiterate Indians from a little village in the hinterlands while on a journey saw a railroad locomotive stalled on the tracks. They began discussing what this strange monster could be. One said, "It is made to go." Another said, "Then let's make it go." So they called some more of their friends, and together they were able to push the engine about six yards down the track. They thought they had done something outstanding.

The next day the engineer came back. He got the steam up and hitched a couple of cars to the engine. When these Indians came along, they were utterly amazed at what they saw. The engineer then offered to take them for a ride in one of the cars. They were wide eyed as with a loud hissing and grinding of wheels he got it in motion and pulled the Indians along. We don't know what they said, but it certainly must have been an eye opener for them. Engines are not made to be moved by an outside power, but by a head of steam within.

So often we try by our own feeble strength to make life go. Life barely moves on; it doesn't always advance in the way we want. We haven't the resourcefulness or the strength alone to move it along victoriously. All the time there is an empty place on the throne of our heart, or perhaps we have let the wrong things have priority in our life. Let God, the true and rightful ruler, come and take His place upon the throne of your heart. Then life will move along with forceful power and wise guidance. Then the direction will always be upward toward God and homeward toward eternity, where men shall live with Him forever. God alone knows the right way and the best way for His beloved children to follow.

PRAYER THOUGHT: *Almighty God, we pray that we may not trust in our own abilities to guide us, but rather that we may wisely look to Thee for the power and direction which will move our souls steadily toward eternity with Thee.*

"Go home to your friends, and tell them how much the Lord has done for you, and how he has had mercy on you." Mark 5:19

Engaged in conversation with a missionary one day, I asked how it was when they began their work in India. He replied, "You can't imagine the utter hopelessness of the conditions we faced on coming here. Here was a people who couldn't read or write. They had very little food to eat or clothes to wear, and no doctors whatever to attend them in illness. They seemed to have no pity for each other; many children and aged were left exposed to die.

I asked, "What were you able to do for such people?" He replied, "By the help of God, I tried to live the gospel. If I saw a baby crying, I would pick it up and comfort it. Did I see a man with a broken limb, I would try to arrange help for it to be mended. When I saw people in distress, I took pity on them. Some I took into my home to care for them. In this way I tried to live the gospel day by day. Finally, these people came to me and said, 'What does this mean? Why are you doing this? Why are you so kind and loving?' That was my chance to preach the gospel, and soon a church was built where they could worship the living God."

Each one has a like opportunity to live God's gospel of love. We aren't living in a heathen country, but in a land of multiplied opportunities. And yet on every street there are those who still are not Christians. I am dead sure that if we would show a little more concern and love for those in need about us, we too could influence them to seek the gospel, which is a matter of life and death to us all. The old adage that says our actions speak louder than our words may be very true in respect to our witness for the kingdom of God. By our actions men shall know that we are disciples of the Lord.

PRAYER THOUGHT: *May we look about us in the immediate area where we live for persons to whom our witness might bring the hope and joy which can come only when a soul has knowledge of Christ.*

"Whatever you ask in prayer, believe that you receive it, and you will." Mark 11:24

One of the sights I observed in India which impressed me, and especially interested me, was to watch the Moslems after they had been to prayer. They would cup their hands as if to ask for a blessing from God. I had two reactions upon seeing this gesture.

My first reaction to this cupped-hands gesture was a negative one. Were these people merely asking for a handout from God? I thought of the prayer life of many Christians. For what do we usually pray? Do we not usually ask Him for things? And are not many of our requests for the satisfaction of our own wants? How much of our prayer time is spent in interceding for the needs of others? How much time do we spend praying for enemies and those who despitefully use us? How much time do we spend praying that God might guide the leaders of the world in these turbulent days through which we pass? Do we spend any time just thanking God for all the things that come our way from the open hands of His provident mercy? How much time do we remain silent to listen to God and to give Him an opportunity to speak to us?

The second reaction to this sight was a positive one. Here are people who have prayed, and after they pray they cup their hands in expectant faith, looking for God's answer. How many Christians have a like confidence? Is our prayer life merely dull routine, expecting nothing whatever to happen? Or is our stance like that of the early disciples who waited in Jerusalem for Pentecost? Do we organize our lives on the certainty that when we pray something always happens? According to our faith God will answer within His will for our lives.

PRAYER THOUGHT: *Merciful Lord, when we pray to Thee, help us to pray not just for our own selfish interests, but let us pray also for others, knowing that whatever we may ask of Thee, Thou dost hear and wilt answer.*

Seek and read from the book of the Lord. Isaiah 34:16

Two poverty-stricken, illiterate men hobbled up to a mission hospital in India one day. The one was blind and the other was physically almost at death's door. They were given modern medical treatment and carefully and lovingly nursed back to health. On leaving the hospital some time later, the blind man asked for a copy of what he called "the Jesus Book." "What use is it to you? You cannot read," said the missionary. "No," he replied, "but I will take it to those who can."

The two men returned to their village happy because now they possessed the gospel, which they had learned to love. Both of them were weavers by trade. Whenever men came to purchase cloth in that little village shop, they were met with this remark, "Before we will do any business with you, you must promise to read us a few pages out of our Jesus book." Even when the tax collector came, he was presented with the same request.

When the doctor from the mission hospital visited the little village nearly two years after these men had been discharged, he learned that the heathen temple there had been closed. Practically the entire village now was worshiping the Christ whom these native converts had introduced to their neighbors.

It is a real inspiration for us to know the power of the Word of God and what it can do to change the lives of people. And yet it is discouraging to know that so few of us use that available power. Within the Bible there is all the dynamic that any of us will need for great living each day. Like a great storehouse filled with adequate supplies is the Bible, for in it God has placed His promises and His instructions for us to lead a life as His own children.

PRAYER THOUGHT: *Lead us, dear Lord, to turn often to Thy written Word, so that we might know the direction and strength which come from increased knowledge of Thy will for our lives.*

"Their mouth is full of curses and bitterness . . . . in their paths
are ruin and misery, and the way of peace they do not know."
Romans 3:14, 16, 17

To understand the land of India better and the challenge
confronting the United States as to this vast part of the world,
America would do well to consider some pertinent facts. A
majority of the people there will go to bed hungry tonight.
Most of these people can neither read nor write. Nearly all of
them live in grueling poverty. Most of them will never have
the benefit of seeing a doctor in their entire lifetime. Many
believe that anything different would be better than what
they now have, and some are determined that changes shall be
made. Many believe that freedom as the western world knows
it, or free enterprise as we sometimes say, means simply the
freedom of western colonial powers to exploit them. Consequently, some of them distrust all people with white skin.
These people are determined that never again will they be
ruled by foreigners.

As we study these underprivileged countries outside the
United States, we must keep in mind the manner in which they
have been treated in the past. Because we were unchristian
in our dealings with them, we are today paying a costly price.
Yet I do not believe at all that it is too late to teach them the
truth they do not yet know. There is only one way out of our
dilemma, and that is to put into immediate practice the gospel
of Christian sharing and love. We must give more than we
have ever shared before, even perhaps with an accompanying
lowering of our own American standard of living. We must
prove that our democratic way of life is the only way that can
lift them out of the depths of despair and need. We must also
share with them the message of God's eternal love.

PRAYER THOUGHT: *Dear Lord, help us by our increased expressions of love toward those who are disillusioned and living
in hopelessness to repair the damage done by mistreatment
and unkindness to men and nations.*

Always be prepared to make a defense to any one who calls
you to account for the hope that is in you. 1 Peter 3:15

A young missionary doctor of Bhimavaram came to this
area when the caste system was still especially prevalent. The
Christians and the untouchables were not allowed to go
through the Brahman streets. This missionary started her work
in a small shed, and people from all castes came seeking her
medical help except the Brahmans. However, occasionally one
could see a high caste person coming as far as the gate of the
mission compound, but no further.

One day an old Brahman man was brought inside the gate.
He had a terrible odor about his body as he had diabetic gan-
grene of the foot. His relatives had taken him to every native
doctor in the town, but there was no improvement in his condition. Finally as a last resort, when his condition seemed almost incurable, the relatives decided to try the young woman
at the mission hospital. When they saw how young the missionary was, they were tempted to go away, but she pleaded
with them to stay and allow her to try to help the man. She
took the matter before the Lord in prayer and asked for His
help. After nine days of treatment the man miraculously became well not only in body, but also in soul, for after considerable study he became a Christian.

Each one of us can be a tremendous witness wherever we
are. We should so live that people might inquire how such
radiant living can be ours. Then we shall perhaps have the opportunity of leading them to the Lord, not discounting the
power of intercessory prayer. In the hands of the Lord all
things are possible, but we so often fail to put our deepest
needs and problems there. Upon the heart of the Lord we
should lay our souls as well as the souls of our neighbors.

PRAYER THOUGHT: *Loving God, may we testify to Thy great
love and mercy by advertising in our lives the joy which is ours
because we are Thy children, and even in this way may Thy
Spirit appeal to the hearts of those who are still outside the
door of faith.*

> They are darkened in their understanding, alienated from the life of God because of the ignorance that is in them. Ephesians 4:18

What a vast difference there is between the people who have heard the gospel of Jesus Christ and those who still live in the darkness of ignorance. Daily I am haunted by ghastly sights I have seen in my travels and the pitiful conditions pertaining to the daily lives of people in so many parts of the globe. We in America have no adequate idea of some of the living conditions abroad, even though we have seen many pictures and read many accounts.

I think of the faces of some mothers whose etched lines spell loneliness and horror. Parents, put yourself in the position of one who has never known the living God. Picture mothers bringing their tender little babies down to the river banks whose waters are filled with hungry crocodiles. Here is a mother about to throw her precious child into the gaping mouths of these fierce reptiles, foolishly thinking that only so can she appease her angry heathen gods. These poor people do not know the truth that sets men free.

By the same token, what a responsibility we Christians have to the world! How will they ever know about the living Christ, if there is no one to tell them? What other plans might there be by which to win the world for Christ? "I have no other plans," said the Lord simply, "I am counting on you." Indeed He is counting on each of us to hold the lifeline of support to those willing to go as missionaries in order that the light of Christ may penetrate the darkened areas of the world. All of us cannot be missionaries abroad, but we can be missionaries at home. We can share in helping to win our neighbors by supporting those who are willing to shove off from home shores and make the sacrifices needed to go in person.

PRAYER THOUGHT: *Merciful Lord, we pray that we may readily accept our obligation as Thy children to bring the light of truth to those of Thy children who still suffer in darkness and despair.*

"Behold, I stand at the door and knock; if any one hears my voice and opens the door, I will come in to him." Revelation 3:20

It was not until after one of my several stops in India that I learned of a certain woman who had come to a Christian missionary after viewing Holman Hunt's painting of the Lord Jesus standing at the heart's door. The artist here depicts the door as being shut and Jesus standing outside knocking. This native Indian convert who was interested in the picture asked the missionary a few questions and then returned to her home.

Several months later that missionary visited the home of the Indian convert. It was then winter when temperatures dip and it becomes quite cold, especially in the foothills of the mountains. Upon arriving there the missionary saw the front door wide open in spite of the cold. The woman was sitting inside, shaking and shivering from the cold. The missionary asked, "Why don't you close the door and keep the little heat you have inside?" Her face brightened as she said, "Remember when I was in your home? You told me the story of that door picture, and the man of the kind face. He looked so gentle and so loving. Such an expression I would never find on any of my heathen gods. So I now leave my door open all the time, lest He should come and find it shut."

How about the door of your heart, my friend? Is it that wide open each day, so that the King can enter and rule supreme? Only He gives that which can really satisfy the deepest hungers of your soul. Does He have a standing invitation to come into your life and thereby use it for His plan? Have you attended to the removal of any barriers of sin that might otherwise keep Him away? Only His power can satisfy.

PRAYER THOUGHT: *Precious Lord, may we be constantly prepared to welcome Thy presence in our lives by always keeping the door of our hearts open for Thy coming.*

All that is in the heavens and in the earth is Thine; thine is the kingdom, O Lord, and thou art exalted as head above all. 1 Chronicles 29:11

My wife and I were visiting in India as this country prepared to welcome Queen Elizabeth of England on one of her tours. For weeks thousands of people were engaged in numerous preparations for such a great event in the history of this newborn nation. It intrigued us to see workers all along the Queen's parade route, as they spread red gravel on the sidewalk. This was their method of indicating the red carpet reception that was hers in the hearts of these people.

As we stood on the route of the parade, we were a part of the hundreds of thousands of people who gathered there. A large number of them came from far distant parts of this great land. Many, no doubt, had ridden third class on the bus, or had walked many miles with their children, merely to get a glimpse of the titular ruler of one of the great countries of the world. As she passed by one could readily sense their warm adoration and profound respect for this titled leader of the British Empire.

Many of us are thrilled when the paths of great human personalities cross ours. Even to have had a glimpse at some world-renowned personality is a memorable experience. But yet we are so ready to forget that the greatest privilege any mortal man can have today is to receive Christ into his heart. To know Him should be our most important goal in life. Here is One who is not only the Savior for eternity, but One also who is a companion and guide along life's way. Here is One who as King of kings is supreme ruler over all the kings and leaders of the earth. He has promised to be our friend and guide this day and every day.

PRAYER THOUGHT: *May we never lose sight of the real privilege which is ours to meet Thee face to face every day of our lives, gracious Lord, realizing that through Thee we know the one power which is truly able to reign eternal over all the world.*

> Have no anxiety about anything, but in everything by prayer and supplication with thanksgiving let your requests be made known to God. Philippians 4:6

Kara, a little orphan girl in India, had a remarkable faith. Kara's greatest wish was to live in the home of her missionary teacher. The teacher had no extra money and no room for her, but she promised to pray about the matter. The next day the teacher received a gift of money from America, and immediately sent for Kara. The little girl, however, met the messenger halfway. Later she explained, "I was praying, too. I was so sure that God would hear me that I started walking toward the missionary's house."

Oh, that we might have the faith of a little child! Their trust in people that they love is so simple and yet so sincere. Children usually have faith in their parents. Under almost any circumstance they trust them. Even at times of great danger a youth knows that his parents' love will protect him. A child rests secure in the knowledge that his parents care for him.

If we have faith in mere human beings, why can't we have faith in our heavenly Father? He has promised us that underneath our lives are the everlasting arms. To be sure, faith is a leap into the unknown; but it is staking everything on God's being there. Sometimes we only see as through a glass darkly. We cannot foretell what the future has in store for us, except this one thing—we believe that God will always be there.

When we pray we do not see God and yet we can be certain He hears us because He has promised that if we ask, we shall receive. We don't always receive what we want, but we will receive what God thinks is best for us. God knows better than we what we have need of. Let us never grow so old that we cannot have the faith of a little child.

PRAYER THOUGHT: *Heavenly Father, we pray that we may attain the simplicity of faith which we see in little children, knowing that the reward of such trust in Thee is everlasting contentment.*

> To the King of ages, immortal, invisible, the only God, be honor and glory for ever and ever. 1 Timothy 1:17

The non-Christian religions of the Orient have many gods, which also means that there are many temples. Now, in Burma these are built as pagodas. In China many temples are built on high hills. In India every village of any size has some structure serving as a temple. To these places the people come for special festivals to hear the beating of the native drums and the ringing of the bells. However, one never hears any singing in these places as one does in Christian churches throughout the world. Many of the children are taken into the temple and there taught about the god in whose honor the temple stands. Looking up into the lifeless face of this statue, they are forced to touch the idol with their hands and to kneel before these gods, making offerings of prayers and gifts to them.

In India a little child who was attending a Christian school returned one day for the holidays. Her parents became quite concerned when they heard her singing Christian hymns. Dressing her in her very best costume, they took her to the Buddhist temple. In the inner shrine they could gaze into the stone-cold face of Buddha. "See," they told her, "we can look into the face of our god and put out our hand and touch him." "Yes," replied the child, "but when we talk to him, he cannot hear us. When a Christian talks to his God, even though he cannot see Him, he knows He hears him and answers his prayers."

No wonder the Lord once said that we must have the faith of a little child. It is a faith upon which we can depend, because it has been proved and tested in the lives of unnumbered followers. Though we cannot see Him, our God hears and answers our prayers.

PRAYER THOUGHT: *Dear Lord, we ask that we might come to Thee with the childlike simplicity of faith which does not require an image of Thee to sustain it, but only trust in Thy unfailing wisdom and strength.*

"I send you to open their eyes, that they may turn from darkness to light and from the power of Satan to God, that they may receive forgiveness of sins and a place among those who are sanctified by faith in me." Acts 26:17, 18

There are many people in the world today who are living in ignorance, burdened with many superstitions. They have never heard of the living God who loves with an everlasting love. They live in fear of their silent idols. They believe they are under the spells of witch doctors and other mystical voices that tell them what they must do.

When I was in Bombay, I learned of a father who had taken his beautiful six-year-old daughter to a religious shrine. There he had beaten her head against the stone altar of that heathen god until he had crushed her skull in death. Why? Because this girl had done something wrong? No! He did this foolish thing simply because he thought some idol's voice demanded that he make this sacrifice to a god that didn't even exist.

The guilt for this dreadful act rests with us. We have failed to answer the challenge of the Lord who long ago gave us the only program that can possibly bring light into darkened hearts. Before He left this world, He instructed His disciples and people of succeeding generations to go into all places, making disciples of all people. He said, "All power hath been given unto me." He faithfully assured us that He would be with us, so that this power would be always available. Because we haven't brought this light of the gospel to people in our own land, as well as to other parts of the world, there are many who are still living in the darkness of superstition and sin.

If we truly know the great love of God that saves us to the uttermost, then we should be compelled to bring His message to all people. How can we help but share the great news which we hold in our hearts today? God's command impels us to live for Him and use ourselves in His service.

PRAYER THOUGHT: *Purge the guilt which rests upon us, O Lord, because we have failed to bring the light of Thy Word into the dark corners of the world.*

"According to your faith be it done to you." Matthew 9:29

One day, in a chance conversation with a mountain climber, I learned a striking lesson. This stocky, fearless guide told of an intensely exciting experience he had faced when he was caught in a terrible storm. He said, "I didn't know what to do. I was frightened half to death. There seemed to be no way out. Then I thought of a prayer I had heard an old colored preacher in my home town give many years before. It went like this: 'God, I just believe you won't allow anything to happen to me today that you and I can't handle together.'" He concluded his account by saying, "Then I was at peace."

All of us can have a like assurance in living, if we would only want it. But we must take the "leap of faith," to borrow the phrase of Kierkegaard. First we use our own resources, and try to do the best with what we have. Yet even our best, built and developed from our own strength, is not enough. We still have a feeling of emptiness. It is at that point that we must believe in a personal, loving God. Then we turn to God with complete confidence that He will be able to supply the assurance and the strength which we need.

The difficulty of so many men is the fact that we don't take God at His word. During our Lord's brief life on earth He repeatedly said to folk with whom He worked and talked, "Great is your faith! Be it done for you as you desire." With God absolutely anything is possible. Even in the dark and cloudy days, when one message of bad news comes hard on the heels of another, we know that He is close beside us, ready to protect us in even the most vicious storms of life. This relationship with God is truly the partnership unlimited.

PRAYER THOUGHT: *Gracious God, we thank Thee that even in those times when we see only clouds and chaos on the horizon of life, Thou yet art able to shelter and protect us, no matter how severe the storm might be.*

> Put on then, as God's chosen ones, holy and beloved, compassion, kindness. Colossians 3:12

Every visitor to the great city of Calcutta leaves with a depressed feeling because of the sights of thousands of people who are literally homeless. They are starving from having no food, and dying because they lack medical care. Wherever you go, you find people squatting on the ground or lying on the steps of public buildings. People pass by without the slightest glance or attention to those of their own land who are in such desperate need.

As one moves away from these heartbreaking scenes, suddenly one confronts a sight that is confusing, to say the least. Down the road there comes a white cow. Around her neck hangs a garland of flowers; her horns are decorated in honor of the Hindu festival which is taking place. The cow is permitted into the bazaar without being molested and can eat all that she wants there of vegetables and greenstuffs displayed. The owner of the food feels honored, because according to Hindu sacred writings the cow is sacred. But for these humans there is no food or shelter. They lie in the filth of the gutter, hoping that a Christian missionary will come by.

All of us need to feel more responsible than we have up to this time, and exert ourselves to alleviate the suffering in the world today. How can we continue to go on our own way so completely oblivious to the tens of thousands of God's children who have nothing with which to exist? We have a responsibility to bring hope into the bare lives of these who, as children of God, have equal significance with us in His sight. Daily we need to remind ourselves of the fact that as we share our gifts, we are sharing with the Lord and letting other men know that we are His disciples. Above all, the work of the Lord will be done among His people.

PRAYER THOUGHT: *May we become more sympathetic toward those who suffer from the diseases of spiritual ignorance, dear Father, and share with our brothers the gifts which we receive from Thee.*

"He that would love life and see good days, let him keep his tongue from evil and his lips from speaking guile." 1 Peter 3:10

While in India one day, an invitation came to me to have lunch with Prime Minister Nehru and his sister, Madame Pandit. I waited with keen anticipation. Finally the moment arrived, and we climbed into the car which had been sent for us. Going to the Cecil House, there in the gardens of this beautiful place, we spoke with two of the world's most influential personalities. After that meeting I was certain that Prime Minister Nehru wants peace for the world. He has sought diligently to develop the economic resources of his country in order to provide food for the rapidly exploding population. At the present time the country is the home of four hundred million people, and is growing at a net increase of two percent a year, or eight million people, which is larger than the population of Texas. Inevitably, there are some grave problems.

Nehru's concern is not alone for his own country, although this weighs heavily upon him, but also for the peace of the world. During our conversation he sketched what might be done with the monies now being spent for war and military equipment, if these could be devoted solely to the welfare of the suffering people of the world.

Each of Christ's followers is called upon to be a part of what must be a rapidly growing movement to help change the climate of the world from one of fear, hatred, and distrust into one of kindness, love, and consideration. We can each begin where we are. If instead of dissipating our own energies by talking falsely about our neighbor, instead of passing rumors, we would place the most charitable construction upon their actions, we should discover that we were building constructively. Good will and brotherhood begin where you are.

PRAYER THOUGHT: *Teach us, heavenly Father, to use our time and efforts not for destructive purposes, but for constructive efforts in behalf of Christlike relationships with individuals and, ultimately, with nations.*

"He is not far from each one of us." Acts 17:27

During my visit with Prime Minister Nehru of India in the gardens of the Cecil House, I was amazed at the absence of soldiers around his estate. I reminded myself that in my own country, when the President travels about, he is surrounded by secret service men. Wherever he goes, elaborate arrangements are made to prepare the way, lest an attempt be made upon his life. As I glanced around at the towering trees, I could see no one guarding this famous world personality. But after the lunch as we were leaving the gardens, I turned and noticed an armed soldier behind almost every tree. They sought skillfully to hide from us, revolving around the trees as our position changed lest they be discovered. Here, all unseen, was a complete guard watching over this man who is so significant today as a policy maker among world leaders.

As I left that garden I thought about how every Christian is surrounded each day by the loving angels of heaven. They are unseen, and yet they are near. They watch over us at the command of our Lord and Savior, who thus keeps a promise made long ago that He would never leave us. These ministering spirits care for us, even though we are not aware of their presence.

Wherever you go in this world, you will find God's presence. He is always ready to communicate with His children in prayer, ready to direct them, and ready to help them make decisions and choices. It is wonderful to know as we live each day that we can carry on in the presence of a great God. As we go about our daily tasks, His love and power are about us. As we lie down at night for rest, He is constantly standing watch over His own, ready to stand at their side again in the new morrow, helping them to live according to His will.

PRAYER THOUGHT: *We Thank Thee, dear Lord, for the comforting knowledge that Thou art keeping an everlasting vigil over our lives, and that no matter where we are or what we do we are never separated from Thy presence.*

Walk as children of light. Ephesians 5:8

In a village church in Travancore, India, there is a wonderful brass lamp. It has about 100 slender arms hanging down from the ceiling. At the end of each is a cup that is filled with oil, and also contains a wick. Each family of the congregation brings its house lamp, and accordingly the church is lighted to the degree of the faithfulness of its worshipers. At the close of evening worship services, people come up to take their lamp to help guide them home through the night. It is a beautiful sight to watch the worshipers depart, and to see the many lights go out in different directions, pushing aside the darkness as they press on.

The Lord has commanded that we walk through life as children of light. How much light does your life shed? Is your light seen by men? Or is it so faint it can be seen by only a very few? The darkness of this world would vanish, if everyone confessing allegiance to Christ would go out into every area of life and let his light of faith shine brightly and unashamedly. Of course, our lives must be in direct touch with Him who is the Light of life. As we worship in His church, commune at the Lord's table and pray and read the Word of God, we bring ourselves to where He kindles and lights the lanterns of our lives. The winds of wickedness and evil will try ever so hard to blow them out. But as we live close to God, He becomes more and more our shield and protector. If we persevere and are faithful, men will know by the steadiness of our living that we have been in contact with Him who is the light of the world. Living as children of the light is our highest calling in this life, for we have been endowed with the blessings of faith according to our faithfulness to our heavenly Father.

PRAYER THOUGHT: *Teach us, God of light, to bring the lamp of our life close to Thy light, so that we may illuminate the world wherever we go and in whatever we do.*

"It is not the will of my Father who is in heaven that one of these little ones should perish." Matthew 18:14

In Ceylon I met a very hospitable bishop who told me something about his activity in the Christian school which he is directing. One of the most vibrant Christian personalities I have ever met, he has dedicated himself wholeheartedly to the work of God's kingdom. He worked for many long hours in order to make Jesus Christ real to the children whom he loved. His personal character had attracted so many children to his school that the walls were fairly bulging.

During his conversation he explained one of his difficulties. Many mornings the children of the school would come early. When he asked them why they had come so early, they replied that they were so hungry they could not sleep. There was no breakfast at home for them to eat, they had brought no food along for lunch, and it was very unlikely they would have anything for dinner. And then the bishop turned to me and said, "How can you teach children that God is love when they are starving to death?"

It would be pure slander for us to blame God. He has left His work in our hands, providing ample resources for us so that if we shared as He would want us to, there would be enough for all. When, however, we are selfish and unwilling to share, then we have become instruments in the hand of the devil. The evil one would like nothing more than to keep Christ boxed up in the church. He becomes disturbed when we take God out into life and put His message into practice every day.

Let us never forget that love is the badge of Christian discipleship. As long as one child is starving on the earth, we have the responsibility toward this individual stamped with the image of God to bring the Father's love to him in a tangible way.

PRAYER THOUGHT: *We know, dear Lord, that it is Thy will that we should share our gifts with all of Thy children. Help us to accept Thy will and unselfishly distribute our abundance with those in want.*

If any one purifies himself from what is ignoble, then he will be a vessel for noble use. 2 Timothy 2:21

Bangkok is one of the most fascinating cities in all the world. It is the city of canals. For many people their only means of transportation are boats that travel through this system of interlocking waterways. The priests visit with the members of their religious groups along the river's edge. People go shopping in stores that have been built for the convenience of these boat riders.

Bangkok is also the city of temples, all of which have been erected to honor the many heathen gods. Surrounding many of these temples are beautiful park areas. Each day dozens of men called sweepers begin work in the early morning hours to clean the streets, so that the grounds which honor these heathen gods might be neat and well ordered and in keeping with the people's reverence for them.

In passing by and viewing these men working so industriously, one thinks of how wonderful it would be, if we would make the same effort to keep our hearts clean and pure for the living God. Rather than allowing an accumulation of unconfessed sins to gather and burden us, would it not be better each day to sweep the slate clear by permitting the Holy Ghost to enter our lives with forgiveness. The Lord cannot exist in a life cluttered with pride, envy, jealousy, and selfishness.

The Lord's power is so great that by using it we may overcome these things, and thereby make our life truly a temple for the Holy Ghost. His promise is that, if we confess our sins, He will be faithful and just, forgiving our sins and indeed cleansing us from unrighteousness. Even though our transgressions against the will of God are as red as blood, yet He will make pure again the hearts of the penitent. God's love is that great!

PRAYER THOUGHT: *Merciful Lord, may we constantly be willing to clean our lives of the accummulation of sins and shortcomings which daily gather and hinder us from presenting a spotless soul before Thy grace.*

We have our hope set on the living God. 1 Timothy 4:10

Many of the sacred temple areas in the city of Bangkok are surrounded by high enclosing walls. There are gates in these walls, however, through which you pass to enter the temple grounds. Outside the gates are many people sitting on the ground who are selling little trinkets and gifts. These are purchased by the religious pilgrims who bring them as sacrifices to their heathen gods. For many of these poor people it is a tremendous financial sacrifice to pay the amount of money necessary to purchase these items.

After he has made his required purchase, the pilgrim takes the gift and enters the temple grounds. In one area he might see a huge figure of the sleeping Buddha, which is the length of an entire city block. To this dumb piece of stone he offers his prayers and rituals, and at its base he places his costly gift. In another area is the Emerald Buddha, where gifts are not only given by the native pilgrims, but they are also sent by world leaders from several nations of the globe.

As one stands in these surroundings, one cannot help but contrast the willingness of people to give to dead idols with the hesitation of Christians to make sacrifices to the living God. The heathen god cannot lift so much as his little finger to help those who worship him. But there is absolutely nothing the living God cannot do. The living God is also a personal God whose love knows no limits. We do not have to appease Him with gifts and sacrifices, in order to know that He hears our prayers and is interested in our lives. We are indeed blessed in having a saving faith in this true God, the Ruler of the universe. Let us then each day count our blessings and remind ourselves of what it means to have God as our Father. Let us prove our love to Him by the way we live.

PRAYER THOUGHT: *Heavenly Father, we pray that we may not follow after the dead gods of this world, but that we will lead lives of devotion to Thee, the loving and living God.*

> Bear witness to the light, that all might believe through him.
> John 1:7

The Buddhists have an interesting way of celebrating their festive days on the many canals. They set adrift small illuminated ships laden with their offerings. As the flaming ships drift down the stream with the current of the water, the priests all chant, "Short is the life of mortals and full of pain; a flame launched upon a deep sea, drifting to the inevitable dissolution. For whatever has an origin also has an end."

We Christians, too, believe that the life of mortals is fleeting and soon over and fraught with pain. However, because of our faith in the living God we have a great hope for the future. The best of life is yet to be experienced, for nothing can be compared to the glory which some day will be revealed in us and to us in heaven.

A missionary in Thailand was reading to a native one day from the Scriptures. She was relating the story of the birth of Christ. "How long has it been since God's Son was born?" the native woman asked. "About two thousand years," the missionary replied. "Why has the news been so long in reaching us? Who has been hiding the Book?" the native then thoughtfully inquired.

Because we have not brought the message of God's Word to the world as we should have done, we face the frustration of an unfinished task. We are not only robbing others of the joy which should be theirs, but by our neglect we harm ourselves, for unless this world becomes a Christian world, we are ever in danger of living in discord and unkindness. Let us resolve to let our lights of Christian witness shine before men, that they might know Him who is the light of the world.

PRAYER THOUGHT: *We pray, dear Father in heaven, that we will take up our task of witnessing for Thee with increased fervor and dedication, so that the light of Thy gospel might shine forth in every land.*

> The Lord is the strength of his people, he is the saving refuge of his anointed. Psalm 28:8

One of the most beautiful islands in all the world is Sumatra. Located on this island is a very interesting church. It is called the Batak Church and now numbers some 800,000 church members. I couldn't help but think of its history as I sat with more than fifteen hundred Batak Christians in worship one Sunday, singing with them the great hymns of faith.

A century ago Ludwig Nommensen, a pioneer missionary to the Batak tribesmen in Sumatra, was told that he could stay on this island for only two years. During that time he studied the customs and traditions that had so long ruled the lives of these people. When the two years had passed by, the chief asked him, "Is there anything in the Christian religion that differs from the laws of the Batak? We too have laws which say that a man must not steal, nor take his neighbor's wife, nor bear false witness against his neighbor." The missionary answered, "My Master gives the power to keep the laws." The chief greatly excited said, "Can you teach my people that?" "No," replied Nommensen, "but God can give them the power, if they ask for it." The fearless missionary was then permitted to stay another six months during which time he taught them about one thing—the power of God. At the end of that time the chief said, "Stay. Your God gives us the strength to do the right and good things."

Our God indeed is sufficient for man's every need. We need Him even during every hour to direct us in the way that we should go through our days. If we follow Him, we shall be victorious over evil. His strength becomes our strength to meet temptation and not let it overpower us. His power is our daily sustenance.

PRAYER THOUGHT: *Almighty God, we thank Thee for the strength which we receive from Thee in order to withstand the temptations of evil, and we pray that we shall remain close to Thee, our source of power.*

"With God all things are possible." Matthew 19:26

During a visit to Nommensen University in Siantar, Sumatra of Indonesia, I had the privilege of speaking to a group of young men studying and preparing for the holy ministry. It was a thrill to hear them participate in the church service in reading Scripture and offering prayer. After I had delivered my address to the group, the seminary choir rose to sing. I declare I have never heard such singing, not any place in the wide world. They sang a very familiar hymn whose melody I immediately recognized. They first sang it in Indonesian, then in Batak, and finally in English: "Holy, Holy, Holy, Lord God Almighty." They came to that phrase, "merciful and mighty," which caused me to think about the power of God. They sang it as if they deeply felt and knew the true significance of this description of our great God.

The Lord is merciful. Constantly in the Bible He is inviting us to come to Him. He is telling us that, although our sins are as scarlet, He can make them white as snow. He has promised all men that, if we will only confess our sins, He will forgive and cleanse us from all inquity. He is the good shepherd who lays down His life for His sheep. "I came that they may have life, and have it abundantly," Jesus once said.

The Lord is also mighty. He is all powerful. "Is anything too hard for God?" This has special significance for each of us, if only we have faith to believe. Then we know that according to His promise we are joint heirs of all His power which is available for us each day that we live. It will carry us through any circumstance and enable us to live the victorious life which the Lord desires for each of us. His promises are dependable and sure.

PRAYER THOUGHT: *Dear Lord, it is wonderful to know that, weak and sinful as we are, with Thy help we can still live a glorious and abundant life.*

"You shall be my witnesses." Acts 1:8

Visit with me today a native Batak Church in Siantar. The congregation of fifteen hundred young people has just been dismissed from the early service. They are exuberantly happy as they go their way, having had the privilege of hearing the gospel. How grateful they are to be children of the light. The second service of the morning is about to begin. The church is filled to capacity by more of God's children seeking to learn of His grace and mercy. These people sing with dynamic fervor and enthusiasm. The preacher of the day is an elder of the church. Many of the lay people must do the preaching because of the shortage of ordained pastors. One of the strengths of this indigenous church is the work of the laymen who backstop their overburdened pastors and who are willing to witness on behalf of their Lord.

Now, every Christian is called upon to be a witness. Once you have committed your life to the Lord, you are not only a privileged recipient of His mercy and grace, but you also assume a responsibility. Every occupation in life can be a sacred vocation. Every place of duty should be a preaching station. Some Christians are ordained to be pastors, but all are ministers. So many in this world look to us for an example to discover a better way of life.

Each day we are teaching souls wherever we go by the things we do or the things we fail to do. As we live our lives to the glory of God, we shall discover a deep joy and satisfaction in living which we have never known before. It is when we come to the end of a day, knowing that we have honestly tried to do everything in our power to make life better for others, that we can lay our heads on our pillows to rest in peace, despite the mistakes that may have been made.

PRAYER THOUGHT: *May we never forget, Lord, that our lives are to be a constant witness to Thy grace and power. We pray that we may keep this witness worthy and faultless.*

I will exalt thee, I will praise thy name; for thou hast done wonderful things. Isaiah 25:1

The Christians in the Batak Church of Indonesia love to sing. They have some of the most musically-pleasing choirs in all the world. They sing in church, at work, at play, and during travel.

One day as I was sitting on the porch of a home in Sumatra, a bus load of Christians came by, all of them singing at the top of their voices the melody, "Praise to the Lord." They reached a dramatic climax as they sang the phrase, "Ponder anew What the Almighty can do."

Right there I concluded that this would be a good daily motto. Too frequently we think only of our own slender resources. We wonder how we shall have the strength to face another day. How shall we find the courage to face prickly problems which block our way? Where shall we find answers to the baffling questions that present themselves? Look away, little man, from yourself and look up to God. "Ponder anew What the Almighty can do."

Immediately I thought of how this great God at the dim far-away beginnings of time caused everything to come into being. He was the architect of this great world. He made everything in it; the crowning point of His achievement was the creation of man. Scripture says simply, "He spoke, and it was done." Such is the power of the Almighty.

I thought of Calvary and God's plan for man's salvation. Before the foundation of our world was laid, there was a council in the circle of the Trinity. "I will go," answered the Son. And God gave His Son unto death that we might live and not die in eternity. I thought of the Holy Ghost and His guiding presence with us each day, imparting to us divine strength in our weakness and infinite power to keep going on. "Ponder anew What the Almighty can do!"

PRAYER THOUGHT: *Lord, may we never lose sight of the infinite power and glory which encompass our lives because of Thy presence.*

> Forgetting what lies behind and straining forward to what lies
> ahead, I press on toward the goal for the prize of the upward
> call of God in Christ Jesus. Philippians 3:13, 14

One of the major crops raised on the island of Sumatra, in
fact in all of Indonesia, is rice. There are rice fields almost
wherever you go. One is amazed at the way these peasant
farmers can bank up the waters and terrace their fields to give
the precious crop proper moisture at the proper time. These
fields are not used only for the purpose of producing a crop,
for it is not unusual to see grown men sitting on the rice fields
fishing in a foot of water. The paradox of the situation is that
not far from them is the rolling ocean, where they could cast
their fishing lines out into the deep.

Sometimes in life we make a similar mistake. We are satisfied with too little. We set our sights too low, and as a result
we don't become that which God has intended us to be. The
Lord once gave us a goal to aim for. He said, "You, therefore,
must be perfect, as your heavenly Father is perfect." No one
can ever perfectly attain this goal, but in striving for it we can
become more than we are. On this earth one should never be
satisfied with what one is.

There is always room for improvement in our lives, if we are
willing to make the effort in that direction. There are sins to
be conquered. There are new victories to be attained. There
are new ways to grow in our appreciation of other people and
the finer things of life. No man's life is built on a plateau. One
either goes downward, or one travels upward. Do not be satisfied with shallow living. Cast out into the deep, and you will
receive blessings the like of which you never dreamed existed.
Once knowing these, you will no longer be content with former
things, for new depths have been added to your life with God
sustaining you.

PRAYER THOUGHT: *We pray, dear Father, that we may not
become complacent with our spiritual progress, but will strive
to plunge ever more deeply into greater devotion.*

"I am the bread of life; he who comes to me shall not hunger, and he who believes in me shall never thirst." John 6:35

My wife and I were invited to dinner at the little food shop operated by a Chinese family. We were once again convinced that people in this whole area of the world are very hospitable. As we sat down to a multi-course dinner, taking some food and barely finishing eating it, our hosts would come to put some more food on our plates. It was the same custom with the tea that was served. As soon as the glass was empty, immediately it would again be filled. There seemed to be a limitless supply of nourishment for our bodies.

The thought occurred to me later that we have spiritual resources even more abundant than these from the hand of Almighty God. He has said, "I am the bread of life; he who comes to me shall not hunger, and he who believes in me shall never thirst."

Each day as we live we reach moments when we think our energies have been spent, and we cannot find within ourselves the resources necessary to carry on. We feel drained of all vigor to face one more crisis, or answer one more problem. But if we keep the channel open to God, there flows through it into our lives the power that we so desperately need at any time we need it. And with the psalmist of old, we shall come to the conclusion that truly the cup of our life runs over. Literally, it is spilling over with the limitless blessings that come to us from the hand of a provident God. He is the only one who is able to give us that which we need for the nourishment and sustenance of our spiritual life. Let us give thanks, then, to our God from hearts that are overflowing with love, because He has first loved us.

PRAYER THOUGHT: *Gracious God, may we always keep the lifeline of love from Thee free and clear, so that we may receive the nourishment of Thy spiritual blessings which enable us to encounter every task in life with fresh vigor and power.*

He has delivered us from the dominion of darkness and transferred us to the kingdom of his beloved Son, in whom we have redemption, the forgiveness of sins. Colossians 1:13, 14

In Sumatra I was told of a certain village where a man much like a soothsayer would make periodic trips into the village to receive the natives and practice his quaint craft. This was a heathen village, so the people followed implicitly his weird counsels. One Saturday night he came running into their town. The strange message was almost unintelligible. He had had some kind of vision, he said, as he ran stark naked about the street. He told the people that in his apparition he was commanded to tell them that they should all become Christian.

No one gave much attention until on another Saturday night the same episode was repeated. The people of the village held a pow-wow, and decided they should do something about it. So the leader marched all his people, some one hundred in number, to the closest Christian mission station and told the workers there what had happened. He said they wanted to receive instruction in the Christian faith. Over one hundred people were consequently received into the church. It was as though this practicer of the black arts had told these people they must put off the dirty rags of their past unrighteousness and put on the new cloak of Christ, and so find the life abundant.

Christ died on the cross that our sins might be forgiven, that the past might be wiped out and forgotten. He rose again for our justification, which means that the spotless robe of His righteousness might be placed on our shoulders as believers, a ring denoting our sonship on our fingers, and the sandals of our new-found mission on our feet. "For," says God, "this my son was dead, and is alive again; he was lost, and is found." This is the wonderful story of penitence, forgiveness, and salvation which are ours to enjoy each day that we live.

PRAYER THOUGHT: *We thank Thee, Lord, that we do not always need to wear the tattered rags of our sin, but that because of Thee we can clothe ourselves in the rich robe of salvation.*

"By this all men will know that you are my disciples, if you have love for one another." John 13:35

While in Siantar, Sumatra, we learned of a tragic bus accident. A group of Christian youth had taken a bus to attend a church convention in a nearby town. On the way home the vehicle skidded over a cliff, with the result that twenty-nine young people were killed, twenty-seven of these from one congregation. Many of them were burned and battered beyond recognition.

There was one young fellow whose life had been spared to him. For weeks, however, he hung between life and death. Nearly all the skin had been burned off his arms and face. The city hospital of this community was so poorly equipped that flies would come through the open windows to feed in the raw wounds. For three months fellow Christian students from Nommensen University volunteered to take shifts through the day and night to stand by his bedside, fanning away the flies. They sacrificed their study time and sleeping time, that they might help this unfortunate fellow in need. What a wonderful example of being our brother's keeper!

Perhaps the opportunities that open up to us each day are not quite so dramatic. But still, opportunities do come in many varying forms and ways. When they do and we resist them, life finally turns sour, and we feel guilty for having let somebody down. But when we accept the challenge of doing what we think our Lord would expect us to do, and extend a helping hand as needed, then we discover the deep-down joys of living, the good feeling inside that Christ has meant us to have when we share His love. Instead of feeling riled and irritated by needs that stare out at you, try putting out a hand of love, and feel the difference it will make in your character. By this shall men know that you are Christ's disciples.

PRAYER THOUGHT: *Precious Lord, we pray that we shall not ignore opportunities to serve Thee, but extend helping hands to others, for we realize that it is in these occasions that our devotion to Thee can be evident and made even stronger.*

"You, therefore, must be perfect, as your heavenly Father is perfect." Matthew 5:48

Our scene is set in a little home in Siantar, Indonesia. A group of young people gather together as is their custom each night for a service of song and prayer. These are dedicated Christians. They have learned to understand what joy there is in walking life's way arm in arm with their Lord. The leader of the group is a very dynamic young man who is as enthusiastic a witness for Christ as one can ever meet. He stands before this group of Christians, leading them in that gospel song, "We are climbing Jacob's ladder." A radiant smile spreads across his face as they sing the phrase, "Every step goes higher, higher."

This is the glory of being a Christian. This is what is called in theological terms "sanctification." We are always seeking to attain, and there is always a power enabling us to strive for the best. No one ever becomes perfect in this world, and yet the Lord urges us on to strive for perfection, saying as He did centuries ago, "You, therefore, must be perfect, as your heavenly Father is perfect."

As we reach for the stars, we make progress. Each day we should take a searching look at our lives to see what gains or losses have taken place. If we have regressed in living, we should take steps immediately to halt the backward slippage. If we have made progress, we should set challenging goals to be attained.

This going forward is not done in man's strength. The first step is to receive Christ into your heart. When we have done that, we receive the promise, "To all who received Him, . . . he gave power to become." The "becoming" process must be a part of every Christian's life. Each day he lives, every step must go higher, higher.

PRAYER THOUGHT: *Lord, may we always seek to grasp that which is beyond our immediate reach, so that we shall not become complacent as we strive toward our heavenly goal.*

"Man looks on the outward appearance, but the Lord looks on the heart." 1 Samuel 16:7

A young Indonesian boy was hired to guard a certain house against burglary while the tenants were on a vacation. Everything went well for a time, without any unusual incidents. Then one day he discovered something. Hurriedly he ran to the neighbor and said, "Miss Nelson, come over quick! There's a burglar in the house!" This happened in the middle of the day, and Miss Nelson couldn't understand why a burglar would be entering then. That would be quite unusual for this part of the world. But she agreed to go with him and he timidly came along.

She opened the door of the house. It was obvious that they were both nervous and afraid. First they examined the living room, and found nothing in there. Then they proceeded to the dining room, the bedroom, and the kitchen in the order of their opening one upon the other. But no intruder could be found. Finally, there was only one room left. Slowly the young Indonesian boy opened the door to the bathroom and shrieked, "There he is! There he is!" Miss Nelson who accompanied him discovered that the lad had seen for the first time his own image in a mirror.

Do you know what you really look like? In America we have mirrors in numerous places in the house. Every one of us can recognize our physical image. But have you taken a good look at yourself? In your heart and mind? What is your thinking like? Do you have high and noble thoughts, or are there things of which you would be ashamed as your mind is exposed to God? What are your desires and ideals like? Are they the kind that the good Lord would want you to have as you live day by day? What about those secret sins? Take a fresh look at yourself, and then take a long look at God. Ask Him to forgive and forget. And friend, He will!

PRAYER THOUGHT: *Dear Lord, help us to hold a mirror to our inner self. We know that whatever is unbecoming we see in that reflection will be graciously forgiven by Thee.*

Thou alone, O Lord, makest me dwell in safety. Psalm 4:8

Living in a free country with the great ocean protecting us, we cannot realize the fears of so many people throughout the world who have lived in war-torn areas. During a certain air raid in China some years back, a native Christian together with his wife and their six-year-old daughter did not have time to escape to their air raid shelter. This particular family finally had to take refuge under their table. As the bombs burst nearby, and their fears for the very safety of their lives mounted, they prayed. "Daddy," said the little girl when the danger was finally past, "the Lord Jesus Christ is the best air raid shelter we have, isn't He?"

Where do we search for a refuge and strength? Do we depend upon material things for security? There are many things in life that money can buy—food, clothing, housing, and physical necessities, which all of us need to survive. Money can be used to seek health, recreation, and pleasure. Yet at the same time, wealth cannot guarantee even these things for us.

Then there are the unpurchasables. Money cannot buy peace or contentment or security. Money cannot make automatic for us happiness and spiritual joy. It does not give us either a trust in the good will of our fellow men or a trust in the love of our merciful God. One need not be rich in dollars and cents to have these qualities of life. These are offered without any monetary cost to us by our Lord Jesus Christ. They are available to all, regardless of circumstances or background. But these things are of no value to us, unless we accept them and use them in our daily living. No man need fear to live, if the Lord is by his side, because he has that which no man can take from him.

PRAYER THOUGHT: *Teach us, Lord of mercy, to accept the security of Thy love for us, and to place our trust in the shelter of Thy everlasting arms.*

Do not be overcome by evil, but overcome evil with good. Romans 12:21

The forgetting of self, and the blessings that then spring from within, is exposed in a sharp light by this story that came out of China some years ago. The missionary parents and three of their children were brutally slain during what were called the Vegetarian Riots. Four other children escaped.

After a short time the four remaining family members were trying to decide what their revenge would be. Being Christian, they agreed they would get the best training available, return to China, and give themselves in devoted service to these people.

This they did. One of the brothers influenced a certain Chinese teacher to accept Christianity. This man later was the father of the mass education movement in China by which literally hundreds of thousands were taught to read, simply because this family knew and loved Christ. By the power of Christ's love, they were enabled to rise above the storms of hatred and revenge and to help those who were in need.

How different would be the condition of our world today, if more people and nations resolved simply to return good for evil. What a difference, if more people and nations would use their energies for constructive measures rather than for the destruction of their fellow men. This is the Christ way of living. Is is the only way that can spare our world from mass suicide. Great storehouses of destructive power have been stashed away by several nations which could wipe us off the face of the earth. Security built merely on bombs will fail. But there is one power that will never fail. "So faith, hope, love abide, these three." "Love never ends."

PRAYER THOUGHT: *Teach us, gracious Lord, to check our desire for revenge when evil is done to us, and instead to return love and understanding through service toward those who would persecute us.*

If sinners entice you, do not consent. Proverbs 1:10

A young Chinese lad was converted to Christ while he was attending a mission school. When the boy's father heard about it, he demanded that his son give up this new religion. Replied the boy, "Father, you don't understand. I am sure if you knew about the Christian way you, too, would want to be a Christian. The Lord is my Savior, and I have promised to follow after Him."

The boy persisted in his faith, and the father persisted in persecuting him. Finally the servants built a box, put the boy in it, and carried him to a stream. Here the father in a final warning said, "Give up this religion, and you will be heir to all my possessions. Otherwise," and with this he pointed to the deep turbid waters below the cliff, "you will be thrown into the water." The boy replied, "Father, I am not afraid. You can kill this body of mine, but you cannot kill me. I belong to Jesus, and He will take care of me."

The box was covered; the servants awaited the order to throw it in the river. But that order never came. Instead, the father uncovered the box and said to the boy, "What has come over you? You have never disobeyed me before. And now you disobey even in the face of death?" The boy replied, "Father, now I belong to Jesus, and He takes all my fears away." Faced with this unflinching dedication, the father yielded and finally gave himself to his Christ.

What a remarkable witness! Should it not lead each one of us to examine ourselves to discover to what lengths we have been willing to go in giving our witness for the Lord? We have never been faced with the sharp alternative of death for our faith. How much more eager, then, ought we to be to share with others the word about the great God who is able to save all men.

PRAYER THOUGHT: *Dear Lord, we pray that we may be worthy of our calling, as opportunities arise in our lives to witness for Thy kingdom.*

> Let us then with confidence draw near to the throne of grace, that we may receive mercy and find grace to help in time of need. Hebrews 4:16

During the course of the last war in China, a missionary shared his message with a congregation in one of the principal cities. He had come straight from the war zone, where he had been put to work at manual labor. His face was wrinkled and weather beaten. His hands were calloused from hard work. When the city where he was working had been attacked, it would have been possible for him to flee to a place of safety. Instead of doing this, he chose to remain with his flock of about three hundred Christian converts. Together they had set out, not knowing what their destination would be.

Great tears of joy rolled down the missionary's cheeks, as with a radiant face he conveyed to his hearers how real God had been to the little group when peril surrounded them. He said the longer the time stretched out, the more completely they had come to rely upon their heavenly Father. In their insecurity they had found security. Before, the faith they had expressed in the singing of the hymns and saying of their prayers was only a mouthed hope. Now they had put it to the test, and had found that God was indeed adequate.

Isn't it unfortunate and indeed very sad that so many of us wait until times of hardship to discover how real God can be in our living? He has promised to be adequate to our every need. And who has ever stepped out on those promises and found that He failed to keep the promises He has given? Each day as we seek His help, we can live in the confident trust that it will come to us, no matter what experience might be in store for us. In the midst of anything, even though it be stormy and foreboding, God is still there.

PRAYER THOUGHT: *Teach us, dear God, to trust fully in Thee in every area of our lives, knowing that in this way we can meet every challenge which comes to us.*

Be doers of the word, and not hearers only. James 1:22

A Chinese Christian farmer had only recently been confirmed into the church as a member. One day he went to see the missionary pastor who had become a very good friend of his. After some moments of casual conversation, he turned to the missionary saying, "I want you to hear what I have memorized." Then he repeated from memory the entire Sermon on the Mount which is more than one hundred verses from the Bible.

At the end of the recital, the missionary turned to the new Christian and said, "This is very good that you have done this. I am very happy about it. But the point isn't only to know the sermon by memory but to practice it." The Chinese peasant replied, "But that is how I learned it. You see, I am only a simple farmer, and when I tried to learn the words by memory I couldn't. So I came upon another plan. I learned a few verses at a time. Then I went out and practiced them on my neighbors until I got them right. I continued to do this to the end of the sermon. That is how I learned it."

Here is a real example of taking Christ seriously. There are many people who go through the formalities of the weekly worship service without being Christian in their everyday living. Indeed, the service of worship begins when the participants leave the church to return to their homes and occupations, when and where they can use the principles that have been taught and explained to them. People memorize sections of the Bible, but yet they do not put into practice what they have learned. If the Word of God is to become the power God meant it to be in your life, you must follow the example of the Chinese Christian farmer who practiced what he believed in his heart.

PRAYER THOUGHT: *We pray, dear God, that we shall not be Christians in name only, but that by Thy help we will be sincere and vital Christians in every area of our lives.*

In all your ways acknowledge him, and he will make straight your paths. Proverbs 3:6

How often men must turn to God and ask Him to forgive their foolish acts. We are frequently guilty of only half-hearted dedication and a meager faith. Many times we are even as foolish as some Chinese peasants I heard about when in the Orient. They were presented with an American-made tractor. They were taught how to operate it, but not how to repair it. As long as it ran, these farmer peasants were delighted with their new equipment. Everything was fine, until one day the machine broke down. Being unable to repair it and not having learned how to put it back in running order, they became angry and took sticks, beating it as though that method could make it run.

Similarly, when life breaks down we whip and cudgel our spirits, or we lose our tempers and become angry, as though this could help the situation. All the time we foolishly ignore our Maker who has the power to make life run again. We fret about what should be the next thing to do. We are impatient, and want our problems to be solved immediately. But then there is God's promise that, if we wait patiently and rest our trust in Him, He will bring us out of chaos in His own good time.

Too few of us are prepared for the inevitable emergencies of life when they come. We are so busily engaged in the mundane things of life that we don't take time to prepare for the things of the spirit. Into every life there come moments when man realizes that he hasn't the strength or the power in himself to conquer a given situation. There is One, however, who stands ready each day to help us at our every point of need. Only in allowing Him to teach us the way that He wants us to go can we find joy and peace.

PRAYER THOUGHT: *Heavenly Father, we pray that when the problems in our lives have caused us nearly to break down, we will wisely turn to Thee for the power to repair what has been shattered and restore us again to full living.*

"No eye has seen, nor ear heard, nor the heart of man conceived, what God has prepared for those who love him." 1 Corinthians 2:9

It is of significant interest to learn that the Chinese word for tomorrow is made up of two separate words which mean "bright day." For the Christian this is supremely true. Scripture reminds us that we should have no concern about tomorrow, since the day's own trouble is sufficient for the day. That does not mean that we should not judiciously plan for tomorrow, for trouble comes to every life. What it will be like depends upon how we spend each preceding day. If we spend today walking close to God, seeking to do His will, then tomorrow will indeed be a bright day.

And the final tomorrow will be the brightest day that we have ever lived! It will be a day in which God has promised there shall be no sorrow, nor sinning, nor suffering, nor sickness, nor separation, nor death. The final bright day will be one beyond description, a day more glorious than ever any mortal eye has looked upon. No mortal mind has the capacity to see what God has prepared for those who love Him. The beauties of this land cannot be compared to anything we have known in this life, even the most beautiful and most precious.

Each day we can live in the anticipation of the surprises ahead in the sure knowledge that, if we live each day with God, the future will hold living more abundant than anything we know now. Said a little girl after she had prayed her evening prayer to God, "Daddy, I am going to wake up again in the morning." Each of us can live with that confident hope. Some day we shall awaken to eternity and move into God's brightest day which He has prepared for those who love Him.

PRAYER THOUGHT: *Almighty God, we are thankful that as Thy children we can look forward to the coming of a day more radiant and glorious than any we have ever known, and that on this day we shall join Thee in Thy heavenly home, and there live with Thee forever.*

"Why do you spend your money for that which is not bread,
and your labor for that which does not satisfy?" Isaiah 55:2

In the Orient there grows a certain plant which has a pala-
table flavor and is satisfying to the appetite. But this plant
has positively no nutritional value. As a result, those people
who continue to eat it slowly die of starvation, without the
usual pangs accompanying starvation.

Now, there are certain types of joy which the world has to
offer that give people a momentary thrill. Just as this Oriental
plant brings on certain death, so likewise do these pleasures.
If you keep on attempting to fill your life with the things that
have no spiritual nutritional value, ultimately you will die a
spiritual death.

There are many people today who follow the crowd down a
dead-end street. The roads they are taking lead nowhere. They
seek the thrill of the moment rather than the lasting joys of
eternity. Most pathetic of all are those who have strayed away
so far they no longer have any desire to know the Lord.

Daily we should re-evaluate the way we are taking. We
should ask ourselves: Am I putting first things first in my life?
What is the most important goal that I strive for? Is it something that all too soon can be taken from me, or is it a treasure
that I shall have forever?

Live your life in the light of eternity. Measure everything
that you do by the fact that at best we spend but a few fleeting
years upon this earth. Resolve to lay up for yourself treasures
in heaven. The Lord stands by our side each day, waiting and
wanting to direct us along a road that leads on and beyond the
horizons of our world. People traveling upon this highway are
the only truly serene and radiant people today.

PRAYER THOUGHT: *Teach us, gracious Lord, to fill ourselves
with the nourishing fare of vital Christian living, so that we
may vigorously press forward on the road to eternal life.*

"They will lay their hands on the sick; and they will recover."
Mark 16:18

Some years ago a young man living in northern China suffered from the tuberculosis of the skin. This malady is a very common disease running through the population. The youth finally was taken to a mission hospital. He was a non-Christian at that time, for he had come from a non-Christian home and a pagan village. After receiving medical care for three months, he was cured through the ministry of those at the hospital. Therefore, the man returned to his village happy and restored in health.

Before long he returned to the hospital, this time to ask to be enrolled for training as a male nurse. These were his words of explanation: "During the days of my illness, it became clear to me that the doctors and nurses who ministered to me were concerned about my sick body because they were Christian. I want to be like them and be a Christian, too, and do for others what they have done for me."

After four years of training there, he graduated. It was his choice to remain as a member of the hospital staff, working along with those who had saved his own life. He offered to use his training in an attempt to save the lives of others.

One can never measure what this type of Christian love and service given by our missionaries can do to influence these masses of people who are living in the lands of darkness. Though all of us cannot settle in these areas to work in the same way, the very least that we can do is to remember daily in our prayers those who are working for us. Also, in our willingness to contribute gifts, we can help in this great ongoing movement of Christ and His church.

PRAYER THOUGHT: *Gracious Lord, may we never underestimate the value of the ministry of service, whether we give of our time or our money to the work of Thy church.*

Riches do not profit in the day of wrath, but righteousness delivers from death. Proverbs 11:4

When one of the ancient kings of China died his son prepared a large mausoleum on a commanding height overlooking the city. Then they dug out two large caves, each thirty-nine by forty feet. Here the body of his royal father, dressed in a robe of satin with a crown resting on his head, was seated upon a marble throne before a marble table. His crown was adorned with costly pearls and jewels. His belt was ablaze with diamonds. A pearl of great value was even placed in his mouth. His feet rested on two gold lions.

Beside the dead king was the body of his queen, dressed in her blood-red robe. She, too, had pearls in her mouth. Jewels were clustered around her head and feet. She reclined on the back of a golden bird. One night robbers broke into the mighty tomb and took as their booty all the treasures that had been so carefully laid away. Only the ravaged bodies were left in the ruined tomb. The entire scene was one of desolation and destruction.

Just so the treasures of this world will in their day also pass away. We cannot take them with us to where we are going. The only way we can claim them forever is to send them ahead while we are living now, to make an investment in the future by our manner of living.

People of high estate and low all discover that life is but a journey. Riches cannot buy an escape from death. For everyone of us there is one day the end of the trail on earth. But for all of us this can be the beginning of a new road that never ends. Whether we shall reach heaven at last by this road will be determined by the choices we make each day. Choose Jesus Christ and you shall live now and for evermore.

PRAYER THOUGHT: *Dear Lord, we pray that we may not choose to carry only the riches of earth on our journey of life, but that we may carry with us an abiding faith in Thee.*

"All things are possible to him who believes." Mark 9:23

There seems to be in the human personality a wonderful built-in capacity to meet crises and to respond to the needs of others. There is a certain amount of pluck and ambition in each of us which, if summoned up by the right opportunity, can become a powerful force to be reckoned with. Every human heart can lay hold of divine powers with which to help others. The entire world witnessed an example of this as the famous Burma Road was built a number of years ago, when a small number of citizens recognized that their efforts could save the life of their nation.

When Chinese ports were cut off from Japan, their source of supply, it became necessary to open this back door. Consequently the seven hundred miles from China to Burma underwent a dramatic change. Marco Polo had traveled this road in the thirteenth century. It was beset with narrow tracks along stony ledges and sharp horseshoe curves, where only sure-footed donkeys could make the laborious journey up and down the mountains. It surely wasn't fit for modern vehicles.

Village clansmen, most of whom had never seen a wheeled vehicle, began the project. They had no modern tools, but hammered the rock with crude implements. Shoulder-slung baskets were all they had to move the tons of earth and rock. Within a year, however, the road was ready for use, but with a fearsome human toll.

When times of necessity come into our lives, it is amazing how resources which we summon up can enable us to do the impossible. This built-in capacity is from God and is His enabling. In the promise of this power the beloved children of God can live each day.

PRAYER THOUGHT: *We thank Thee, almighty God, for the reserves of strength and courage upon which we can draw in times of necessity, and which are present in all of us because of Thy divine power in our lives.*

Thanks be to God, who gives us the victory through our Lord Jesus Christ. 1 Corinthians 15:57

On a visit to a native village, a missionary found a little lad all alone, stretched out on a simple straw mat. His eyes were closed; apparently death was near. The man whispered in the boy's ear, "God so loved the world that he gave his only Son, that whoever believes in him should not perish but have eternal life." He repeated it five times without any apparent response. The boy did not seem to hear. On hearing it the sixth time, however, the boy opened his eyes and said, "And I never even thanked Him, but nobody ever told me before."

We live in a land where there are churches on many street corners. We have been raised in a Christian country with the democratic form of government "under God." There are very few people in America who have not heard again and again the greatest story ever told—that of God coming to earth in the form of His Son to die on the cross, that men might have eternal life. This is God's greatest gift to man.

Yet, how about us? Are we simply beggars, asking God for the gadgets of life, begging handouts for every single day? Or do our prayers also include themes of thanksgiving, especially for the new resurrection life which is ours through Him? Do we thank Him merely with the glib words of a prayer, or do we also thank Him by the giving of our lives in trying to do what must be done, if His will is to be accomplished for His children on this earth? No one who appreciates the gift of eternal life should live a day without giving thanks to God for the supreme victory which came through Jesus Christ—the victory that overcomes the world.

PRAYER THOUGHT: *Dear Lord, may we not come to Thee in prayer only to ask that our requests be fulfilled, but may we continually offer our prayers of thanksgiving for the victory which is ours through Thy grace.*

I wait for the Lord, my soul waits, and in his word I hope.
Psalm 130:5

An amusing fable is told about a certain Chinese peasant. At the right time of the year he planted the seed for his annual crop. Eagerly he watched each row, waiting for the seed sprouts to push through the surface of the soil. When the shoots finally appeared through the crust and started to point heavenward, the farmer became impatient and decided that he would help them grow even faster. Therefore, early each morning he went out in the field to pull the plants a little farther out of the ground. At first it appeared that his crop was ahead of that of his neighbors. But one day he discovered to his great disappointment that every plant was drooping and withered. Finally they all shriveled and died.

The parable for our own lives here is evident. We become anxious. We think that God doesn't act quickly enough. We follow our own foolish ways. We pull away from God. Finally, when we have parted from Him, we discover that all is lost. Even our own power which we thought was good enough to carry us on is not adequate. Under stress, it soon crumbles away. Unless the vine is connected with the branch, it, too, will shrivel away and die. The secret is to stay close to the Presence with His power to help us grow.

We must learn patience. God's ways are not man's ways, nor are they always readily understood by men. But ultimately, if only we give God time, He will fulfill every promise that He has made to us. He is our only friend who never fails. Sometimes we cannot understand the isolated events and happenings of a certain day. Let us learn to take the long look and see what the years have to say against the days. In that trust we can advance and face life.

PRAYER THOUGHT: *Almighty God, may we not pull away from the power of Thy presence because of our impatience to know Thy will, but instead, may we trust in the ultimate wisdom of Thy plan and purpose.*

Whatever was written in former days was written for our instruction, that by steadfastness and by the encouragement of the scriptures we might have hope. Romans 15:4

Some time ago the wife of General Chiang Kai-shek came into the General's room and found him repeating to himself the words of one of the Psalms as though he were trying to memorize it. She asked him why he was doing this. His reply was, "Because it satisfies my soul during these dark days. I like the Psalms. They are among the great classics of all literature, and I have memorized thirty of them already." "Why memorize them, if you have them in the Bible?" his wife again asked. "Why memorize them? Because I want to have those Psalms in my soul and not outside. Then I can carry them with me wherever I go into any crisis of life," was her husband's earnest reply.

Now ask yourself this question: How much of the Bible do I carry with me? When a special need or crisis comes into your day, do you have at memory's fingertip a comforting assurance of the Lord's presence? When you are challenged by the ideas of an unbeliever, do you have a defense of your faith from the Word of God in your mind? As Christians we need to go to our Bibles often, to learn more about our Lord and His teachings, and to grow in our faith-relationship with Him. Indeed, this is the letter of God to His children.

Why not set aside a portion of each day for the Lord? Let nothing interfere or take these moments from you, for this is sacred time and to be used only for fellowship with the Master. Carry Him with you in your heart each day, and listen to His faithful promises. Yours will then be a more abundant life, a richer life of trust, and a more influential life in the service of your Lord.

PRAYER THOUGHT: *Gracious Lord, we pray that we will increase our knowledge of Thy Holy Word, so that we may be further strengthened and comforted throughout times of crisis by a deeper understanding of Thy will and way.*

Have unity of spirit, sympathy, love of the brethren, a tender heart and a humble mind. 1 Peter 3:8

A former communist, who had recently escaped from the interior of China, told me of some of his experiences there. He mentioned in particular his observations concerning a mission hospital operated by a dedicated group of Christians. "What I saw there was hard for me to believe," he confided. "There was barely a space anywhere that wasn't occupied by some sick Chinese man or woman or child. Yet no one was turned away. Some space was found to care for everyone. And what care they got! Every person was treated with tender and tireless devotion."

The missionaries who were in charge of the hospital obviously were European, but this Chinese man wasn't quite sure from what country they came. So he asked them one day, "To what country do you people belong?" Without hesitation he received this reply: "We belong to no country. We belong to the world. We are brothers and sisters in Christ."

The ex-communist concluded: "Until we can echo the conviction of these workers, until we can say that we are brothers and sisters in Christ with all men, the world will never know a lasting peace."

This kind of peace begins right at our own back door and on the street where we live. It begins in our daily association with all manner of people. All of us are a part of the great brotherhood of God and fellow members of His kingdom. It is then our opportunity to love others as one great family of the children of God. Let us resolve to follow Christ in being kind and loving and tender hearted to all men, regardless of their social position, profession, or skin color.

PRAYER THOUGHT: *Teach us, Lord of love, to show Thy love toward us by truly living in brotherhood with all men, and by extending the truth of Thy gospel throughout the world.*

312

"The Lord is my rock, and my fortress, and my deliverer." 2 Samuel 22:2

As one sees Red China today, apparently entirely conquered by the godless politics of communism, one thinks of many true stories that have come out of the past history of the mainland. Fifteen hundred years ago the great wall of China, for example, stood unbreached. Then on a certain day one of the guards of the wall foolishly became intoxicated. As he stood by the gate a harmless-looking shepherd came along, engaged the guard in conversation, and finally by an enticing bribe persuaded the guard to run an errand. This left the gate unattended for a moment. This was the moment of moments, and on a pre-arranged signal hundreds of barbarians poured through the gate. These people were not able to conquer China by bringing up force to batter against the wall. But they were able to gain entrance to the otherwise well-guarded area because of one man who was weak during one moment, and therefore an easily-conquered victim.

We who belong to the Lord by His mercy have a great wall of strength surrounding us. In fact, no power on earth can conquer us, for we walk through life in the greater strength of our God who lives and moves within us. Man himself is the gatekeeper of his own heart. He has the ultimate right to choose who can gain entrance into his life. All the enemies of the world are powerless, unless we give them the opportunity to come into our lives. When we fall before temptation, we discover that the power of God is able to help us to our feet again and anew to set us straight on our journey. No man need be defeated in life, if he will only stay close to the Lord. With Him as our companion, our fears can vanish away, and our hearts be set at peace.

PRAYER THOUGHT: *Whenever we allow sin to break through the wall of love which Thou hast placed around us, O God, may we remember that if through penitence we come to Thee for forgiveness, Thou art gracious and powerful to close the breach.*

"If the Son makes you free, you will be free indeed." John 8:36

On a beautiful sunlit day I stood at the border between Hong Kong and communist China. A little narrow bridge separates the two territories. On the side where I was standing the British flag was waving. On the other side the red flag of the hammer and sickle was plainly in view. I could observe the communist guards as they interviewed the people who were attempting to move across into the free world. The situation was filled with suspense and pure terror.

A minister's papers were examined. He was reluctantly allowed to come across the line. For months some fellow pastors in Hong Kong had come to this post praying that he would be allowed to come across the bridge. What a reunion they had on that day!

Next there came a lean, gaunt man. Receiving the approval of the border officials, he ran and threw his arms around his waiting wife. All in one breath he cried, "I'm so sick! I'm so tired! I'm so hungry! But I'm so happy!"

The third person was an old woman who carried in a little bag the only possessions she was allowed to take with her. Being granted her freedom, she dropped her bag and turned to the communist officials in the distance as if to taunt them, as she prayed, "Thank God, I'm free!"

Our hearts rise in prayer for those who live in lands of slavery today. But worse than those who must bear physical torture are the people who must live in the chilling shadows of fear and never know the truth that Christ can set them free. You who are weary of sorrow and sadness, remember that God's truth can set you free. His peace is everlasting, and yet fresh each new day. Freed from sin, we are assured that one day we shall enter the heaven prepared for the faithful.

PRAYER THOUGHT: *Dear Lord, we pray that we may always remember how wonderful it is to be free in the love of Christ.*

Now may the God of peace . . . , equip you with everything good that you may do his will, working in you that which is pleasing in his sight. Hebrews 13:20, 21

Hong Kong is one of the great shopping centers of the world and a free port. People who take extended trips around the world wait to do much of their shopping for themselves and for friends back home until they have come here. On one of my trips I stopped at a tailor shop in Hong Kong that had been highly recommended to me, and was measured for an over-coat. The next day I went back for a fitting. The Chinese tailor made some adjustments, and then told me to come back the following day.

Three days thereafter I was again asked to return. The tailor did not expect any extra pay for the special care which he was evidently giving me. He was the kind of fellow who was satisfied with nothing less than perfection. As I left his shop with my coat over my arms, I couldn't help but think of how we spend so much time in perfecting the things pertaining to the body, and yet spend so little time in perfecting those things which pertain to the soul.

Famous is the story about Michelangelo. One day he saw a rough partly-hewn block of marble which had been cast aside by some sculptor after a careless worker's hammer had chipped it. He said, "I see an angel imprisoned in that piece of marble, and I am going to set it free." He proceeded to work until he had gloriously accomplished his task. The good Lord sees "a possible you" in each one of us, a person capable of becoming ever so much more than we now are. If we will only allow Him, God will work in our life each day, perfecting us more and more as we journey along. However, we must daily open our hearts to Him and, surrendering all claim to ourselves, allow our lives to be so altered that they fit into His pattern.

PRAYER THOUGHT: *Almighty Lord, we ask Thee to mold our lives into more perfect proportions by Thy guidance and direction, so that we may be able some day to enter into the glory of eternity.*

[There are] "men who have risked their lives for the sake of our Lord Jesus Christ." Acts 15:26

Few of us realize the sufferings that faithful Christians have had to endure behind the Bamboo Curtain. A missionary after his escape from communist China into Hong Kong told about how his beard literally had been torn from his face, and how another religious leader had been forced to sit in a squatting position on his heels for eight days. Both were falsely accused of organizing and leading a spy ring in Peiping. They had been tortured for almost fourteen months before their escape. Their joints were nearly paralyzed, and running sores covered their bodies. After months of such torture, they said that sleep was possible for only a few minutes at a time.

One of the reasons why it was so difficult for them to escape was the fact that the communists in China are becoming sensitive to the publicity which follows when half-starved human scarecrows stumble out of this godless country. They want to present a good picture to the world, rather than to let evidence of the real way they are treating these helpless people leak out for all the world to see.

It is comfortable for us to live in relative ease and complacency each day, unaware of the sufferings that other people have to endure who are born, and live, in other circumstances. How grateful we should be for the place of our birth, and for the fact that we can live in a country where there is still freedom of worship. To keep these liberties, however, calls for a greater measure of dedication than we've ever shown before. The price tag on this freedom may very well be help freely given to needy folk around the face of the globe and out-and-out sacrifice on their behalf. This is the command and will of God for us who are His disciples.

PRAYER THOUGHT: *Help us, dear Father, to alert ourselves to the great need of those children of Thine who suffer in countries of oppression and ungodliness, and may we sacrifice from our abundance that they may be comforted.*

I sought the Lord, and he answered me, and delivered me from all my fears. Psalm 34:4

When in Hong Kong, I thought of the many Chinese Christians and missionaries who fled from Red China to seek refuge in this already overpopulated area. A group of these Christians was crossing an area, when halted by gunfire. It seemed as though death surrounded them at every turn. As they marched along hoping to find safety, they kept singing, "I will not be afraid! I will look upward and travel onward, and not be afraid!"

There is deep meaning to this little song. One of the most rampant and insidious diseases is that of fear. It causes many a sleepless night. It can ruin our days. It depresses the soul, and lays waste our powers. It burdens and taxes the heart.

There is, however, an antidote to fear, and that is faith. Someone has aptly put it, "Faith is fear that has said its prayers." Now by this I do not at all mean faith in one's self, although we must have confidence in the resources at hand. What I am talking about is faith in a Power above us. The secret of the overcoming life is to keep looking upward.

The hymn writer knew the problems that surrounded man, for he said, "I look not back, I look not forward, I look not round me, but I look up into the face of Jesus for there my fears are stilled." The reason? God gives power to conquer every cankerous care and fear. There is no force in the world which He cannot help us overcome. There are many people who say that one might as well give up in this business of living. We Christians know better. Discover that God has the power available to handle all your fears and worries. Resolve by His enabling grace to keep traveling onward.

PRAYER THOUGHT: *Merciful Lord, it is so comforting to know that, no matter how overwhelmed we are by fear, we can never be defeated as long as we trust in Thy wisdom and saving power to deliver us.*

317

Therefore, my beloved brethren, be steadfast, immovable, always abounding in the work of the Lord, knowing that in the Lord your labor is not in vain. 1 Corinthians 15:58

Church World Service is a central department of the National Council of the Churches of Christ in America. It is devoted to providing a ministry of relief to those in need, particularly to those who are refugees. In Hong Kong the Council consists of representatives from many church agencies and organizations. This is a partial picture of what it does: Every day fifty-two thousand children receive milk and biscuits through one of nine milk stations. Once a week mobile squads go to eleven Church World Service food stations to distribute rice, pork, corn oil, or whatever other commodity is available. Twice a month these mobile squads go to twenty-two church distribution centers to parcel out food rations. In one church distribution center alone there is a case record of having provided for almost 4,500 individuals. In 1960 this organization distributed 12,500,000 pounds of foodstuffs. Some 130,000 individuals here alone are dependent upon this agency of love.

As one walks about and observes the work of even this one organization, one can sense the presence of the Master. It was He who long ago said, "As you did it to one of the least of these my brethren, you did it to me." Not all of us can go to Hong Kong or to other places where this agency operates in order to give our help and time. But all of us even here at home can contribute our money to these worthy causes. Moreover, there are those right in our own community who need our prayers and help. Let us resolve not to become so busy with the trivial and the petty matters of our own life as to forget our central purpose for living. "For to me to live is Christ," said Paul, and this surely means to be like Him in all that we do, giving of ourselves in a willing spirit for the welfare of our brethren and fellow members of God's family.

PRAYER THOUGHT: *Dear Lord, keep us always mindful of the true purpose of our lives. Help us to be generous contributors to the cause of Thy kingdom.*

You shall not harden your heart or shut your hand against your poor brother, but you shall open your hand to him, and lend him sufficient for his need, whatever it may be. Deuteronomy 15: 7, 8

In spite of the extensive building program in Hong Kong, there are still 500,000 people living in shacks, another seventy thousand on roof tops, and again fifteen thousand people sleeping on the streets. Refugees enter the free world from communist China at the rate of one hundred a day or thirty-six thousand a year.

On a recent visit there I interviewed a few who, at the risk of their lives, had just come across the border. They had been living in a commune of seventeen thousand people. They had no independence whatever of their own. They were forced to become slave laborers, and were assigned jobs without reference to health, capabilities or likes, and wherever the commune felt they were needed. Men, women, and children worked hard through a long day, and then were expected to attend training meetings every night. At the time they fled they were actually starving to death, receiving a ration of only one ounce of rice per meal. "Do you want to go back?" I asked. "No, never!" they replied.

When they came across the borderline to the free world, the refugees had nothing. To whom then did they turn? To the church! Thank God, the church does support agencies which help those who cannot help themselves. Surely, this is the Lord's will, and a real part of what it means to be a disciple of His. We must not only receive the blessings of God, but we must share these with our less fortunate brothers.

There hangs a sign over a little bank at the airport in Hong Kong. Its purpose is to ask for contributions for refugees. It reads, "Your small change will make a big change for them." Let us give as the Lord has given to us.

PRAYER THOUGHT: *Lord, keep us ever aware of the desperate need of others. Help us to be generous as we share Thy gifts.*

The prayer of a righteous man has great power in its effects.
James 5:16

In interviewing the Chinese refugees of whom I wrote yesterday, it was quite easy to discover the difference between our democratic way of life and their system of communism. In the way of communism man is a slave to the state. The state has little concern for the dignity of the human individual. In the democratic way of life everyone is considered important, regardless of the number of his talents and regardless of his skin color or religious creed.

Communism, however, utilizes a person like one would a machine or a tool or an animal. True democracy counts man as its most precious resource, and is willing to pay any price to develop all the potential within each single person.

These attitudes are reflected in the position these two systems take on God and the church. In the communist state they teach their youth in the schools that there is no God, that there is no life after death. In America, at least nominally, most people believe in God as Creator and in Jesus Christ as Lord.

Each one of us can make a real and meaningful contribution to the cause of the Lord's kingdom, as we give ourselves more fully to becoming more Christian in all our relationships. The world will never be captured by communism as long as there is a vital, energetic Christian church. It is only when we fail to do our part to make the church a living power that we are in danger. "The Lord hath need of you!" The church is made up of its people. You are a part of the real bulwark against a godless system. The more dedicated you become to the Lord and His kingdom, the more certain it is that the world will come to know God's will, and that His way will prevail.

PRAYER THOUGHT: *Help us to live our life, Lord, so that others may see in us a little of Thee, and be drawn into the fellowship of Thy kingdom.*

The steps of a man are from the Lord, and he establishes him
in whose way he delights. Psalm 37:23

Among the experiences related by missionaries in Hong
Kong was the story of a little Chinese boy who worked on a
naval vessel. He wasn't aboard long before he had won the
love of the crew. Soong admired the captain above the rest.
Captain Jones became his hero. One day the captain told
Soong about the Lord Jesus. The Chinese boy responded by
placing his faith in the Lord. He became a deeply committed
Christian, and later received his education in America.

Then Soong went back to China to tell the good news of
what Christ had done in his life. He began to translate and
publish the gospel in his language. Soong married a Chinese
girl. They became the parents of six children. One girl was
Mrs. Sun Yat-sen, the wife of a Chinese liberator. Another
was the wife of the minister of finance. Another is the wife of
Chiang Kai-shek, the latter known not only in China, but
throughout the world. The one son became a member of the
Cabinet. Think of the wide and tremendous influence set loose
by one Chinese boy called by God to do the Lord's work. Only
eternity will reveal its extent.

Sometimes one soul may seem insignificant, but always it is
of incomparable value. One never knows when another John
Wesley, or a Martin Luther, or an Albert Schweitzer might be
born and won for Christ, and then used effectively for His
kingdom. There is always the latent possibility of the wonder-
working miracle of God's regenerative grace and power
through a single soul, and then His use of this soul to bring
about a widening circle of tremendous results for His kingdom.
It may very well be that such a soul is growing up in your
home today. Since faith is more often caught than taught,
make sure that you are staying close to God and receiving
His grace.

PRAYER THOUGHT: *Dear Lord, may we ever be conscious of
the possibilities for doing Thy will through encouraging and
sustaining others who share our faith in Thee.*

"Let your light so shine before men, that they may see your
good works and give glory to your Father who is in heaven."
Matthew 5:16

In cubical 410, Block D, in a residential area of Hong Kong
lives the Yonge family. They are seven in number, having fled
from the communist regime in north China several years ago.
Much of this time the father has been unemployed. But the
family has loyally stayed together, obtaining food and clothing
whenever possible. Recently the mother's health broke as the
result of their struggle. The oldest girl, a very intelligent student, gave up her schooling in order to help the family. Marie,
the next oldest, still dreams of becoming a nurse. The three
youngest children, all boys, never complain and make the best
of the situation.

When a church relief agency needed a shipping clerk, Mr.
Yonge was suggested. Though the salary was pitifully low according to American standards, the family has now found new
life and new hope. Merely to visit the tiny cubicle where all
seven individuals live, eat, sleep, and cook is to receive a benediction.

Many of us gripe and complain because of the things that
we do not have. Yet there are many people in the world today
who are content with so little of the physical necessaries. The
chief reason why the Yonge family is so happy today is because
they have finally found freedom. We in America accept so
many of life's extra benefits with hardly ever a thought for the
millions who do not have even the basic needs. And, of course,
our greatest freedom is to know the truth that sets men free,
which is to know Jesus Christ. Are you a living example of the
peace that comes into one's heart from knowing Christ? When
people are in your presence can they sense the difference this
makes? Do they receive a benediction from knowing you?

PRAYER THOUGHT: *Help us, O Lord, to realize fully our re-
sponsibilities as Thy children, and to live our lives as worthy
examples to others of the peace which comes to those who
know Thee as their heavenly Father.*

Beloved, let us love one another; for love is of God, and he
who loves is born of God and knows God. 1 John 4:7

On a certain day in Hong Kong the director of Church World
Service discovered forty-seven refugees who had just arrived
from Red China. They were dreadfully bewildered and confused after a frightening night on board an overloaded junk on
which they had managed to make their escape. The director
arranged for them to receive food, and gave them clothing,
blankets, and toilet articles from the Church World Service
supplies. In co-operation with another mission, he provided
housing and care for them until all could locate work and
places to live. At the end of their first day of freedom one
refugee said, "We have never known of such love from strangers!"

The Lord once said, "A new commandment I give to you,
that you love one another; even as I have loved you, . . . By
this all men will know that you are my disciples, if you have
love for one another." Love becomes the badge of discipleship.
As we continue our support and interest in the worthwhile
agencies of our community and world that are there to help
others, we are actually doing the Lord's work. He has no hands
but ours to do His work today.

When Jesus was on earth, He showed us how to live. His
own life was a personification of love. No one was ever excluded. No matter how busy He was, He would always stop
to help someone in need, even though it were only to answer
the cry of a little child.

There are many voices in the world that are literally crying
for our help and attention today. Let us keep our hearts attuned to the causes of the world, resolving to love even as God
himself has loved us. We have been appointed to be messen-
gers of the great love of God for fallen men and for those in
distress and unrest. Let us carry out our appointment now.

PRAYER THOUGHT: *Help us, Lord, to be instruments of Thy
love. May we always show to others a face of love and hands
of comfort, especially to those who do not yet know Thee.*

"These are they who have come out of great tribulation." Revelation 7:14

A young mother carrying her six-month-old son on her back approached the Church Relief Office in Hong Kong one day. As she entered the door, she turned to one of the workers and with obvious hesitance said, "Do you help people? I mean, children?" She was assured that they did help anyone who needed it. Then she began to tell the story of her plight as she said, "Look at me. I have no education. I am unable to support my children and give them proper schooling. They have insufficient food and clothing and none of the ordinary things of life. I have two other sons besides this baby. Their ages are thirteen and eight. Can you help them get an education? I want them to become useful and self-supporting citizens." Between sobs she added, "This is the reason I risked the journey, and brought them out of communist China."

In further investigating the case, the social service worker walked up the steep and narrow stairs of a tenement house. Here she found a windowless room, six feet square, which these people now called their home. A little straw mat spread upon the floor was the only bed. Needless to say, these people were promptly given help and encouragement to seek a better life.

This assistance came because there were Americans who saw fit to contribute of their means to relief work supported by the church around the world. Think of the multiplied advantages of your life today compared to the millions who have so much less than you. Then surely you will resolve to do more than ever before for them, that they might be relieved of misery and know a happier life. These our brothers are looking to us for help and hope in their plight.

PRAYER THOUGHT: *Lord of mercy, may we resolve to give more of our abundance to the cause of relief work, so that even through us the unfortunate people of this world might come to know Thy compassion and love.*

As each has received a gift, employ it for one another, as good stewards of God's varied grace. 1 Peter 4:10

Tsang Mou is an eighteen-year-old boy student. His family had been widely separated. He decided to make a break for freedom in the hope that he could go to Indonesia. He reached Hong Kong, and then was stranded there, due to difficulties in obtaining a visa. After living on the streets for two weeks with little food to eat and no money, he went to a church relief agency in search of help. His example of determined courage persuaded the workers there that the boy should be encouraged and helped. As a result, students of a university there were enlisted to underwrite his support for a year. From the church organization he has received food and clothing, as well as temporary employment. He is now enrolled as a student. There is probably no happier boy in Hong Kong, even though life is still uncertain and full of danger for him.

As I have traveled about this world, and have seen the many places where the church is at work, the thought often comes to me, "What would happen to people, if those who were followers of Christ withdrew all their help?" And yet, in spite of all that we have done, there is so much yet to do! We need to be laid hold of by the power of God. He gave everything He had for us. We become selfish, and seek to hold on to our possessions, thinking that they are our own. But we are simply stewards. All that we have has been given us in trust by God. Some day each of us will have to stand before God the Creator to give an account of our stewardship of what really belongs to Him. Let every one of us take a daily look at our lives, to see how we are using that which God has given to us. Ruskin kept a stone always before him on his desk inscribed with but one word: "Now!" Let that be the watchword of our personal examination.

PRAYER THOUGHT: *We pray, dear God, that we may in even some small way be worthy of Thy investment in us, and that we will return to Thee a full measure of service.*

325

"The Lord will reign for ever and ever." Exodus 15:18

While talking to a missionary in Hong Kong, I was greatly interested to hear his appraisal of the future of Christianity in Red China. In spite of the fierce drive of the communists, he feels that the Christian church there will survive. There is no doubt but that the church in the Far East has faced great trials and persecutions. None of us has ever experienced anything like what our fellow Christians behind the Bamboo Curtain have passed through. But what we must always keep in mind is that the Christian church was born in persecution. The Lord himself was despised and rejected by those about Him. His disciples were ridiculed and set upon. Once they had regained their composure after the crucifixion, and after meeting their risen Lord, they were ready to go and preach, in spite of the fact that they faced certain death.

It will again be true, despite the new persecution flaming in the world today, that the church will only be greatly strengthened. In spite of all the designs of the communists in seeking to eliminate the church, a police state can never stamp out the Christian faith. Again men must learn that God has not abandoned His world. There have been other periods of history when the horizons for the church's very existence were dark. But God's way has ultimately prevailed.

So shall it be in the future. No mere man can ever overcome the plans of the Almighty. Whenever we are engulfed by fear, we should remember that God is greater than all the forces of darkness that can be arrayed against Him. In God's due season He shall reign for ever and ever. The most important thing of all is that we ever remain faithfully on God's side. That is the place of ultimate victory.

PRAYER THOUGHT: *Almighty God, when fear threatens to overwhelm us, we are comforted by the knowledge that Thou art more powerful than any force of evil, and that if we remain true to our pledge of faith, we shall some day see Thee reign forever more.*

I always take pains to have a clear conscience toward God and toward men. Acts 24:16

A young Chinese gentleman had been converted to the Christian way. His newly found faith meant more to him than he could possibly express. He had resolved that he was going to be true and loyal to this faith, no matter what it cost him, because he had finally found a peace in his heart that he did not know before.

One day one of his acquaintances laid before him the temptation to cheat. When he refused to do it, his countryman asked him the reason for his standing firm in the right way. "Because if I do this, three will know that I have cheated," replied the Christian. "You will know, I will know, and heaven will know."

This is a good thought to remember as we face each day and all of the temptations that come. You cannot hide from God, nor run away from yourself. The Lord has given us an inner guiding voice called conscience which, if properly cared for, will tell us what is wrong and what is right. God is speaking to us through that sense of good and evil, but we must make certain that the channels of communication and fellowship are open and clear. Satan takes great delight in standing as a block along that channel and telling us what he wants us to do.

When a little boy was told about the voice within his heart, he turned to God when temptation faced him and said, "Lord make that voice loud." "The righteous shall prosper but the wicked shall perish." We can take either way as we live each day. No one forces us to choose the path which we travel. Each one of us is free to make that choice according to his own will. In that momentous decision, however, we choose either death or life.

PRAYER THOUGHT: *Teach us, heavenly Father, to listen carefully to the voice of our conscience, when we are tempted to leave the road going home to Thee and to follow instead the path of evil which will lead us only to darkness and death.*

Enter his gates with thanksgiving, and his courts with praise! Give thanks to him, bless his name! For the Lord is good; his steadfast love endures for ever, and his faithfulness to all generations. Psalm 100: 4, 5

A missionary tells us about a very boisterous Buddhist harvest festival held in the valley near his home. The natives carried on their celebrations for five days and five nights. After every span of five years the Buddhists celebrate a harvest festival just after their last crop of rice has been gathered. Every tenth year, however, the celebration seems to be the super-colossal variety. This particular time happened to be the tenth year.

Strings of lights brilliantly illuminated the valley all night long. A loud band played at frequent intervals throughout the night and the day. Firecrackers exploded from time to time. Farther down in the valley statues of Buddha commanded the entrance to a certain area where a drama was being enacted to the accompaniment of weird-sounding music. These people were worshiping according to the religious customs familiar to them. It was all they knew how to do in response to the deep soul stirring within. In spite of all the activity, there was a pathos of sadness reflected on their countenances, because in their hearts they did not know the true and living God.

How different such a celebration is from that on our Thanksgiving Day! We address ourselves to the living God, to whom we are grateful for all that comes to us each day. Yet, ought not every day be one of thanksgiving? Let us begin each day by counting our blessings, yes, even naming them one by one, to see what the Lord has done for us. Then let us in gratitude resolve to share our faith and our knowledge of God with all people.

PRAYER THOUGHT: *Living God, we thank Thee that our prayers are not offered to a lifeless statue, but that in Thee we have the one eternal God who blesses us with all good gifts.*

Let all who take refuge in thee rejoice, let them ever sing for joy. Psalm 5:11

There was a certain prominent Chinese businessman who was not willing to be convinced that he should attend a Christian worship service. The missionaries called on him many times, but he would have nothing to do with them or their message. However, he lived close to the missionary's home, so one day, much to the surprise of the worker, he came to her house and said, "I have now decided I want to learn something about your religion. I have heard very little about it and the reason I am requesting information is this: I have heard the laughter in your house and also in the houses of my countrymen who have embraced your faith. You must have something special that makes people so happy, and I have decided that I want to find it and have it, too."

The Christian must witness with a joyous life. He is able to be happy because he has in his heart the peace that goes far beyond all human understanding. If we pretend to be Christians, and go around worried and anxious and fretful, we are very poor examples of the triumphant faith that is supposed to be ours. This does not mean that we should feign joy and plaster our faces with a false smile. Our joy in the Lord's love goes much deeper, as its roots are made firm in our hearts. Problems will come, but this faith will enable us to face them and overcome them. Indeed, our joy will then have even more substantial depth.

The Lord was always telling the people with whom He associated to be of good cheer. There is nothing of which to be afraid in life, if you are on the Lord's side, because He has told us that He has overcome the world. Everyone that belongs to Him is more than a conqueror. Let us give evidence by our living that there is this abiding joy in our hearts.

PRAYER THOUGHT: *May we give witness to our faith in Thee, gracious God, by allowing the abiding joy and hope which is ours to shine brightly before all men.*

He will give his angels charge of you to guard you in all your ways. Psalm 91:11

One day I had the opportunity along with eleven other men to enjoy a luncheon in the American ambassador's home over there in Taipeh, Taiwan. It was my privilege to sit next to the son of Chiang Kai-shek. We started conversing about his father, who has spent some very difficult and trying years in holding together the forces of the Nationalist Chinese on this island.

During the meal we discussed an incident concerning the General that took place when China was being overrun by the communists. Chiang and his wife were always in the midst of those who were in battle. One day two Chinese recognized them as they were walking arm in arm around a devastated area, seemingly unaware of the lurking dangers to their persons. "Look," said one to the other, "they don't even have a bodyguard." The second replied, "They don't need a bodyguard—they have God!"

This does not imply that we should throw ourselves into unwarranted danger, with the hope that in some miraculous way God will spare our life. But it still is true that God is the best bodyguard in the world. As we allow Him to mount guard about our lives, we can be spared from the possibility of losing life's battle. He is our personal bodyguard against the many temptations and sins that daily threaten us. And if we are wounded and broken by the enemy because we have wandered too far away from God, He is right at hand to pick us up again and to bind up our wounds and to help us get on with our living. God has the only power that is capable of resisting the opposing forces that surround us each day. Wise indeed is the man who stays close to this Presence.

PRAYER THOUGHT: *May we always be surrounded by the protection of Thy power, Almighty Lord, and never separate ourselves from the security of Thy presence.*

"When you walk through fire you shall not be burned, and the flame shall not consume you. For I am the Lord your God." Isaiah 43: 2, 3

During the time I spent in Japan, I had the opportunity of being with people who at various times related incidents from the years of World War II. One of these was an incident which occurred in the city of Okayama in June, 1945. On that particular night the city was burned. When the fire was raging at its worst, a certain man offered himself as a leader. Soaking a heavy blanket in water, he covered his body with it. Immediately he darted through the hot searing flames. After reaching safety outside the city he ran back again to the fire where scores of people were trapped and helpless. "It is all right," he told them. "I have run through. Hurry and wet your blankets or whatever else you have to cover yourself. Follow me, there is no other way of escape. You will surely be burned to death if you stay here." Those who followed his instructions and ran with him through the raging flames were saved. But those who hesitated and did not want to follow later perished in the ashes.

In the long ago there was One who came from heaven to earth to live as the Son of Man and the Son of God. He was despised and rejected and seriously misunderstood by men of His own day. In spite of His goodness, men ultimately led Him to His death. This man died on a roughhewn cross on the hill of Calvary, going first through the darkness of the valley of the shadow. But let us note that He went all the way through and then arose again. Now He stands beckoning to us each day with His outstretched and nail-pierced hands, saying, "Follow me; there is no other way of escape. If you neglect My way, it will surely mean your destruction. If you do choose to go with Me, that commitment will mean for you everlasting life."

PRAYER THOUGHT: *Divine Redeemer, we pray that we may not hesitate to follow Thee in order to escape from the scorching flames of evil; but that we shall willingly accept Thy plan of salvation.*

You yourselves have been taught by God to love one another.
1 Thessalonians 4:9

He is known as Mr. Atom Bomb I. He is called this because
he has survived the largest number of surgical operations after
the fall of the first atomic bomb in Hiroshima. One day I stood
there, talking to him about the events of the past years and
about mankind's hopes for the future. He did his best to hide
his gnarled hands, and hunched his welted back into his ki-
mona, as he told me the story of the morning of August 6, 1945.
At 8:15 a.m. a bluish-gray cloud rose over this peaceful city
of several hundred thousand people. Before it cleared more
than half of them had been killed or injured by the fall of one
bomb. He described vividly the horrors that followed, telling
of the many young people who would have to go through life
crippled because of this incident. Then he concluded his re-
marks with this prayer: "Lord, please don't let it happen
again!"

We are either going to have a future world of peace, or one
that is in pieces. The road to peace begins at your doorstep
and mine. It begins right on the street where you live. What
is your attitude toward your neighbors and friends? Toward
people of other races and creeds? Hatreds begin in the hearts
of individuals, and then spread to community life, and then finally explode into international strife.

The Lord once said, "Blessed are the peacemakers." Everyone of us is called to be a part of this peace corps. We have
no ammunition or weapons, but we travel in the company of
those who have courage to resist temptation and to follow
Jesus in being a brother's keeper. Each day countless opportunities present themselves for us to walk the way of the
Lord. If we accept them and use them properly, we are on our
way to building stronger foundations for world peace.

PRAYER THOUGHT: *Gracious God, help us to show grace and
understanding to every fellow traveler in this journey of life.
May our attitude toward others reflect the warmth and kindness which we receive from Thee.*

"I will restore health to you, and your wounds I will heal," says the Lord. Jeremiah 30:17

One is surprised on visiting Hiroshima today to discover that the entire city has already been rebuilt. As one thinks of the horror and destruction that came upon that city, because man dared to destroy other men in a minute's flash of ammunition, one would think it would be very different from other cities in Japan. Walking through the downtown section of the city, you find a new Hiroshima. A few blocks away from its center, however, stands the skeleton of the industrial exhibition hall. It has been left unrepaired as a permanent reminder to the world of the horror that came from the fall of that one fearsome atomic bomb. In front of the building, now in ruins, there bloom clusters of scarlet flowers making a mockery of predictions that an atom-scorched earth would bear no plants for generations. A blasted building and defiant blossoms—these are symbols of man's power to destroy and nature's irresistible demand for rebirth.

Sin, too, has the power to destroy our spiritual life. It can bring to ruin a man's entire future, for it can maim his character and deprive his soul of any chance for growth into the saving knowledge of God. And yet, within each of us lies the possibility for spiritual rebirth because of the love of Jesus Christ our Savior and Lord. The devil, the world, and our own flesh batter at our lives and leave the ruins behind. But if we take these remnants and place them in the hands of God, a miracle is sure to follow. Man can be born again as a child of God. For the Christian there is no such thing as living in hopelessness, for where God is there is hope. Even when sin has crumbled a life and to all appearances it is beyond restoration, there still exists the unconquerable power of God which can put a new spirit into that life. God in the world means hope for His followers.

PRAYER THOUGHT: *Almighty God, we are grateful that in Thy powerful hands the wreckage and ruin of our lives can be rebuilt to endure throughout a glorious eternity.*

Let each man take care how he builds. 1 Corinthians 3:10

The Imperial Hotel in Tokyo has a very interesting history. It once was a dream in the mind of its builder. People thought its construction would be an impossible task. No construction project like this had ever been undertaken before. With great wisdom and much pain, the architect laid plans for a building that would be impervious to shattering earth tremors in a land of earthquakes and tidal waves.

After carefully viewing the situation, he found that eight feet below the surface of the ground lay a sixty foot bed of soft mud. The idea came to him to float this great structure on the bed of mud which would then act as a shock absorber to the earthquakes.

After four years of hard work, much ridicule and jeers by skeptical builders and onlookers, this amazing building was completed. Soon the day arrived which proved the genius of its construction. The worst earthquake which Japan had witnessed in 52 years caused well-built houses and buildings to tumble into rubble and ruin. But the Imperial Hotel stood firm and unshaken, because its foundations could adjust to the earth's sharp tremors.

Now, here is a parable: Our lives are buildings. They are the most important buildings that we can possibly construct, because life is not meant only for this day, but for the eternal future. How careful we should be in how we build! Only with the Lord as our architect can we construct a life which will be able to stand firm when the storms of life descend. God's master plan is the safest for us to know, as it will have our best spiritual development as its goal. He has planned an eternity for those who have loved and trusted Him.

PRAYER THOUGHT: *Dear Lord, our prayer is that we may wisely employ Thee as the architect for our lives, so that they may be grounded in Thy love, and with Thy guidance and direction may be able to withstand the trials and temptations of this life.*

"Man does not live by bread alone, but . . . man lives by every-thing that proceeds out of the mouth of the Lord." Deuteron-omy 8:3

It is a wonderful inspiration to know the dedication of new-born converts for Christ throughout the world. A good ex-ample of these people is a little Christian boy in Japan who came to the mission school one morning and told the teacher that he hadn't eaten any breakfast. In surprise the teacher asked him, "Didn't you have any food in your house?" The boy replied, "Yes, we have plenty of food, but this morning I got up late. I didn't have time to eat any breakfast. I only had time to feed my soul, so I read my Bible and came to school without my breakfast."

Do we have a like sense of values? If it is a choice between receiving food for our bodies or providing food for our souls, which do we take first? The Lord reminded us in the long ago that man does not live by bread alone. Bread is impor-tant. I have seen enough hungry and starving people in the world to know the truth of this. All of us should dedicate ourselves each day through a sharing process, so that people everywhere might have the same opportunities to satisfy their physical needs as we have in our country. But so often we are tempted to put the things of the body ahead of the things of the spirit. Because we do not see the latter in tan-gible form, we seem to forget them easily.

God's Word is a lamp unto our feet. How dare we go forth into any day without consulting Him who alone knows the way that we should travel? Scripture says that man lives by what comes from the lips of the Lord. How dare we deprive ourselves of our blueprint for life? God is the only one who is able to bring us safely to the final destination of life which we seek.

PRAYER THOUGHT: *Teach us, gracious God, to nourish our-selves with Thy Word, knowing that in this way we receive sustenance for the deep hunger of our souls.*

"You shall love the Lord your God with all your heart, and with all your soul. and with all your mind, and with all your strength . . . , You shall love your neighbor as yourself." Mark 12: 30, 31

On a beautiful Sunday morning I was invited to attend a worship service in the United Church of Japan. It was a thrill to join with those Japanese Christians singing the great and familiar hymns of faith like, "Rock of Ages, cleft for me, Let me hide myself in Thee," and "Must Jesus bear the cross alone, And all the world go free?" In their midst that day I thought of these people, the victims of the first atomic bomb and of all the crosses they had to bear because of the sin and iniquity of the world. And yet in spite of all this, they were willing to remain Christian, because they had learned that the Christian way of life is far superior to anything they had ever known before. They were convinced that their joy must still be found in their following the Lord.

The standard of living has been raised tremendously in recent years in Japan. But in spite of this fact, there are still multitudes who are destitute and in extreme need. As I left the church that day, I noticed two men sitting outside. One of them asked for alms, so I took out a coin and gave it to him. Then he looked at me and said, "How about my buddy?" I couldn't help but be impressed by this poor man's concern for a fellow sufferer, who had his brother's need on his heart.

What if we who have been so bountifully blessed were as concerned about each other? So often we think only of number one and forget all about our neighbors around the globe, many of whom are so desperately in need. The greatest commandment of all is this: "You shall love the Lord your God with all your heart, and . . . your neighbor as yourself." Let us not forget that every man is our neighbor, regardless of where he lives and what the color of his skin may be.

PRAYER THOUGHT: *May we never cease to be concerned for the welfare of our neighbors, gracious God, and show mercy and love toward every child of Thine.*

Grow in the grace and knowledge of our Lord and Savior Jesus Christ. 2 Peter 3:18

Visitors to Japan have the opportunity of beholding in the many public and private gardens samples of the remarkable little dwarfed trees which have made Japanese beauty so unique. They may wonder how such stunted growths are produced. The trees which are called bon-sai are dwarfed in this way: A gardener sets a young pine in a small amount of soil in a shallow dish. As the tiny tree begins to grow, he trims back each root and also cuts the branches. When he dies, then it becomes the responsibility of his son to tend the tree. This same thing is done on down through many generations, as the dwarfed trees are trimmed and given special care.

Today standing in any one of the Tokyo gardens, a visitor can see any number of these plants which have never outgrown that original shallow dish. Hundreds of years old, the plant yet stands only about twenty inches high. A skillful job has been done here in hobbling a tree until it has missed its destiny. There is life, but no strength in that life.

A good parable which we can apply to life is found here. The mind and the soul of a man can be cut back, too, just as the Japanese pine tree can be cut back and made into little else than a dwarf. If our spiritual needs and desires are thwarted and neglected day after day, we are doing nothing more than cutting back the tree of life that God has meant to grow in our soul. Day by day we are expected to become more than we have been, but with a willing and receptive spirit according to God's desire for our lives. To as many as receive Christ, to them He gives the power to become—to keep growing. That is the promise from His own words. Take care, my soul, lest you miss your eternal destiny with Christ. Reap, instead, the harvest of the abundant life as a child of the living God.

PRAYER THOUGHT: *May we never stunt our spiritual growth by refusing to grow in faith, dear Christ, but daily seek to strengthen our spiritual stature through fellowship with Thee.*

Your iniquities have made a separation between you and your
God, and your sins have hid his face from you. Isaiah 59:2

Standing one day at the harbor of Yokohama, I was on the
brink of another memorable experience in my visit to Japan.
The friends who had come there by car to meet me said, "As
we drive along, we might be able to see Mount Fujiyama, at
least one side of it." But as we drove down the road there
was no mountain in sight. Only a thick haze of cloud hung
low on the horizon. Just as we were about to turn our attention away in disappointment, the sun suddenly came
through the cover of fog. The clouds were parted like a great
celestial curtain, and there stood before us the snow-capped
heights of Mount Fujiyama, the spiritual symbol that speaks
to the soul of Japan. It had been there all the while, but the
lifted clouds revealed to us its presence.

God is always present in life, too. But sometimes clouds
come and hide Him from us. Our vision is clouded, and the
way ahead seems uncertain. However, we can be very certain that He does not cause this thing to happen. Clouds of
doubt arise from our own minds. We wonder if God loves us.
We have been told that He is a personal God who is interested in the life of each of us. Yet when we feel that all is
not going well, we blame God and accuse Him of not really
being interested, after all. And suddenly because we lose our
faith, we can no longer see God.

Then, too, the clouds of sin cause separation from Him. If
we are not willing to repent of our evil ways they remain as
great storm centers in our soul, causing us nothing but distress. Our sense of guilt builds up within our soul, until we
must seek relief by forgiveness from God. The most wonderful thing of all is that God is always there, waiting for us to
ask for the sun of His love to break through, and when it does
the clouds all vanish away.

PRAYER THOUGHT: *Help us, gracious God, to repent and so
remove the veil of sin which prevents us from seeing Thy face
of love.*

"I am the light of the world; he who follows me will not walk in darkness, but will have the light of life." John 8:12

During the last World War, a Christian missionary was living in an area where displaced Japanese people had been assigned to a relocation camp. A group of Christians came from the nearby city to spend a day in this camp to lead the group in Bible study, in prayer, and in the singing of the great hymns. They brought with them a collapsible setting for a little chapel.

The focal point of the worship service was a large painting of Christ praying in the Garden of Gethsemane. Jesus was kneeling there in prayer. Fervently He was pouring out His heart to God. Darkness and anguish were in the air that night, for Christ knew that He would soon be led to His crucifixion. Then came that faith-filled prayer, "Father, not my will, but Thine, be done."

The missionary explained to the group that it was here that Jesus knelt to pray before His crucifixion in the darkest part of that night of betrayal. Pointing to the halo around the Master's head a boy said, "But there is light here." When the missionary tried to explain the reason for the halo, the Japanese lad suddenly interrupted him, "Now I understand. It is always light when God is near."

This is the truth that millions of Christians should know, because they have heard the good news but do not always believe, because they have not built an adequate faith. The day may be ever so dark, and the way beset with many difficulties, but there can always be a light in the soul, if one has faith to trust that God is near. There is no darkness that will not disappear in the face of His light. "I am the light of the world," He said, "he who follows me . . . will have the light of life."

PRAYER THOUGHT: *Lord of light, we thank Thee for the abiding contentment and trust which we have because we have seen Thy light, and know that it is powerful enough to dispel the darkest gloom.*

"All the peoples of the earth shall see that you are called by the name of the Lord." Deuteronomy 28:10

It is amazing to discover the wonderful faith of the new Christians in foreign lands. When a citizen of many of these non-Christian lands embraces Christianity, he does it only after very careful study and examination, for it is not easy for him to give up the old time-honored native rituals and superstitions. When it comes time for the baptismal service, he is then given the privilege of choosing a new name. At one of these baptismal services in Japan, the first to come forward was an old man. The missionary asked him his name. He had chosen the name Simeon. Then he smiled and added, "For mine eyes have seen the salvation of the Lord."

The second man was young and strong. "The name?" asked the pastor. "Cornelius," he replied. Then the pastor looked at the man who was so courageous and healthy and understood why he had chosen this name.

The third who came to the baptismal font was a little child clinging to his father's hand. "And the name?" asked the pastor. The father replied, "His name is Isaac, for I now give him to the Lord."

We wonder and marvel at the faith of these new Christians. They are good examples of the kind of vibrant faith and deep joy that God wants all of His children to have when they sincerely commit their lives to Him. Regardless of what our given name is, we all have an obligation because we carry the name Christian. And what does this mean? We carry the mark of a follower of Jesus Christ and are to walk in the pathway upon which He travels and to do good, just because He has done so much for us and because we love Him so!

PRAYER THOUGHT: *Dear Jesus, we pray that we shall always honor the name we bear as Christians, and that Thy will might be done in our lives as we follow along Thy pathway.*

Do not neglect the gift you have. 1 Timothy 4:14

In Kyoto, Japan, is located a Christian school where today thousands of students are studying, simply because one man put the gospel of love into practice. Many years ago a Japanese youth named Neshima became a Christian. In some way he had come into possession of a much-worn Bible. Now, in the day in which he lived it was a crime punishable by death, if it could be proved that one was a Christian. Fearful that his life might reveal his Christian convictions, Neshima tried to conceal himself aboard a ship as a stowaway. Before long he was discovered and brought to the captain who said to him, "We will have to take you back to port." Neshima, shaking with fear, fell down on his hands and knees pleading, "Please don't! For then I shall be killed!"

Deeply touched by the youth's earnest plea, the captain gave him a job as a cabin boy. On the long voyage across the Pacific Ocean, Neshima succeeded in converting that captain to Christ. Out of gratitude for what the boy had revealed to him, the ship captain helped Neshima to acquire both a college and a seminary education. Alone this Christian youth went back to Kyoto, and there established a Christian school with eight students enrolled.

What power there can be in the witness of one person! Perhaps we all do not have the abilities necessary to win the world for Christ, but we do have the capacity to witness personally. In witnessing we may win someone who in turn will have an outstanding influence on many others. The chain of lives that may be affected by the example and constant witness of even one person is endless. Such is our responsibility as bearers of the gospel of love.

PRAYER THOUGHT: *Dear God, help us to let Thee shine forth in our lives, for we do not know when our witness may strike a responsive chord in the heart of one who can have great influence upon others.*

"Blessed is the man who trusts in the Lord, whose trust is the Lord." Jeremiah 17:7

Unique ways of expressing ideas may be observed in nearly every native dialect and national tongue. In relation to common things and everyday experiences from their way of life, people put into their language certain phrases which have special meaning for them.

When in Japan, I was particularly impressed by one of these many quaint sayings which one finds so often. One day I happened to be conversing with a Japanese who could speak English. He told me that the bamboo meant security. I was puzzled by what he was trying to tell me. He went on to relate that the bamboo is one of the farmers' chief crops there. If he has a bad crop or a failure, he is in trouble. But if he has a good crop, he is ready for the winter. Accordingly, then, the bamboo is a symbol of security.

In a spiritual sense now, let us think of the blessings we have because of our faith as Christians. We can say faith is for security. Sometimes, in fact quite frequently, we cannot see the pathway which is ahead of us. Although we may complain because the way is dark, yet even this darkness can be a blessing in disguise. Many people would break down and quit striving, if they could see before themselves in one sweep all the happenings of a single year or even a single month. God has told us that we need be concerned only about the day at hand. If they would only have faith, they would receive the capacity to endure. Indeed, faith is for security. We can trust perfectly in the One who is our leader. If we will but follow Him, there is absolutely nothing of which we need be afraid. We are in possession of an eternal quality that no power on earth is able to take from us. We know finally that even man's last enemy—death—will be conquered.

PRAYER THOUGHT: *Dear Lord, we pray that we may increase our store of faith, so that we may receive the security of full trust in Thy wisdom and guidance for our lives.*

If there is any excellence, if there is anything worthy of praise, think about these things. Philippians 4:8

In Japan one lovely spring morning, when the cherry blossoms were unfurled in all their splendor, a light snow wrapped the entire landscape in a mantle of white. The delicate tints of the cherry blossoms against the pure white snow made an unforgettable picture. On this same morning, since he was thinking of the damage to the blossoms and the resulting loss of fruit, a Japanese gentleman wrote his neighbor a letter of sympathy. He was unhappy because of this misfortune in the loss of the crop through this untimely freeze. He recevied an immediate reply which read, "You have offered me a gross insult. You have written me a letter expressing sympathy, but you have not even mentioned the beautiful snow."

What a different and more beautiful life all of us would lead, if we could see the blessings which can come out of any situation. There is a lesson of gratitude which can be learned, no matter what fate befalls us. Two people can look out of the same window but with a different reaction in their thoughts and opposite expressions in their voices. One can say, "How terrible it is today, it's snowing!" The other can respond, "But look at the beautiful blanket of snow with which God is covering His earth!"

So it is in life. One individual sees mud, and the other individual sees stars. The man who keeps on looking up will be the first to find the break in the clouds or the glory of the stars. There is hope forever shining behind whatever temporary darkness there might be. The promise of God himself is that all things will work out for good in the lives of those who love Him. Hope for the better tomorrow is never dead when we trust in the loving mercy of God.

PRAYER THOUGHT: *May we always look for the rainbows in life instead of complaining about the rain, dear Lord, so that we may see the beauty that is present in every burden.*

"Thou art a God ready to forgive, gracious and merciful, slow to anger and abounding in steadfast love." Nehemiah 9:17

The Japanese people have some very interesting customs which seem to us to be quite strange. One of many examples that could be mentioned is that one in which the women set aside a day of mourning for their broken sewing needles. The school girls in Tokyo on that day also mourn for their broken dolls. A regular Buddhist ceremony is held for this strange occasion which is attended by all the girls and their mothers. All the dolls that have been broken during the past year are buried in a certain grave by a Buddhist priest. There is great mourning and much lamenting over both the broken dolls and the broken needles.

So often we are upset because of the loss of material things. We need to get our sense of values straight. Ask yourself for an honest answer to the question, "What is most important in my life?" In the final analysis it is certainly not the things that can be destroyed, but the things that are eternal which must be the most important in life.

Only God can reveal to us the true values in life. Are we concerned about these things that matter most? The heavenly Father has said that those who mourn over their sins are blessed, for they shall be comforted. Sin separates us from God. Sin breaks life down. But God comes to us with the promise that He will bury our sins as in a great grave, if we are sincerely penitent over them, and confess them. This, then, becomes a day of victory for us, as we find that we are not only forgiven by our great God of love, but that our sins have also been forgotten. This is God's sure promise to us: "Even though your sins are like scarlet, they shall be as white as snow." Putting aside the errors of the past, and burying them in His love, let us strive to lead holier lives for the service of our Lord.

PRAYER THOUGHT: *God of love, we come to Thee in penitence for the sins which beset us, knowing that Thou wilt bury them in Thy loving forgiveness.*

> We can confidently say, "The Lord is my helper, I will not be afraid; what can man do to me?" Hebrews 13:6

One of the great Christian saints of this generation was a man who suffered bitterly in many ways because of the deep convictions that were his. These grew out of his love for the Christian gospel. The man's name to whom I am referring was Toyohiko Kagawa. In the area of Kobe in Japan he rented a room measuring six feet square which he planned to use as his headquarters to help the poor. There he lived among them and shared his all with them. When I visited with him on one of my tours to Japan, it almost seemed to me as though one could see the Master standing by his side. Without a doubt the Lord was there.

One cold morning Kagawa's heart almost broke at the sight of a little Japanese girl, thinly clad, going to work at a nearby factory. Her mother had pawned the few warm clothes the girl possessed for foolish things. Later Kagawa was put in prison by the powers that were in control, since they opposed his organizing the people into Christian co-operatives. At night he looked through the bars of his cell, and saw the stars shining overhead. He rejoiced that now he had even more time to think of God, and to know the strength and courage that only God can give His children. Kagawa became more convinced that the love of God never fails, and that it is stronger than any other power on this earth.

Do we have that same conviction in our hearts? If we possess it, then we will willingly suffer the various taunts of our fellow men as we seek to exemplify our Lord in our daily living. In spite of whatever evil may surround us, we can be certain that if we will only keep going God's way, we are following along the victorious way.

PRAYER THOUGHT: *Almighty God, keep us strong in the conviction that it is only by living each day lives of dedication to Thee and by trusting in Thee that we can be victorious over the forces of evil and corruption.*

"Yield yourselves to the Lord, . . . and serve the Lord your God." 2 Chronicles 30:8

One of the great Christians of Japan that I have had the privilege of interviewing during my visits there was Toyohiko Kagawa. He was a most gracious person with deep rock-ribbed Christian convictions. On one occasion he was asked this question, "What is the first thing in knowing the will of God?" Kagawa answered in a single word: "Surrender."

One's thoughts go back to the early Christian disciples. The Master turned to them and in very simple language said, "Follow me." This was His will for their lives. Scripture tells us that they left all—their homes, their families, their friends, their businesses—to follow Him. They surrendered all to obey the call of the Lord to serve Him in a special way. They were willing to give up their personal ambitions and possessions and desires.

There was another individual mentioned in Scripture who came to the Lord, but who was unwilling to do this. He was filled with questions about his soul, for he asked, "What must I do to inherit eternal life?" When the Lord told him, "Surrender, give up what you have in life," he was unwilling to obey. Rather than surrender, he wanted to keep what he had. Scripture says that he walked away sorrowful.

We are challenged each day by the Lord to follow Him. Each new dawn reminds us of the fresh opportunity to answer that challenge and use the day to the Master's glory. When we ask, "Lord, what do you expect of us?" He replies, "Surrender. Above everything else, give me your life, and I will remake it into a life of lasting glory." Take the leap of faith, yield all to Him, and you will discover how adequate your God is, and how faithfully He loves you.

PRAYER THOUGHT: *Precious Lord, help us willingly to surrender our lives into Thy keeping, forsaking all the vain pleasures of personal possessions and ambitions, and instead consecrating ourselves totally for Thy use.*

"He is not God of the dead, but of the living." Matthew 22:32

Buddhism is regarded as the religion of the Japanese people. But it offers no vital faith for youth. Typical is the incident reported by one of the Protestant missionaries in Japan. This pastor was leading a young businessman's Bible class, when he asked them whether or not they believed in Buddhism. No one knew what to answer. One could see by the puzzled look on their faces that they were in effect saying, "You can see he doesn't know what the score is!" Finally a spokesman answered for the group: "You see, teacher, no one believes in Buddhism any more. Buddhism is only the customs that we observe. When someone dies we call in a Buddhist priest. Otherwise we don't need him. You might say that Buddhism is a religion for dead people."

The world is longing for more than a religion for dead people. In Christianity God has given men the answer to satisfy their need for an outside strength and hope. Ours is a religion of the living God for living people. Our God does not offer us life only in the world to come, although this is a part of His great promise, and no one can minimize the joy of believing for certain that there is an eternity. But more than that, our faith offers us a way of life here and now. It teaches us how to live today, and it teaches us how to live abundantly. It not only gives us the assurance of a Savior from sin, but also an example for living. Our ideal is the Lord who himself during His own life on earth knew no sin. He is the one who stands before us this very day and says, "You therefore, must be perfect, as your heavenly Father is perfect." Though we cannot by our own strength reach our goal, we can aspire by the help of God to live as He would want us to, and follow His plan for our life. In His victorious conquest of evil we shall live as redeemed saints of the living God.

PRAYER THOUGHT: *We thank Thee, heavenly Father, that Thou art the living God who givest us the perfect example by which we can live abundantly in this life, and also prepare for the eternal life to come.*

"Put away the foreign gods . . . from among you, and direct
your heart to the Lord, and serve him only." 1 Samuel 7:3

Shinto is even a less vital force in the life of the Japanese
people than Buddhism. Its sheer animism and nature worship make it irrelevant to the needs of its adherents. A large
boulder in the river running through the city of Yamaguchi
is crowned with the familiar braided rope and dangling white
papers, symbolizing this object as sacred and to be worshiped.

In the same town is a shop which opens to the street, so that
one can see the trunk of a huge old tree which grew out of
the floor of the shop and up through the roof of it. The count-
ers of this store were built around it. Again it was decorated
with the rope and the white paper which designated it as a
divine tree to be revered.

On a survey trip into the mountains, a missionary one day
found an old country woman struggling down the road with
a heavy burden piled upon her back. After she was given a
ride in the automobile, she couldn't thank the missionary
enough for his unheard-of act of kindness. She then called
the car "tasuke-gami" or "helping god," speaking of it with
great reverence, and considering it to be a god. This happens
today in modern, enlightened, and highly cultured Japan.

And yet, before we criticize and look askance at what we
call strange superstition, we had better look searchingly into
our own lives to see honestly what our relationship is to the
living God. Have we crowded Him out with things of secondary importance? Have we neglected our worship of Him
for other things that seemed to need more immediate attention? Let us beware of those appealing false gods which seek
to draw us each day. God alone is the true and sovereign
God of the world. Has He not said, "I am the Lord your
God, . . . You shall have no other gods before me."

PRAYER THOUGHT: *Teach us, precious Lord, to examine the
things in our lives which we place first in importance, and then
to hold them up to the light of our faith where we may see
them in a proper perspective.*

348

> Keep yourselves in the love of God; wait for the mercy of our Lord Jesus Christ unto eternal life. Jude 21

One of the most unsightly places I have ever visited is the land of Korea. How my heart ached for the young men of our country who sacrificed their time and their lives during the war that was recently fought there! Wherever one goes, one is surrounded by poverty and filth.

The difficulties that faced the soldiers during those desperately cold winter months must have been nearly unbearable. I remember the story told about a Marine who was asked, "If you could have anything you wanted, what would you ask for? Blueberry pie, or a chicken dinner, or what?" The Marine immediately replied, "Give me tomorrow!"

There are many people living today under oppressive burdens. They surely must keep asking themselves the question, "Is there any hope?" All of us have certain Gethsemanes to go through. But none of us will ever have to suffer as bitterly as did the Lord. Of one thing we can be sure, and that is that if we remain faithful to Him, some day we shall inherit the crown of eternal life. There is ahead a glorious tomorrow, when we shall be rid of suffering, sickness, and death, and shall be with our loved ones in God's eternal home.

Heaven is a prepared place for a prepared people. Each day, then, we must grow in grace and in a saving knowledge of our Lord. Jesus has meant that life should be progressive. The longer we live, the closer we should draw to God. Thus we shall discover that the greater will our strength be. The longer we live, the more we should anticipate life's final journey which will be a most wonderful journey, if only we have put our trust in the Lord. Let us anticipate that glorious day when we shall hear all God's trumpets sounding in the resurrection morning!

PRAYER THOUGHT: *Lord Jesus, help us to use these fleeting days on earth to prepare ourselves for a glorious tomorrow with Thee in Thy heavenly mansions.*

"Man shall not live by bread alone, but by every word that proceeds from the mouth of God." Matthew 4:4

In many countries of the world human life is so cheap. People are put away simply because of lack of food and medicine. Even parents have been known to barter away the precious life of their children.

When in Seoul, I visited a number of orphanages. The matron of one of these explained to me where many of these babies had come from by saying that the social workers went out at night and looked for them in garbage cans. Many parents, having wrapped little ones in dirty newspapers, had thrown them into the garbage cans, there to die from exposure. What an inspiration it was to go through this orphanage and see these well cared for little babies, God's children, being nursed and loved back to health again. Somebody was now tenderly caring for their babies, because somebody loved even as Christ commanded us to love.

There are many parents in the world today who are saying, "Well, I am giving my children nourishing food to eat and good clothes to wear and well built and furnished homes in which to live." But still, I wonder if spiritually they are doing to their children something akin to what these Korean parents did physically. They are tossing their children aside and not giving them the spiritual nourishment which they need and deserve.

Some years ago, when a certain father lost his child in death, he grieved for her deeply in spite of the fact that his girl was a Christian and greatly loved her Lord. Through his tears he said, "Just think, my little girl never heard her father pray!" The greatest inheritance which we can give our children is a Christian faith.

PRAYER THOUGHT: *Heavenly Father, we pray that the youth of the world may be given the opportunity to know Thy enriching love and that their entire lives may be sustained by such a close relationship with Thee.*

"Therefore you also must be ready; for the Son of man is coming at an hour you do not expect." Matthew 24:44

While in Korea I was told about a youth serving in the army under the most difficult of circumstances. One day he received notice that he soon could go back home, for his period of enlistment was nearly finished.

Finally the long-anticipated day came. The embarkation boat was to leave at 2:30 a.m. Put yourself in the soldier's place and feel the tingle of excitement that must have been his, for now at long last he could turn his back on the war. One of his friends asked, "What if you should oversleep and miss the boat?" "Oh, no," he said, "that could not be. I bought two alarm clocks. I have one set at 1:30 a.m. and one at 1:45 a.m." "Well, at that time of morning you might oversleep both clocks," said his friend. He replied, "I have that figured out, too. The switchboard operator is calling me at 2:00 a.m." "Yes," his friend, being a pessimist replied, "but isn't it possible that she could forget to call you?" "Yes, but I have that all figured out, too. I have decided not to go to sleep at all!"

The moral of the incident is obvious. Be prepared! The greatest journey that any of us will ever take is the final journey of life to our eternal home. Scripture gives us this warning, "Watch, therefore, for you don't know on what day your Lord is coming." There is nothing at all to become frightened about, unless we are living lives that are apart from God. If we remain in His presence, leading a godly life, there is nothing to fear. He knows the way home, and has promised to guide us safely to our destination, if only we continue to have faith in Him as our Lord and Savior.

PRAYER THOUGHT: *Gracious Lord, may we not be found spiritually asleep when at last we are called to our eternal home, but may we be continually awake and watchful, lest we fail to be prepared for the final journey of this life.*

As we have opportunity, let us do good to all men. Galatians 6:10

It was during the war days in Korea. The American troops had received their Christmas gifts from home. This was the day they had all looked forward to with eagerness. There would be something different to enjoy from the rations they had so long been eating! One soldier opened his package and found a fruitcake. His mother knew that this was a favorite. Longingly he anticipated the joy of eating it. As he imagined that savory taste, there came a starving mother and her famished child near where he was. He looked at them, and then he looked at his cake. He could no longer resist. He gave the whole fruitcake to them. How the angels in heaven must have rejoiced as under circumstances so trying this G. I. went about doing good, even as His Lord had asked him to do.

In our selfish blindness and egocentric manner we must admit that there are too many people in this world who say, "What I have is mine, and I am going to keep it to myself." Their lives are like the bogs and swamps, for they don't go anywhere. Their stagnant waters breed selfishness, and cause discomfort to those surrounding them.

There are others who say, "What is mine is God's." Their lives are like rivers, having a source and a destination. Constantly they willingly give of themselves to make the pathways of life easier for their fellow men, causing flowers to spring up in barren desert-like lives, and bringing comfort into aching hearts. Each one of us must realize our responsibility to be our brother's keeper. At the same time we are called to let that obligation of responsibility send us into action, using opportunities inherent in our daily lives to spend our love on others.

PRAYER THOUGHT: *May we willingly offer whatever we have to others in need, dear God, so that they may be eased and comforted even more by Thy mercy.*

"Watch therefore, for you do not know on what day your Lord is coming." Matthew 24:42

The city of Honolulu and the islands surrounding it together make one of the most beautiful places on the face of the globe. As one travels around the world from east to west, this is a choice stopping place for relaxation and rest from the rigors of travel. Relaxing on its white sand beaches, and enjoying the balmy climate of this select area of God's world, the weary traveler's energy and love for life are new born.

One question which people always ask when they come to Honolulu concerns the volcano there. If it is erupting, the question is, "How soon will it stop?" If it is dormant, the question is, "When will it erupt?" The answer is always the same in both cases, for the natives say, "We are one day closer to it."

The longer we live and the longer we travel on this journey of life, the more sharply conscious we become of the fact that some day we must face our Master in judgment. When will this be? When will life's journey end? When will Christ come again? These are questions which the minds of men have been asking and pondering for centuries, but which they still cannot answer. For years people have tried to unscrew Scripture and prophecy to get an answer, in spite of the fact that Christ said He would come as a thief in the night, and that no man could know the hour. His admonition was that we watch and always be ready. That man is wise who daily prepares himself for his eternal future, for with each passing day we are one day closer to it. God's judgment day is inescapable, but we need not fear when Christ our Savior, whom we have walked with on earth, stands at our side to claim eternal life for us.

PRAYER THOUGHT: *Precious Lord, we pray that we may be constantly prepared for Thy coming again, knowing that each day brings us closer to our day of eternal judgment.*

That thy way may be known upon earth, thy saving power among all nations. Psalm 67:2

About one out of every three people in the world today belongs to the Christian church. It is a thrill to travel to various areas of the world, and see church spires everywhere pointing heavenward, surmounted by a cross proclaiming that here live people who have dedicated their lives to God. From the far-flung reaches of the Orient to the deepest jungles of Africa men have proclaimed the gospel of redeeming love that has made us one family under God. Scripture says of these, "How beautiful upon the mountains are the feet of him who brings good tidings." These are the heralds of the great good news that God has visited and redeemed His people.

But there is so much work undone. Many there are who have yet not heard of this gift of the Savior. These millions still live in their sin and degrading idolatry. One cannot travel far in the world today without thinking what a different world this would be now, if men throughout the ages had been more faithful in carrying out the Master's command to make disciples of all nations. How much better, if we had brought them Bibles rather than bombs. How much greater gain it would have been for the kingdom of God, if we had sent bread instead of bullets.

Throughout the world where the gospel message has reached the hearts of people, it has made a visible influence in their lives. They have been released from their fears. Their lives have been given hope and purpose. The skin color of the Christian makes no difference, nor do his meager circumstances. When a person is in possession of the gospel, he feels rich beyond measure, because he knows that he is a child of the eternal King. With such a conviction in his heart, he finds that unmeasured joy and hope are his.

PRAYER THOUGHT: *May we seek continually to carry out Thy will in our lives, dear Lord, bringing the joy of Thy gospel and the good news of salvation to our brothers in the family of God.*

I have learned, in whatever state I am, to be content. Philippians 4:11

It isn't at all easy to be a missionary for the Lord in any area of the world. And yet I have never heard one of these courageous people complain about the hardships they accept. When asked how they maintain the vibrant spirit they manifest, they always answer that it is because they know the lift of the presence of their Lord. He is so real to them. "How can you endure all your burdens?" I asked one. "Because Jesus is always as near to me as this brother," he replied, as he put his hand upon the shoulder of a native standing next to him.

When we become that sure of the presence of the Divine, and when we become that certain of the presence of His power, we shall be ready to do what the world would otherwise call the impossible. However, so few of us take time to develop a friendship with God. We are involved in being busy with the goings-on of life. Perhaps we should more closely follow the plan of an old Christian woman who lived alone. Each day she opened her hymnbook and sang hymns of praise to the Lord. In reading her Bible, she let the Lord speak to her. When she was tired of reading and singing, then she would just sit in quiet meditation and enjoy the blessings all about her. "I know then how much the Lord loves me."

It is in the presence of the Lord that we can feel an incoming strength, even when we need Him most desperately. It is in His presence also that we feel the challenge and the command to go out into life and share our faith with others who need it. Our blessings indeed daily surround us; but in many other ways also the Lord tells us, "Fear not, for I am with you." Such a friendship with the Eternal cannot be shaken.

PRAYER THOUGHT: *Dear Lord, may we never fail to appreciate the marvelous blessings which are ours because we are Thy children and because we possess the priceless gift of Thy continual companionship.*

"I have come as light into the world, that whoever believes in me may not remain in darkness." John 12:46

One of the most apt descriptions of today's world situation is to call it a turbulent world. Temporary peace among nations is not secure. The forces of the evil one sometimes seem to have gained the ruling hand. We shall see many pictures of the world as we journey on, which will not be pleasant to look at. And yet, in the midst of apparent chaos and suffering, it is my hope that we will all see the eternal light. If we put our resources to work in making it become strong enough, it can cause all the darkness of the world to vanish.

As I think back to some of the places where I have been, there are some sights that remain forever etched upon my memory. I find myself in Africa where, in the heart of the jungles, I discovered a group of dedicated Christian natives. I have heard them singing, even though they are blind, "What a friend we have in Jesus, All our sins and griefs to bear."

I find myself in India, where people are steeped in starvation and misery. These masses want more than the mind of western man can imagine. In spite of their poverty, the Christian raises his voice in song, "O God, how great Thou art!"

I find myself in Hong Kong. A little church there is crowded to the walls with faithful Christians. I hear their voices unite in another hymn of faith, "Day by day Thy mercies, Lord, attend me."

I find myself in Japan. Christian leaders of all backgrounds are gathered together, and I hear them singing, "O God, our help in ages past, Our hope for years to come." This is indeed the only faith that can overcome the turbulence of the world.

PRAYER THOUGHT: *Almighty God, we are grateful that Thy light shines brightly in even the darkest regions of the earth and is not dimmed, no matter what desolation and destruction mankind brings upon itself.*

"Am I my brother's keeper?" Genesis 4:9

Throughout the several years that I have traveled abroad, I have come back home to America each time with two conclusions made more firm in my heart. Wherever I have gone, America has stood as a golden symbol of hope for the downtrodden. On the other hand, I have also discovered the ugly truth that this nation has not measured up to its image in many of these underprivileged countries. People seem convinced that we are more interested in materialism and in gaining things for ourselves through exploitation than in sharing things with others.

In this day in which time seems to be quickly running out for the survival of mankind, all of us need to take a searching inventory, in order that we might get the house of our life in proper readiness for the Lord's coming. This whole process of keeping a Christian democracy vital and generative involves sharing, the like of which we have not even begun to do. If we would give more than mere lip service to being our brother's keeper, then we had better become in real fact our brother's keeper, letting him know by our deeds that we really care.

This great country of ours has been blessed in more ways than any other area in the world in all of history. We have the technical know-how to teach others to make for themselves a better way of life. We have the wherewithal to help create better living conditions. And then add to all this our being blessed with the knowledge of the light of the gospel which urgently demands our passing it on to all people until the darkness of the earth is vanished. America can remain the symbol of hope to all the world's distressed, if only we will let the love of God spill out generously from our hands and hearts to all people.

PRAYER THOUGHT: *Gracious God, may we as Christians and as Americans resolve anew to discharge our responsibility of bringing the light and hope of Thy gospel into the lives of all men.*

"All who call upon the name of the Lord shall be delivered."
Joel 2:32

For years civilizations have searched for answers to the perplexing questions which confuse the minds of men. We are still searching for satisfactory solutions to such problems as hatred among nations, bitter prejudice among races, and jealousy among all classes of people. The pat theories of men up to this point have all failed. What will men do now? What solution will we try? On our answer hangs our destiny.

In this desperate hour, the Christian is certain beyond all doubt that the world has been given the answer in the person and the life of Jesus Christ. God has for nearly two thousand years provided the one solution. As is so often the case, it takes a desperate situation to turn a man to God. We try by our feeble methods to save ourselves, but finally in utter despair we realize that only God is able, and then turning to Him for help, we also find Him willing.

The power that has changed the lives of men throughout all centuries is the same power, still available today. It can transform the lives of all people. The umbrella of God's providence and power is raised over all His creation, and His sun rises over good and evil. His goodness is not confined to a certain people. Throughout His earthly life, Jesus talked about the whole world. The words "the world" and "all" were frequently in His speech. In His earthly activities no one was too insignificant to be remembered. All the nations were included in His last will and testament. When He left the world to return to His Father, He told His disciples that He would not leave them alone. He is in the world today, ready to help. What God waits for now is the total commitment of the life of each of us. When that day comes, almost unbelievable things will happen.

PRAYER THOUGHT: *Gracious God, we pray that we may have the wisdom to commit ourselves totally to Thee and to Thy will, so that we may know the power of Thy goodness in our lives.*

Thanks be to God for his inexpressible gift! 2 Corinthians 9:15

Walking along the streets of Moscow one day, I met a Russian carrying what I had always known as a Christmas tree. When we stopped for a moment's friendly conversation, I referred to it as a Christmas tree. He said, "Oh, no, this is a New Year's tree." On talking further with him, I learned that because of their atheism, people behind the Iron Curtain do not celebrate Christmas, but instead their big festival is New Year. There are no worship services arranged, but instead this is the time when they put up their tree, gather families together, and exchange gifts.

Suddenly it flashed through my mind, "Suppose there were no Christmas! Suppose that Christ had never come into the world. What a difference it would mean for our lives!"

Assuredly, there would be no forgiveness of sins, for man does not have the ability to forgive himself. If Christ had not come, we should have to go through life burdened with our transgressions and guilt. But because He came, surely He has borne our grief and carried our sorrows.

Again, suppose that Christ had not come. There would be no abiding companionship along life's way. Man would then walk alone, fight his own battles, and have no Presence by his side to encourage him on and to guide and direct him. But there is a Presence beside you each day. For the Lord forever keeps His promise, "Lo, I am with you always, to the close of the age."

If there had been no Christmas, we would have no hope for eternity. Christ came into the world to save us from our sins and to give us the shining hope of everlasting life. Thank God, then, that we live in a country where there is a Christmas! Thank Him for joy and hope. Thank God for Christ!

PRAYER THOUGHT: *Heavenly Father, we have no words which can adequately express our gratitude for Thy matchless gift, Thy Son, whom Thou didst send to us on Christmas to take the burden of our sin upon His shoulders, enabling us to walk into the heaven which Thou hast prepared for us.*

Once you were darkness, but now you are light in the Lord;
walk as children of light. Ephesians 5:8

Today even more than ever before, we must have confidence
and trust in what we believe. Everyone seeks security. We
must bring correct answers to the life-and-death questions that
face men.

It was the Master who once said, "Ye will know the truth,
and the truth will make you free." Today more than ever before we must let the original freedom bells continue to ring out
the good news of the gospel to all the world. People everywhere are hungry for salvation. Many live in darkness simply
because we have not brought them a knowledge of the power
that can set men free. Many are burdened with their sins, because they do not know Christ as their Savior. Many live in-
secure lives, not knowing the power that can steady and un-
dergird them in their daily living. Many are very lonely, because they have not been introduced to the Presence with
whom they can walk and talk with burning hearts each day.

We who know the Christ must be willing to share and to
sacrifice, that the inner light we live by might be in the lives
of others, too. We who have been born in freedom, and therefore know the truth that sets men's hearts free, are invested
by God with powers to do great things with this inheritance.
Properly harnessed and moved by a great Christlike compassion, we could do great things for Him. The gloomy darkness
of the world would ebb away. There is only one Physician
who has the power to bring healing to the world, and that is
God's holy Son, our Lord Christ. We have tried man's way
these many centuries, and it has consistently failed. Isn't it
about time that we resolve to try every possible aspect of God's
way? And if we do, He himself has already promised us that
we shall be victorious over the weariness of life.

PRAYER THOUGHT: *We pray that we may carry our knowledge of Thee, the Light of the world, into shadowed corners
where the joy of Thy gospel of salvation can dispel the darkness of ignorance and misery.*

All the ends of the earth shall remember and turn to the Lord.
Psalm 22:27

Most of us have not been serious enough about this one life
we have been given. In this game of life we find ourselves in
the last quarter. Up to this point it appears that we are losing.
There continue to be wars and rumors of wars. There are vast
areas of human need opening up to us all around. In my jour-
neyings about, I have been appalled by the masses of people
who are starving for lack of food, dying for want of medicine,
and living in spiritual darkness, because we have lagged in
bringing them the good news of Him who is the light of the
world. Many have grown weary in the repeated failure of mere
man-made efforts to win. Our hope is in the fact that people
are probing as never before to find other more constructive
and lasting solutions to problems.

These times demand our very best efforts. The stakes are
high, and we dare not lose. For too long we have been playing
with the second team in the line while the regulars sit on the
sidelines. We dare not procrastinate any longer. The time has
come to make some substitutions.

Now then, what solution do I propose in order to help solve
the problems we face? Generally speaking, the dynamics of
God must be substituted for the mechanics of men. Our forces
are large enough if, linking ourselves to the living God, we
unite them to pull the game out of apparent defeat. Our sole
hope is that we allow God to develop out of such unity a giant
soul which can control the minds and hearts of men in order
to use these new powers for good rather than for destruction.
The only way of escape is to put our faith in Almighty God
and in His power to change the lives of men. We must accept
the responsibility of carrying this faith to all nations, so that
all men might have that same opportunity.

PRAYER THOUGHT: *Dear Lord, we resolve to strengthen our
witnessing for Thee, so that the world might come to know
Thee and to place its trust and faith in Thy will for the future
of man.*

"You are the light of the world." Matthew 5:14

Do we really believe as we should in the power of God? We glibly confess, "I believe in the power of God the Father Almighty." And yet we live our days as if we had to depend upon our own puny strength. God intends us to be heirs of Christ the King, and yet we act as paupered orphans. We read in His Word that we are more than conquerors through Him, and yet each day we live defeated and despairing lives. We need a workable faith more than anything else.

For all too long we have confined God's power to formal worship. The challenge of this day's hour is to encourage all believing Christians to take the Master from out of the stained glass windows of our churches and bring Him out onto the streets of life. Being a Christian is not merely a devotional exercise; it involves the total realm of life. Each one of us is individually responsible for all he thinks and says and does. Each is important in the sight of God and has a task to do. The forces of darkness will not be defeated by a few towering characters shining like lights, but rather by the multitudes of individual Christians who brighten the corners wherever they are. Darkness cannot tolerate the light. It flees its presence. If each of us would reflect the light as God has bidden us do, the darkness would soon disappear.

We Christians hold in our possession the power that can change the world. For too long we have been sounding our message through muted flutes. It is now time for the sound of trumpets to come forth joyously and triumphantly with the best news the world has ever heard. Our Christian faith must ever be a living, growing, dynamic movement, and then it can reform the world. "All power has been given to me in heaven and on earth," said the Lord. Now we must serve Him in making His power known in all hearts.

PRAYER THOUGHT: *Dear Lord, let us so live that our lives may testify to the glorious victory which we have through Thee, and that as children of Thy light we may dispel the gloom of hopelessness.*

"He knows that a day of darkness is ready at his hand; distress and anguish terrify him." Job 15:23, 24

There are some conclusions we should arrive at before we complete our trip around the world. For too long now we have been willing to save ourselves and our society by a type of inventive science divorced from God. Take a good look at today's world. Every place you go, people are afraid and nearly on the verge of panic at the thought of total destruction. Many nations have powers within their grasp such as man has never before possessed. What we face today is the stupendous fact that, while science can give us power, science alone cannot determine how we shall use it. Science alone cannot save us. We desperately need the gospel to transform our personal lives. We need it for the renewal of society.

A glance at the world's time clock finds it standing at five minutes to twelve midnight. We stand now at the crossroads. Either we are not far from the frazzled end of civilization, or we are on the threshold of life's more glorious day. There is very little time for us Christians to usher in the life-saving and the life-giving gospel to the world.

In other areas of life we have been willing to make great sacrifices. We have poured billions of dollars into aircraft with which to deliver atomic and hydrogen bombs. We have worked around the clock on experiments in jet propulsion and guided missiles. We have discovered power that can destroy the world. The choice is self-evident. If we fail to heed God, we can be eliminated from the earth. But I feel that yet there is time! Wake up, O world, and listen to the only voice that can lead in the way of peace! It is God's voice that speaks the truth.

PRAYER THOUGHT: *Precious Savior, we pray that we may turn to Thee, so that the world will not come to destruction, but that people might know Thy plan of glory and peace for all mankind.*

> And a highway shall be there, and it shall be called the Holy Way. Isaiah 35:8

We are almost at the end of our journey. We have visited many of the places in God's wonderful world, and have seen how people live and act and worship. We have observed some of the staggering problems which face us today, frightening because of their complexity and yet these are the problems that we must recognize in this turbulent world. What solutions will be needed, if it is to become the kind of world that God can approve?

Men have tried various roads. Some have turned out to be blind alleys; others have failed to bring us to a better world. There still remain many arid desolate places that must be cultivated until they become gardens. Hopeless people need help. Hatreds cry to be replaced by love. Starving people need bread. The dead-end streets of man bring us trouble and lead nowhere. But this is God's world, and He is its planner. To come out right, we must live according to His commands.

There is one road that we can take that will lead us through. Someone has called it the "road of reconciling love." It will lead you from your home today into the deep South of our country, where so many unsolved problems still are found. It will lead behind the Bamboo Curtain and the Iron Curtain, and take you into Africa, India, China, and to other parts of the earth.

It is also called the King's highway. The guide is the Prince of Peace. Walking with Him is a radiant company of people. They are convinced that only by loving one another, by sharing and believing and trusting, can we find a way out of our dilemma. This is a road that never ends. It goes on through the valleys of life into the eternity of heaven where some day people shall gather from East and West and North and South. There shall be one flock and one Shepherd.

PRAYER THOUGHT: *We pray, dear Lord, that we will travel on the one road that is really going somewhere, so that we may reach the destination of an eternity with Thee.*

"The time is fulfilled, and the kingdom of God is at hand."
Mark 1:15

Today we approach the home-coming landing and the end
of our journey. We have been in many strange places, and
have seen many wonderful as well as heartbreaking things.
No matter how enriching a journey has been, the best part of
any trip is the arrival home, where once more you are surrounded by friends and loved ones.

Just so, the final journey of life will be the most wonderful
leg of our trip. And the arrival will be the most exciting, for
we are destined to travel to a place that has been gloriously
described in Scripture. There shall be no night there, neither
sinning nor sorrow nor death. It shall be a place of song and
joy and everlasting life. It will mean reunion with our loved
ones.

The landing will be as sudden as is the landing of our plane
dipping down from the sky to the airport landing strip below.
There will not be a trying period of waiting, nor a protracted
period of sleep. Did not Jesus say to the penitent thief on the
cross, "Today you will be with me in Paradise"? This statement tells us all about heaven that we need to know. We shall
be with the Lord in a beautiful place which He has now gone
to prepare. There nothing—absolutely nothing—shall separate us from the love of God which is in Christ Jesus.

So live each day to the fullest with God, and heaven has already begun for you. Keep walking life's way with Him, and
He will lead you into fairer pastures, until finally you shall go
with Him to the other shore. There will be rejoicing in heav-
en over another soul who has won through by repentance and
faith, being redeemed by the blood of the Lamb. As a child
of the King, you will be with Him even after time is ended
and eternity has begun in His heaven.

PRAYER THOUGHT: *Heavenly Father, we pray that when our
journey of life is ended we may come home to Thee where we
shall find joy and peace beyond our present comprehension.*

DATE DUE